NATIONAL SERVICE

Pergamon Titles of Related Interest

Sarkesian BEYOND THE BATTLEFIELD: The New
  Military Professionalism
Taylor DEFENSE MANPOWER PLANNING: Issues for the 1980s
Tropman NEW STRATEGIC PERSPECTIVES ON SOCIAL POLICY

Related Journals*

BULLETIN OF SCIENCE, TECHNOLOGY & SOCIETY
INTERNATIONAL JOURNAL OF INTERCULTURAL RELATIONS
SOCIO-ECONOMIC PLANNING SCIENCES
SPACE SOLAR POWER REVIEW
TECHNOLOGY IN SOCIETY
WOMEN'S STUDIES INTERNATIONAL
WORLD DEVELOPMENT

*Free specimen copies available upon request.

PERGAMON
POLICY   ON SOCIAL POLICY
STUDIES

NATIONAL SERVICE
Social, Economic and Military Impacts

Edited by
Michael W. Sherraden
Donald J. Eberly

Pergamon Press
NEW YORK • OXFORD • TORONTO • SYDNEY • PARIS • FRANKFURT

Pergamon Press Offices:

U.S.A.	Pergamon Press Inc., Maxwell House, Fairview Park, Elmsford, New York 10523, U.S.A.
U.K.	Pergamon Press Ltd., Headington Hill Hall, Oxford OX3 0BW, England
CANADA	Pergamon Press Canada Ltd., Suite 104, 150 Consumers Road, Willowdale, Ontario M2J 1P9, Canada
AUSTRALIA	Pergamon Press (Aust.) Pty. Ltd., P.O. Box 544, Potts Point, NSW 2011, Australia
FRANCE	Pergamon Press SARL, 24 rue des Ecoles, 75240 Paris, Cedex 05, France
FEDERAL REPUBLIC OF GERMANY	Pergamon Press GmbH, Hammerweg 6 6242 Kronberg/Taunus, Federal Republic of Germany

Library of Congress Cataloging in Publication Data
Main entry under title:

National service.

(Pergamon policy studies on social policy)
Bibliography: p.
Includes index.
1. National service--United States--Ad-
dresses, essays, lectures. 2. Youth--
Employment--United States--Addresses,
essays, lectures. I. Sherraden, Michael W.
(Michael Wayne), 1948-   . II. Eberly,
Donald J. III. Series.
HD4870.U6N37   1982   331.3'412'0420973   81-19954
ISBN 0-08-027531-1   AACR2

HD
4870
.U6
N37
1982

Printed in the United States of America

Contents

Foreword

Since my college years, almost forty years ago, I have watched the fluctuations in public interest in implementing some form of national service. Clearly, the initial years of the decade of the 1980s have produced and intensified national discussion as to whether national service in one format or another is desirable and feasible. The moves taken to establish a presidential commission on national service have reflected this level of increased concern.

In my view, there are three different but converging sources of interest and concern; one is relatively new and the other two are of long standing. First, the new dimension in the debate is the pressing question of military manpower; that is, the difficult and almost intractable problems of an expanded all-volunteer military. Could a form of national service improve recruitment and make the all-volunteer force a more viable military establishment? Powerful political leaders have reached the point where they are prepared to examine the national service option. Second, renewed interest in national service derives from the traditional concern to handle more effectively the socioeconomic ills of an advanced industrial society. To the recognized problems of inner city and low income families have been added an immense increased demand for health services and a range of problems labeled as "ecology" or the "environment." The fiscal strains of the welfare state and ecological issues have served to strengthen interest in the potentialities of a national service system.

Third, national service also has been defined traditionally as a form of youth education. Currently it is seen as a supplement to correct the defects of contemporary education. In this view, participants would benefit from national service in terms of personal development and increased maturity. The campuses are quiet while the students pursue the specific requirements of obtaining a good job, with little involvement in civic education and citizenship obligation. Such criticism of education, especially of higher education, is widespread without improvement either in academic instruction or in increased participation in community and public affairs. The idea of national service is pressed with increasing vigor as a device for enhancing the emerging generation's sense of collective responsibility.

To assist this debate on national service which is certain to last during the years ahead, Michael W. Sherraden and Donald J. Eberly have produced a comprehensive and very useful sourcebook on national service. They have had the cooperation of a group of interdisciplinary experts in presenting an overview in depth of our knowledge and of the available alternatives and policy issues which must be confronted. They offer penetrating exposition of the rationales of the different forms of national service, and of the experience of the United States with national service precedents, as well as the experience of other nations. Alternative forms of national service are examined, and the difficult issues of effectively linking national service to the requirements of the military are extensively evaluated.

Carefully reasoned estimates of the impact of national service on youth employment, education, and the all-volunteer forces are examined with exacting thoroughness. Research on the effects of previous and existing national service type programs in the United States is reviewed, and the available research on youth attitudes is summarized. In short, with the publication of this volume we have passed from the phase of broad sketches of national models to organizational and policy analysis in detail.

From my point of view, both as a teacher and as a person interested in the consequences of research on policy, the enterprise is striking for its direct confrontation of the "hard" and "unsolved" problems. The development of national service is seen in its full complexity and difficulty by the contributors.

Thus, the volume helps clarify the basic issues of voluntary versus mandatory national service. The attitudes of young people, and the goals of national service, lead the editors in their policy analysis to conclude that for civilian assignments only a voluntary system would be effective. I agree. In fact, I believe that the military option should and could also be voluntary. A mandatory system would have to offer extensive opportunity for exemption, especially on the basis of personal conscience.

In the contemporary scene, there is considerable convergence between a volunteer and a mandatory system; the greatest difference would be symbolic, and in the minds of men and women such symbolism is important. Only a great national debate will resolve the issue, although I am convinced that "peacetime" mandatory service—civilian or military—is not needed and would be counterproductive and tension producing. It takes only a very tiny concentration of oppositionists to cause extensive disruption and agitation. Nor does a democratic society require a tyranny of the vast majority. And I am convinced that a national service with vigorous leaders would attract a majority of young people, as the United States develops the notion that each young person "owed" the nation a contribution of work and service.

But a voluntary system faces the complex problems of linking civilian service with military service. In this volume, the scope of the problem is made clear and reasonable solutions are offered, solutions which center on educational benefits for both military and civilian service. On the basis of the materials presented, in fact, my conviction is reaffirmed that voluntary national service would enhance the ability of the all-volunteer force to recruit the required short-term personnel with appropriate educational background. The national service concept would reinforce the sense of civic obligation in the youthful population. Serving the nation for a limited period of time would be a norm which would be strengthened. As a result, military service would to a great extent be seen as a legitimate expression of civic obligation or duty and not solely or primarily as a job. By emphasizing such appeals—national obligation and educational benefits—the pool of potential recruits for short-term service would be increased.

The fact that the organizers and contributors to this volume are inclined toward national service does not distort their understanding of youth attitudes and youth culture. The typical young male or female is reluctant to lose one year in the struggle to find a place in the occupational structure; this is a very important and dominant attitude. The powerful counterfactor is the professed willingness of youth to do national service if most others also serve. Such an attitude pattern bespeaks the need for a rapid buildup of certain types of national service to make visible the relatively widespread base of participation. But the administrative difficulties of rapid buildup are immensely dangerous and could be self-destructive.

In fact, the reader of this volume will quickly discover that the "administrative factor" is likely to be the limiting element in implementing national service. We are dealing not with administrative problems specific to national service, but a dilemma of contemporary society. Our national institutions—both public and private—face immense defects in organizational effectiveness. National service would be particularly vulnerable unless creatively organized. The publication of this valuable volume is an important step in coming to face directly the problems of organizational format which remain to be solved. If the nation should move toward a national service, fiscal constraint will dictate a gradual buildup strategy which appears, in my view, to be the sounder approach.

Basically we are dealing with the fundamental issues of citizenship in a democratic society. Citizenship implies a balance between rights and obligations. The last half century has seen the increased scope and importance of individual rights, while the concept of citizen obligation has not been clarified and made effectively operational. In part, we are dealing with the contemporary search for a modern version of the tradition of the citizen soldier. We are dealing with a much broader scope of the tasks of citizen obligation than service in the armed forces, although such service remains fundamental. If national service has meaning which will endure, it involves the notion that the society needs more than taxpayers. It needs active and responsible citizens. A democratic society needs appropriate and realistic means of educating each new generation in the meaning of citizenship. National service is one form of such education for a political democracy.

Morris Janowitz
University of Chicago
October 1981

Preface

National service is an idea which recognizes that individuals can and should contribute to the larger society and that society should be structured to facilitate and encourage such activity. The editors of this volume support the development of a voluntary and diversified program of national service in the United States.

Michael Sherraden has directed a rural program for emotionally disturbed adolescents and has seen first hand that the operations of an 1800 acre ranch with cattle, horses, hogs, and chickens, with a garden and hay fields, with fences to mend and machinery to repair, can all be managed with a group of "disturbed" teenagers. From this and other experiences, both urban and rural, with "normal" as well as disturbed teens, Sherraden has come to the view that nearly everyone has something to contribute. Moreover, the majority of young people respond positively, often with pride and satisfaction, when they are in a situation where something is genuinely expected of them. With the contraction in demand for teenage labor in the post-industrial era, the real shortchanging of America's young people is that they do not have sufficient opportunities to assume responsible roles in society.

Donald Eberly's interest in national service developed from both a global and a personal perspective. It was global in the sense of the stark contrast he perceived between America's commitment to winning wars and her commitment to winning the peace. As a high school student during World War II, he was aware of vast resources of men, money, and materials being expended in the war effort. As a college student right after the war, he was amazed at the Herculean effort required to raise $30,000 for a mission of peace. Led by Earl W. Eames, Jr. and Lloyd Haynes, a group of MIT students, of which Eberly was one, sought to bring 80 graduate students from the war-torn countries of Europe for a summer of study and fellowship at MIT. The effort finally succeeded, but the experience left an indelible impression.

Eberly's personal impetus came from being called up in the draft shortly after the outbreak of the Korean War. He believed he could better serve his country in a peaceful role rather than in a military one, but ruled out the Conscientious Objector route since he was prepared to use force to protect someone who was endangered. As it turned out, testing the national service idea made two years of military service more livable for Eberly. He decided to treat it as an experiment. If he survived, he would seek a job in Africa and assess which experience was of greater value to the United States.

He did, and concluded that his African teaching experience was not only of greater value to the United States than his military service, but also of value to several hundred Nigerian students at Molusi College, Ijebu-Igbo, and to himself.

The editors' view is that national service should be voluntary and that the need for national service transcends military recruitment policies, but these and other issues are more complex than they may seem on the surface. In this book, such issues are addressed head on. Diverse perspectives are weighed against one another. Most of the authors are generally in favor of national service, but individual views vary substantially. In all cases, the views presented are those of individual authors and do not necessarily represent the positions of any private firm, organization, university, or government agency through which authors earn their livelihoods or are otherwise affiliated.

We would like to acknowledge the support of The George Warren Brown School of Social Work, Washington University, St. Louis, and the National Service Secretariat, Washington, D.C., in facilitating the writing of this book. Special thanks to Keith Morton for his excellent typing of the manuscript and Louise Eberly for her assistance at several points along the way.

In general, the book presents a framework for considering national service. It begins in Chapter 1 with a rationale for national service, describing several national needs which might be addressed simultaneously by a national service program. In Chapters 2 and 3, the book offers an historical framework for national service, including both theoretical views and experimental programs. Comparative examples of national service are presented in Chapters 4 and 5, with descriptions of youth service programs in Africa, Asia, and Europe. Chapters 6, 7, and 8 describe several different frameworks for national service itself, with an attempt by the editors in Chapter 6 to provide the reader with a set of dimensions that may by used in judging national service proposals in relation to the reader's own value system. Chapter 7 is a proposal by the editors, and Chapter 8 offers alternative models for the administration of a national service program. Chapters 9 through 11 address potential impacts of national service on youth employment, education, and the military, respectively. Because of the constitutional mandate to provide for the common defense, the military impact is a special case. Should national service prove to have other than a positive or neutral impact on the nation's defense capability, it may be assumed that national service would be altered to correct the situation. Chapter 12 addresses the economic value of service projects and Chapter 13 examines national service impacts on participants. In Chapter 14, the voices of young people themselves are heard. The final chapter attempts to weave together many points from the rest of the book into a future scenario for national service.

As we write this preface just before the book goes to press, newspaper headlines remind us of the variety of persons and interests perceiving national service as a good idea. On July 5, 1981, the Gallup Poll reported that public support for compulsory national service for men had risen from a ratio of 60:33 in 1979 to 71:24 in 1981, with the greatest growth in support for compulsory national service coming from persons 18 to 24 years of age. At the same time, the Gallup Poll reported that a majority, by a ratio of 54:40, supported compulsory national service for women.

On August 17, 1981, the Attorney General's Task Force on Violent Crime, co-chaired by former Attorney General Griffin Bell and Illinois Governor James R. Thompson, suggested "that some form of national public service might be appropriate as a means to provide a portion of the structure now lacking in many young people's lives and thereby reduce the likelihood of their involvement in criminal activity." This recommendation was particularly noteworthy because the Task Force deliberately went outside its mandate by concerning itself with the root causes of crime.

On August 19, 1981, *The Wall Street Journal* reported that Senator Sam Nunn (D., Ga.) planned to submit legislation that would "introduce for the first time a legally mandatory period of national service for all young Americans." Approximately 100,000 18-year old men would be conscripted into military service while the remainder of the age group, upwards of four million persons, would be required to perform unpaid charitable or civil defense work for one or two weeks per year.

In a speech at Washington University, reported in the September 6, 1981, *St. Louis Post-Dispatch*, Senator Bill Bradley (D., N.J.) suggested that all young people ought to spend a year in some capacity, but not necessarily the military, in service to the country. Students interrupted Bradley's speech to applaud this proposal.

On September 16, 1981, Brown University announced the creation of a National Service Scholarship Program funded by a one million dollar grant from the C.V. Starr Foundation. Eligibility for scholarship aid will be open to students who have completed a year or more of full-time work at no pay or subsistence level pay in public or private agencies that provide service to the elderly, disabled, ill, or other disadvantaged people; or similar work for agencies involved with conservation of national resources; or voluntary military service.

However, at a time of increasing public sentiment and leadership calls for some form of national service, opportunities for voluntary public service by young people appear to be drying up. On September 16, 1981, the Federal Office of Personnel Management announced that it was scrapping its intern program that placed over 1,000 college students in professional government jobs each summer. We have also been told to expect the demise of the Young Adult Conservation Corps in 1982 and VISTA in 1983. The Youth Conservation Corps, a summer program, is to be cut back as well. These cuts in service opportunities run counter to public opinion which supports increased service commitments among young people.

In the context of this book, national service is presented as a program for young people, but there is no reason why national service could not be adapted to older adults as well. As the population of the United States ages, and especially as the baby boom population bulge enters retirement age in the next century, there will be a tremendous need for older adults to contribute to society in every conceivable way to help compensate for the great expense in supporting this older population. A flexible and diversified national service program would be an ideal way to meet this challenge.

It is too soon to know whether public opinion will be transformed into a national service program in the 1980s, or what form such a program would take. There is, however, reason to believe that national service will be seriously considered and debated in the years ahead. This book is written to stimulate, facilitate, and inform that debate.

M.S. and D.E.

NATIONAL SERVICE

Part I:
Perspectives on National Service

Chapter 1

Why National Service?

Michael W. Sherraden and Donald J. Eberly

National service can be defined in many ways. As a general term, it refers to a period of service given by the individual to the nation or community. National service embodies two complementary ideas: one, that some service to the larger society is part of individual citizenship responsibility; and two, that society should be structured in ways which provide citizens with opportunities to make meaningful contributions. The idea of national service has been around a long time and, over the years, many thoughtful and prominent people have called for a national service program. Some national service experiments have taken place in the United States—the Civilian Conservation Corps (CCC) of the New Deal is the most prominent example—but to date the United States has never undertaken a permanent and large scale national service effort. Even the CCC, although it lasted nine years from 1933 to 1942, was always viewed by the Congress and the American people as a temporary program.[1]

National service has had different meanings at different times. During World War II, national service was the name of a plan, never put into effect, by which the U.S. government would have mobilized the civilian work force, assigning workers to those jobs which contributed the most to the war effort. At the same time, national service in Great Britain was synonymous with military service. In 1962, national service was the name that President Kennedy gave to a small program in the planning stage that emerged in 1964 as Volunteers in Service to America (VISTA), part of President Johnson's plan for a war on poverty.

Since the mid-1960s, national service in the United States has come to mean a program in which a large number of young people would participate in a wide range of service activities, including such areas as conservation, health, education, energy, and public works. Some also include military service under the national service umbrella. While recognizing military service as a part of national service in the largest sense, and while devoting a chapter to the impact of a national service program on the armed forces, our emphasis is clearly on the nonmilitary aspects of national service. We can foresee a time in the all too distant future when there may be no need for military service; we cannot, on the other hand, foresee the time when there would no longer be a need for health and education and conservation work, nor when the involvement of young people in meeting such needs would not contribute significantly to their growth as persons and as citizens.

It is this long-range perspective that leads us to suggest national service for the 1980s and beyond. We believe that postindustrial America is becoming a society in which many young people no longer have opportunities to shape and build a future for themselves or to contribute to the world around them. To an ever increasing extent, young people are not needed in the labor force of the market economy. Ironically, the talent and energy of young people are very much needed outside the market economy to provide care for the very old, the very young, and the disabled; and to contribute to the conservation of energy and other natural resources. Schools have served as holding tanks to keep young people off the job market; but schooling, although it has been extended remarkably over the years in duration, scope, and extent of the population attending school, has not absorbed all of the labor force slack. The military is the other major alternative; but the military, because of the very poor incentives it offers and its negative image in the post-Vietnam era, is attractive primarily to those who have no other choice. In the United States, the military operates on what Roger Landrum has called "conscription by unemployment."[2] It is not an exaggeration to say that the military is the biggest public employment program for disadvantaged young people.

Altogether, the society does not provide responsible and respectable opportunities for a great number of teenagers and young adults. The message to young people is that they are not needed by society; they are extraneous, perhaps even a burden. As a result, youth populations are culturally, socially, and economically drifting apart from adult society.[3]

SIGNS OF A PROBLEM

What are the symptoms of increasingly disengaged youth populations? The negative signs are grindingly familiar. They include high unemployment rates; high rates of alcoholism and drug use; large numbers of school dropouts, truants, and functional illiterates; rising homicide, rape, robbery, and other crime statistics; and, perhaps most telling of all, record numbers of suicides among young people. As we pause to look more closely at some of these problems, it is apparent that something is happening to America's young people, and it is not encouraging.

Unemployment

For several years, youth unemployment has been in the forefront of public discussion. The unemployment rate for 16 to 24 year olds has been about double the overall unemployment rate throughout the decade of the 1970s.[4] The unemployment rate for teenagers 16 to 19 years of age has always been higher. During 1980, the teenage unemployment rate held steady at around 19 percent, and the overall unemployment rate at about 7.5 percent. Nonwhite teenagers experienced much higher unemployment rates, then around 35 percent. In the cities, it was not uncommon to find nonwhite teenage unemployment rates as high as 50 or 60 percent.

There are a variety of contributing factors to the high unemployment rates among young people. Most significant over the long term have been (1) the baby boom population bulge of 1946 to 1965 which in 1980 covered the age range of 15 to 34, (2) increasing entry of older females into the labor force, and (3) a relative decline in demand for unskilled and low skilled labor, especially agricultural labor.

Some analysts point to the population bulge and predict that the high rate of youth unemployment is a passing phenomenon. For example, Richard Freeman suggests that there may be a shortage of youth available for employment in the future. According to Freeman, "the problems of teenage and youth unemployment, which have been especially severe for blacks, ought to diminish, though to what extent is not clear."[5] This forecast, hesitant as it is, may be optimistic. It is quite possible that other trends will overshadow in significance the change in youth population. To be specific, there is reason to believe that adult women will continue to enter the labor market in record numbers, competing for available jobs. And because many adult women are burdened with lack of training and work experience, they compete directly with young people for low skill jobs, primarily in the service sector of the economy. Moreover, we cannot be very optimistic that the number of low skill jobs will increase. While it is true that many service sector industries have been expanding, and some service sector jobs are low skill positions open to young people, there is reason to doubt whether the expansion will continue at a rapid rate.[6] Already, 69 percent of paid workers in the United States produce services, while only 31 percent produce goods.[7] If the United States is entering a period of rebuilding its economy, investment, and hence jobs, will flow toward production. And if the United States fails to address economic difficulties and continues in a prolonged period of sluggishness, then demand for labor in general will be slack; and young workers, always among the more marginal, will continue to bear a heavy load of unemployment.

Why is unemployment among young people a problem? In 1961, James Conant wrote a report entitled *Social Dynamite*, which identified an explosive, unemployed, and out-of-school urban youth population.[8] Since the writing of Conant's report there have indeed been explosions in our central cities and there are continuing fears that riots will break out again. The federal government has attempted to respond to this situation; most youth employment programs initiated during the 1960s and 1970s have been rooted in this fear of explosion in our cities. In one sense, therefore, Conant's prediction has been angrily substantiated. In the 1960s, cities were torn by riots; but the "explosion" itself has been only a small part of a much, much greater destruction. U.S. cities are burning constantly from within, like underground coal fires which burn for decades. Only rarely is an explosion heard at the surface. Unemployment is like oxygen for these subterranean fires. Unemployment eats away at whatever sense of community once existed. Business declines. Crime increases. Anyone who can possibly afford to leave does so. Buildings are abandoned. Local businesses and governments throttle services—financial services, garbage services, retail stores. Everything declines. Because any kind of business is perceived as a hazardous undertaking, consumer prices are higher than in the wealthy suburbs. Residents become poorer than ever and the process continues. This is the vortex of poverty, and it is very much connected with unemployment.

As part of the Vice President's Task Force on Youth Employment, which functioned during the final years of the Carter administration, M. Harvey Brenner conducted a study estimating the social costs of youth unemployment.[9] Brenner found substantial evidence linking youth unemployment with a wide range of social problems. When youth are unemployed in unusually high numbers relative to the number of unemployed adults, social pathologies among youth also increase. Among those increased pathologies are homicides; motor vehicle mortality; residence in a mental hospital; and arrest rates for assault, criminal homicide, auto theft, robbery, forcible rape, prostitution, and narcotics. Brenner's study confirms that youth unemployment is not a harmless phenomenon. The nation pays a high price when young people are seeking work and cannot find it.

Crime, Violence, and Vandalism

The frequency of most crime has increased in the United States, and much of the crime, including violent crime, is committed by young people. "According to the Federal Bureau of Investigation, young people under the age of 21 account for 59 percent of all arrests for serious crimes."[10] Table 1.1 presents some data on percent change in arrest trends for a ten year period from 1969 to 1978.

During the 1970s, the United States witnessed dramatic increases in arrests for violent crime and major property crime. In general, these increases tended to run across the entire population. As with most other types of crime, arrests of females increased significantly more than arrests of males. (Regarding the differences in arrest trends between males and females, the reader should bear in mind that the total number of arrests is much higher for males in virtually every category of crime.) The percent changes in violent

Table 1.1. Selected Total Arrest Trends, Percent Change 1969 to 1978

Offense Charged	Males		Females	
	Total	Under 18	Total	Under 18
Murder and Nonnegligent Manslaughter	+15.6	+13.6	+8.9	+14.1
Forcible Rape	+35.6	+12.2	—	—
Robbery	+32.6	+33.3	+62.4	+48.7
Aggravated Assault	+48.1	+57.9	+58.0	+106.5
Total Violent Crime	+40.0	+40.6	+55.5	+82.6
Burglary	+31.7	+29.0	+92.1	+90.6
Larceny–Theft	+47.1	+23.3	+95.2	+58.6
Motor Vehicle Theft	−18.9	−27.3	+38.1	+41.0
Total Major Property Crime	+31.5	+16.6	+92.6	+60.2
Forgery and Counterfeiting	+20.6	+49.1	+85.7	+121.3
Fraud	+63.5	+44.3	+218.7	+148.4
Embezzlement	−20.6	+231.3	+4.5	+154.4
Stolen Property; Buying, Receiving, Possessing	+87.2	+95.4	+157.8	+148.5
Total Nonviolent Income-Related Crime	+56.2	+86.6	+164.0	+139.1

Source: U.S. Department of Justice, *FBI Uniform Crime Reports for the United States, 1978* (Washington: U.S. Government Printing Office, 1978) p. 189.

crime and major property crime, although very large, are not surprising to many observers. With crime growing so fast, a large number of American households have had first hand experience with some form of violent crime or major property crime.

Perhaps more surprising are the high increases in arrests for nonviolent income-related crime—forgery, counterfeiting, fraud, embezzlement, and handling stolen property. Again, these increases tended to run across the entire population; and, again, the growth in arrest rates for females was outpacing the growth in arrest rates for males. During this ten year period, there was a more than 50 percent increase in nonviolent income-related arrests among males, and about a 150 percent increase among females. These data indicate that many more people, including young people, are engaging in purposeful illicit income-producing activities. They are disengaged from the legitimate economy and are making a living outside the law. The economic costs of all crime, but particularly these types of crime, are very great. The high increase in arrests for income-producing crimes is a danger signal. This is not a group of weirdos engaging in senseless violence. Instead, it is by and large a group of intelligent and rational people who have systematically planned, prepared, and carried out schemes to make a clever living off of other people's effort. The remarkable growth in the number of such people, as indicated by arrest increases, is as great a threat to the social fabric as the increases in violent and major property crimes.

Also increasing among young people are vandalism and physical violence. George Gallup recently assessed these trends: "Vandalism is an enormous problem in our schools, and so is physical abuse. One child or teenager in five says he or she is fearful of physical abuse in school. That's an incredible finding. It would suggest that children are better off on the streets than they are in schools!"[11] Mr. Gallup is quite correct that many children are better off on the streets than they are in school. We have talked with quite a few high school students who avoid going to the bathroom all day because it is not safe to go into the bathrooms at school. Senseless destruction of property is also widespread in schools: "School vandalism alone is estimated by the Senate Subcommittee to Investigate Delinquency to cost $500 million a year, an average yearly cost of $60,000 per school district."[12]

An Educational Imbalance

Schools have been blamed for a problem—the imbalance between passive and experiential education—that is really not the schools' fault but is primarily due to a series of societal changes during the twentieth century. Schools have always emphasized formal learning. In the early days of formal education, books, blackboards, and recitation served to balance the largely experiential nature of the students' lives. Then, beginning early in the twentieth century, a series of laws, technological advances, and economic changes effectively removed many opportunities for experiential education from the lives of young people. Child labor laws were enacted. Schooling became compulsory to age 16 or 17. Automation arrived in the kitchen and on the farm. Traditional youth jobs disappeared. As a result of these changes, young people were much less in demand by business and industry, by farmers, and by parents. Young people moved from active participation in the factory, the farm, and the home to a more passive position. They literally took their seats in the classroom, in the automobile, and in front of the television set.

Alienation and Political Apathy

Possibly related to the passiveness described above, there is substantial evidence that more and more young people are becoming disengaged politically and culturally. Low rates of participation in the electoral process by youth is one indicator. In general, there has been a decline in the percentage of young people ages 18 to 24 voting in presidential elections since 1968. Table 1.2 presents these data. The decline has occurred among all races, with the exception of blacks in 1980. In 1976, when asked why they did not vote, 30 percent of the youth surveyed reported that lack of interest was a major reason for not voting.[13]

Table 1.2.   Reported Percent Voting in National Elections of 18 to 24 Year Olds, by Race

Race	Civilian Noninstitutional Population			
	1968	1972	1976	1980
White	52.2	51.9	44.7	41.8
Black	38.1	34.7	27.9	30.1
Spanish Origin	NA	38.9	21.8	15.9
All Races	50.4	49.6	42.2	39.9

Source: U.S. Bureau of the Census; adapted in part from Committee for the Study of National Service, *Youth and the Needs of the Nation* (Washington: Potomac Institute, 1979), p. 79; the 1980 figures are from *Current Population Survey* (November 1980).

Young people are also demonstrating, as a group, limited commitment to the activities and responsibilities they assume:

High rates of failure to complete activities is an additonal factor to note. Over a third of young people who enlist in the armed forces are discharged before the first term of enlistment is completed. Dropout rates in the Job Corps are over 50 percent. Dropout rates in the Peace Corps have gone from the lowest of any overseas assistance program in the early 1960s to almost a third of enrollees. Just how to interpret these rates of leaving activities before completion is uncertain, much like the confusion surrounding the causes of widespread illiteracy levels among high school students. A certain amount of "threshing around" and an unwillingness to make and keep commitments characterizes the identity-searching of youth, but why have dropout rates accelerated in almost all the formal activities for youth during recent years?[14]

Another sign of alienation is the high number of young people, largely middle class, who have joined charismatic communal religious organizations or, as they are commonly called, cults. Dr. John Clark, a psychiatrist on the faculty of Harvard Medical School, has studied cult membership. He is quoted in an article in the *Wall Street Journal*:

"About half the kids who join cults are what we call 'seekers', people with troubled histories who are looking for causes that might give structure to their lives, but the other half has no such background," he says. "They are trusting kids whose minds have been opened by their parents to the play of ideas. The cults take advantage of their naivete and openness to hook them. They can't do that nearly as easily with streetwise kids who know a con when they see one."

Dr. Clark estimates that cult membership in the U.S. has climbed to more than three million. It is a development that he calls "frightening." He warns that "the mind-changing process involved in cult conversions can seriously alter a person's mental and physical makeup with long-term implications we're only beginning to learn."[15]

Regarding the link between alienation and cult membership, we can turn to evidence from an extensive analysis of one of the larger Jesus movement organizations:

> These young people who collectively were not particularly politically–oriented (in terms of activity) before joining became even less so after joining. Most had not been very involved in politics in their society, or in vigorous attempts to challenge or change the system before joining. . . . Eighty-six percent were totally unconcerned with politics, only 17 percent indicated any political identification, and most of these identified as either moderate or conservative. None were then active in any political organizations or activities.[16]

Alcohol and Drug Use

Alcohol and drug use among young people is at high levels. The latest evidence from the Institute for Social Research at the University of Michigan indicates that drug use may be leveling off after rising for many years, but this news should not be interpreted to mean that drug use is not prevalent. "American young people use more drugs than the young people of any other industrialized nation. During the 1970s, drug use among high school students increased steadily. By 1980 nearly two-thirds of American high school seniors reported that they had used an illicit drug at some time."[17] Drugs are commonly available in almost all high schools and junior high schools, and in many grade schools; and alcohol use is at record levels.

> We're fully as much a drug culture today as we were in the 1960s. We just did a survey on college campuses, and the use of drugs—barbiturates, amphetamines, and hallucinogens as well as marijuana—are as high as they were back in the late 60s. We find the use of marijuana is up tremendously. Alcohol is a tremendous problem. The top problem in the minds of young people today, in terms of the biggest problems they feel are facing their generation, are problems related to alcohol. One in six deaths among young people today is alcohol-related.[18]

Crime statistics related to alcohol and drug use also indicate that these problems have grown more serious during the 1970s. Table 1.3 demonstrates that arrests for drug abuse violations doubled for males and also increased significantly for females between 1969 and 1978. Certainly these data do not indicate a decline in drug use—especially in light of a growing acceptance of drugs in most communities. For example, it is now uncommon for police almost anywhere to arrest someone for possession of a small amount of marijuana, whereas in the past a person could easily be arrested and sent to prison for having so much as one marijuana cigarette in his or her pocket. The fact that drug related arrests increased in spite of the growing accep-

Table 1.3. Arrest Trends for Drug Abuse Violations and Driving Under the Influence, Percent Change 1969 to 1978

	Males		Females	
Offense Charge	Total	Under 18	Total	Under 18
Drug Abuse Violations	+104.5	+105.8	+76.1	+46.5
Driving Under the Influence	+80.0	+265.4	+154.8	+842.8

Source: U.S. Department of Justice, *FBI Uniform Crime Reports for the United States, 1978* (Washington: U.S. Government Printing Office, 1978), p. 189.

tance of drug use is a sign that drug use was definitely not declining during the 1970s.

More striking than drug abuse violations is the dramatic increase in arrests for driving under the influence of alcohol, especially in the under 18 age group. Such arrests for this group increased 265 percent for males and 842 percent for females in this ten year period. This is an alarming trend by any standard. And it is becoming increasingly clear that alcohol and drug problems, including hard drug use, are phenomena which cut across all social classes.

> Most past studies showed that teenagers from poor or blue-collar families were more likely to drink or smoke marijuana than those of the middle class, and that use of more potent drugs was largely confined to lower–income groups. But recent studies indicate that better-off kids are catching up.
>
> Last year, for instance, the University of Michigan Survey Research Center's annual national poll of high-school seniors showed that drinking among seniors who were college-bound, a rough measure of middle-class status, stood at 88%, almost the same as the figure for seniors who didn't plan to attend college. Rates of increase for marijuana use were about the same for both groups, but the use of cocaine rose among the college-bound while leveling off for the others.[19]

Vagrancy

The increased use of alcohol and drugs and large numbers of teenage runaways have led to great numbers of young people who are on the social and economic fringe of society. Vagrant and transient, many teenagers live by handout, petty crime, or prostitution; many have had their psyches scarred by chemicals and their bodies aged prematurely by the hardships of street life. The widespread effort to "deinstitutionalize," i.e., place mental patients in community settings rather than in large institutions, has contributed to this phenomenon because patients are often dumped out of institutions without appropriate planning or funding for their care in the community. They end up on the streets. "More and More Young Men Ending Up on Skid

Row," reads one headline; the story documents that the average age of home-less alcoholics has fallen.[20] Today, many young men in their twenties have joined older vagrants on skid row. This situation is in some ways reminiscent of the "youthful tramps" of the 1930s, which was the term then applied to the large number of unemployed young people who took to the rails, high-ways, and hobo camps during the Depression. Because of the prevalence of alcohol and drug use, however, today's youthful tramps are probably more debilitated than their Depression-era counterparts.

Suicide

Suicide is now the third most common cause of death among young people ages 15 through 24. Accidents and homicide are number one and number two, respectively. Among white males in this age group, suicide is the second leading cause of death, exceeding homicides. The suicide rate among young people has at least doubled since 1960. Without doubt, these suicide statistics are the bleakest of all possible comments on the place of young people in our society.

THE UNEQUAL BURDEN ON NONWHITE YOUNG PEOPLE

Many of the problem areas described above have a greater impact on non-white young people than on white young people. Two of the most striking areas are unemployment and crime.

The unemployment rate for young nonwhites is much higher than for young whites. This holds true in suburbs and nonmetropolitan areas as well as central cities, and for nonpoverty areas as well as poverty areas. Moreover, the long-term trend is toward increasing disparity. As the labor market has become less hospitable to young workers in general, nonwhites have been squeezed out of employment at a much higher rate than whites. Table 1.4 illustrates the trend from 1954 to 1979. In 1954, the nonwhite unemployment rate for 16 to 19 year olds was 136 percent of the white unemployment rate. By 1979, the nonwhite unemployment rate for this age group had reached 241 percent of the white unemployment rate, nearly two and one half times greater.

For those who may be inclined toward a victim-blaming analysis of these unemployment statistics—that is, that nonwhites lack motivation, are inher-ently less intelligent, do not dress or talk appropriately, or any of a thousand other variations on this theme—it might be illuminating to look at some inequalities in the way black and white children grow up in America. Marian Wright Edelman and Paul V. Smith of the Children's Defense Fund have

Table 1.4. Unemployment Rates for White and Nonwhite 16 to 19 Year Olds, Selected Years

Year	White	Nonwhite	Nonwhite as a Percent of White
1954	12.1	16.5	136
1959	13.1	26.1	199
1964	14.8	27.2	184
1969	10.7	24.0	224
1974	14.0	32.9	235
1979	13.9	33.5	241

Source: *Employment and Training Report of the President, 1980* (Washington: U.S. Government Printing Office, 1980), p. 230.

published a book entitled *Portrait of Inequality: Black and White Children in America*, which clearly and succinctly details differences in the social and economic conditions faced by blacks and whites when they are children.[21] There is not sufficient space here to report all of the relevant data, but a few examples may begin to describe the problem: Less than half of all black children live in a two parent household, while more than four-fifths of all white children live with two parents. The per capita family income for blacks is 55 percent that of whites. One in four black chidren has no parent in the labor force, while the ratio is one in sixteen for white children. Almost half of all black families are headed by a person who has not graduated from high school, while only one quarter of all white families are headed by non-high school graduates. The infant death rate for nonwhites is twice as high as for whites. Teenage childbearing rates are much higher for blacks than for whites, and larger percentages of blacks have out-of-wedlock births. As a percentage of population, more black children are not immunized against major preventable diseases. More black children have nutritional intake below established standards. More than twice as many black children as white children live in inadequate housing. Twice as many black children as white children live in some kind of institution.

This is a portrait of racism. With disadvantages so deep and passed along from generation to generation, it is not surprising that nonwhite young people have not competed successfully in the labor market. Nonwhites contend not only with outright discrimination, but also with backgrounds of poverty, inadequate housing, poor health care, inadequate schools, and all of the other negative effects of accumulated and institutionalized bigotry. These effects will not easily disappear, especially in the political and economic climate ushered in by the 1980 elections. Nonwhites will face the same disadvantages as in the past and quite possibly worse. Moreover, the percentage of nonwhite young people is projected to increase. In 1980, 15.8 percent of all 18 year olds were nonwhite; in 1990, 19.1 percent of all 18 year olds will be nonwhite.[22] As the percentage of nonwhite young people increases, we may also project increasing percentages of disadvantaged young people facing a discriminatory labor market.

Crime is another area in which nonwhite young people bear a disproportionate burden, as both criminals and victims. With such severely restricted employment opportunities, anger and economic necessity are evidenced in crime statistics at very young ages. Table 1.5 presents arrest rates by race for persons 11 to 17 years of age for violent and major property crime.

It is startling that youths under 17 years of age already exhibit marked differences in arrests for serious crime by race. Part of the difference in statistics is probably due to preferential treatment of whites by police, i.e., whites are probably reprimanded and released to parents without criminal charges more frequently than blacks. But greater leniency for whites does not explain all the difference. Many nonwhites react at young ages, through crime, to the dismal future which lies ahead of them. The message is burned into the brains of black babies that society doesn't have a place for them.

The violence which results also disproportionately affects black children and teenagers as crime victims, especially in the number of homicides. Table 1.6 documents that nonwhite persons under the age of 20 are approximately five times as likely to be murdered as whites of the same age.

Table 1.5.   Arrest Rates for 11 to 17 Year Olds by Type of Offense and Race, 1975

Type of Offense	Arrests per 1,000	
	White	Black
Murder, Nonnegligent Manslaughter	0.02	0.20
Negligent Manslaughter	0.01	0.01
Forcible Rape	0.07	0.44
Robbery	0.52	5.63
Aggravated Assault	0.74	3.12
Total Violent Offenses	1.36	9.40
Burglary	6.55	14.40
Larceny–Theft	11.94	28.28
Motor Vehicle Theft	1.87	3.37
Total Major Property Crime	20.36	46.05

Source: U.S. Department of Justice, *Sourcebook of Criminal Statistics, 1977* (Washington: U.S. Government Printing Office, 1978), Table 4.7; U.S. Bureau of the Census, *Current Population Reports*, Series P-25, No. 721, "Estimates of the Population of the United States by Age, Sex, and Race: 1970 to 1977 (Washington: U.S. Government Printing Office, April 1978), Table 2; calculations by the Children's Defense Fund; adapted from Marian Wright Edelman and Paul V. Smith, *Portrait of Inequality* (Washington: Children's Defense Fund, 1980), Table 58.

Table 1.6. Death Rates from Homicide by Race and Sex for 1 through 19 Year
Olds, 1975

	Rate per 100,000	
Sex	White	Nonwhite
Male	8.2	47.8
Female	3.2	14.6

Source: U.S. Department of Health, Education and Welfare, *Health, United States, 1976-1977*
(Washington: U.S. Government Printing Office, 1977), Tables 26, 27, and 28; calculations by
Children's Defense Fund; adapted from Marian Wright Edelman and Paul V. Smith, *Portrait
of Inequality* (Washington: Children's Defense Fund, 1980), Table 57.

National service would by no means eliminate the accumulated effects of
racism, but it would provide one additional setting in which nonwhites could
stand on equal footing with whites. It is a step in the right direction.

WORK THAT NEEDS TO BE DONE

In the early 1900s, William James envisioned sending young men "to coal
and iron mines, to freight trains, to fishing fleets in December, to dishwash-
ing, clothes washing, and window washing, to road building and tunnel making, to foundries and stoke-holes, and to the frames of skyscrapers. . . ."[23]
James assumed that there was plenty of work that needed to be done. But
in careful consideration of national service, the question must be more
thoroughly examined. What work needs to be done? National service cannot
realize its potential unless participants engage in work that both participants
and the public perceive to be needed.

Various surveys in the past two decades have pointed to a need for some 4
million unskilled or semiskilled people in public service work. The most
recent survey, completed by the Urban Institute and American Institutes for
Research in 1978, identified 233 areas of activity and then reported on the
need for workers in 115 of these areas. Claiming that the estimates are
conservative, the survey found a need for 3 million work years in these 115
areas.[24] Eberly has analyzed this report according to skill levels and concluded that two thirds of the jobs could be done by young people in national
service. From this and other studies, Eberly has formulated a likely distribution of persons in national service, by type of work and by level of education.
This distribution is presented in table 1.7 which assumes a national service
enrollment of 1 million at the end of the third year.

Table 1.7 is a conservative estimate of useful work that could be done by
young people in national service. To take one category, parks and recreation,
as an example, the backlog of maintenance alone in U.S. National Parks has

Table 1.7. Anticipated Distribution of Persons in Types of Civilian National Service by Educational Backgrounds, End of Third Year

	High School Dropouts	High School Graduates	College Graduates
Conservation, Energy, Environment	110,000	90,000	30,000
Day Care	10,000	25,000	15,000
Education	20,000	70,000	90,000
Health and Mental Health	15,000	25,000	60,000
Housing	20,000	20,000	10,000
Libraries, Museums, Arts	10,000	15,000	25,000
Service to Children, Youth, Elderly, Disabled, Probationers, Prisoners	45,000	70,000	75,000
Parks and Recreation	15,000	15,000	10,000
Protection (Fire, Police, Highway Safety)	15,000	20,000	15,000
Public Works	20,000	20,000	20,000
Total	280,000	370,000	350,000

Source: Analysis by Donald Eberly, based on data from The Urban Institute, *Assessing the Feasibility of Large-Scale Countercyclical Public Job-Creation*, three volumes (Washington: The Urban Institute, 1978).

been estimated at $1.6 billion.[25] Because much of this work is labor intensive, this figure translates into at least 125,000 national service work years. Other federal recreation areas, such as U.S. Forest Service lands, and many State Parks are in equally desperate need of maintenance work. Moreover, we know from prior experience with the Civilian Conservation Corps of the 1930s and programs such as the Youth Conservation Corps and Young Adult Conservation Corps that young people can do this work very effectively.

Another area with nearly limitless potential is energy conservation. The high cost of energy is choking the American economy and there is tremendous potential for easing this burden through conservation. Sam Brown, while Director of ACTION, pointed out that energy-related national service projects would strengthen the nation and broaden the meaning of citizenship as well:

A program of national service that would enlist young people in the national effort, for instance, to conserve energy, is in my view as important to protecting our national interest as any effort now being made to improve the combat readiness of our military forces.

Clearly, one way to avoid confrontation in the Persian Gulf is to find alternatives to reliance on Middle Eastern oil. My own very strong view is that if we look only in that narrow context, young people whose inclination is to work in conservation efforts, whose interests lie there, whose skills could be applied to helping the country conserve the now estimated 40 percent of the energy that we

currently consume, would help as much in our national concern about reliance on the Middle East as any military preparedness ever could.

What seems to me to be important about a serious study of national service is the possibility that it can help us develop a new concept of citizenship which in turn can give a new depth of meaning to patriotism.

We have limited too severely the ways in which Americans can express affection for their country. In doing so, we have made shallow the meaning of patriotism, narrowed the scale by which we measure love of country, and restricted how that affection can be expressed.[26]

Service is sometimes viewed in terms of concrete products—trees planted, bridges repaired, railroad beds rebuilt, houses insulated—and sometimes in terms of human service. In recent years, the human service emphasis has been prominent. For example, Adam Yarmolinsky has suggested that "the greatest unmet needs in the United States today are for human services delivered by relatively untrained but caring people at the local community level."[27]

> Yarmolinsky points out that the human services professions (doctors, nurses, teachers, lawyers, social workers) are not in short supply, although some are not well distributed geographically. But "people like home health care aides and classroom aides and playground counselors and helpers in community centers" are lacking. Services once provided by neighbors and friends when communities were more cohesive and stable are missing, and various new services are required by new social conditions.[28]

In 1970, Eberly conducted a study for the Russell Sage Foundation which identified a need for 4 million nonprofessional service years,[29] a figure consistent with studies in other years.[30]

Given the continuation of the 1981 climate of reduced federal expenditures for social services and the move toward block grants to replace specific programs, the need for social services at the local level will be even greater. Block grants will inevitably lead to service gaps in many communities. With specific services no longer mandated by federal direction, some states will drop or severely curtail essential services. A national service tailored to local community needs is one way to fill some of these gaps.

Another service area with great potential is emergency and catastrophe relief services. The experience of the Civilian Conservation Corps (1933-1942) offers an excellent lesson:

> CCC camps tended to engage in emergency projects as needed, ranging from fire fighting to winter storm rescue to flood clean-up efforts. According to CCC records, over two million man-days were devoted to emergency work other than fighting forest fires. Forest fire fighting accounted for an additional six million man-days.[31]

The CCC was always ready in time of need to lend the aid of both men and equipment whether the emergency took the form of a lost hunter or child, flood, hurricane or fire. It was the emergency service as well as work on projects large and small, which played an important part in gaining approval for the enrollees by the people of the state and nation.[32]

Emergency and catastrophe relief is an ideal area for national service for at least three reasons: (1) the services could be very valuable in reducing both economic loss and human suffering; (2) the work offers an immediate sense of purpose and is tremendously gratifying to participants; and (3) there is no better way to get favorable coverage in the press and public appreciation of the program.

YOUNG PEOPLE ARE READY TO SERVE

We began this chapter with some rather dismal statistics about youth in America. We would like to conclude by looking at the other side of the coin, which is that young people, when given the chance to contribute, have almost always responded positively. And there is reason to believe that many teens and young adults are hungry to hear the message that society has a place for them to serve others. We close this chapter with some observations by George Gallup, Jr.:

There is certainly much to be said on the positive side about young people. Through the Gallup Youth Surveys we're able to measure the dimensions of these various good points about youth. One of the most striking points about youth is that they are more tolerant of persons of different races and backgrounds and religions. The differences between teenagers and older persons are very dramatic.

Secondly, they appear to be extremely candid and realistic about themselves. . . .

Three, there's a strong desire to serve others. I think the youth population has been misnamed the self-centered generation. Many of them want to go into the so-called helping professions: medicine, teaching, and so on. We found among 18-29 year olds in a study in Dayton, Ohio—which is a barometer county—that fully one-third of persons there said they would like to go into the social services as a life's career. I think that's an incredible finding.

Four, young people are extremely religious. They are more spiritually inclined if you will, than are their elders. The only thing they don't do is go to church as regularly, but in terms of levels of belief and religious practice, in terms of prayer, they tend to be a very religious sector of the population. That's sometimes overlooked. Certainly one of the roles of leaders, particularly religious leaders, is to join the will to believe among young people with their desire to serve others.

Five, young people are surprisingly traditional. There's very little difference between teenagers and older persons in terms of favoring stronger family ties, in terms of the importance of attitudes of hard work, and in terms of the importance of authority in society. I was quite surprised by those findings. . . .

Our teenage population is clearly frustrated. They want to be a part of society. They do not want a free ride. The problem we face in America today is not a lack of willingness to serve or to help others, but to find the appropriate outlet for this zeal to help others.[33]

NOTES

1. John A. Salmond, *The Civilian Conservation Corps, 1933-1942: A New Deal Case Study* (Durham, North Carolina: Duke University Press, 1967).

2. Roger Landrum, "Serving America: Alternatives to the Draft," *USA Today* (January 1981).

3. James Coleman, *Adolescent Society* (New York: Free Press, 1961).

4. *Employment and Training Report of the President, 1980* (Washington: U.S. Government Printing Office, 1980), p. 228.

5. Richard Freeman, "The Work Force of the Future: An Overview," in *Work in America: The Decade Ahead* edited by Clark Kerr and Jerome Rosow (New York: D. Van Nostrand, 1979), pp. 28-79.

6. For an excellent discussion of the service sector see Emma Rothschild, "Reagan and the Real America," *New York Review* 28, no. 1 (February 5, 1981): 12-18.

7. U.S. Department of Labor, *Employment and Earnings* (Washington: U.S. Government Printing Office, June 1980), cited by John McKnight, "A Nation of Clients," *Public Welfare* (Fall 1980), pp. 15-19.

8. National Committee for Children and Youth, *Social Dynamite*, Report of the Conference on Unemployed, Out-of-School Youth in Urban Areas (Washington: National Committee for Children and Youth, 1961).

9. M. Harvey Brenner, "Estimating the Social Costs of Youth Employment Problems," in Vice President's Task Force on Youth Employment, *A Review of Youth Employment Problems, Programs, and Policies*, three volumes (Washington: U.S. Government Printing Office, January 1980).

10. Committee for the Study of National Service, *Youth and the Needs of the Nation* (Washington: Potomac Institute, 1979), pp. 77-78, citing U.S. Department of Justice, *FBI Uniform Crime Reports* (Washington: U.S. Government Printing Office, October 1978).

11. George Gallup, Jr., "Who's for National Service?" in *National Youth Service: What's at Stake?* (Washington: Potomac Institute, 1980), pp. 15-22.

12. Committee for the Study of National Service, *Youth and the Needs of the Nation*, p. 78.

13. U.S. Bureau of the Census, *Characteristics of American Children and Youth: 1976* (Washington: U.S. Government Printing Office, 1978), pp. 54-58.

14. Committee for the Study of National Service, *Youth and the Needs of the Nation*, p. 78.

15. Frederick Klein, "Losing the Way: Teen-Age Suicide Toll Points Up the Dangers of Growing Up Rich," *Wall Street Journal* (May 14, 1981), pp. 1 and 19.

16. James Richardson, Mary Stewart, and Robert Simmonds, *Organized Miracles: A Study of Contemporary Youth, Communal, Fundamentalist Organization* (New Brunswick, New Jersey: Transaction Books, 1979), pp. 220-21.

17. "Teenage Drug Use," *ISR Newsletter* (Institute for Social Research, The University of Michigan, Summer 1981), p. 10.

18. Gallup, "Who's for National Service?" p. 16.

19. Klein, "Losing the Way," pp. 1 and 19.

20. Harry Atkins, "More and More Young Men Ending Up On Skid Row," *Ann Arbor News* (January 30, 1975), p. 28.

21. Marian Wright Edelman and Paul V. Smith, *Portrait of Inequality: Black and White Children in America* (Washington: Children's Defense Fund, 1980).

22. U.S. Bureau of the Census, *Current Population Reports*, Series P-25, no. 704 (July 1977).

23. William James, "The Moral Equivalent of War," *International Conciliation*, No. 27 (New York: Carnegie Endowment for International Peace, February 1910), p. 17.

24. The Urban Institute, *Assessing the Feasibility of Large-Scale Countercyclical Public Job-Creation*, three volumes (Washington: The Urban Institute, 1978).

25. James Watt, Secretary of the Interior, testifying in a Senate Hearing, reported in the *Wall Street Journal* (May 8, 1981), p. 1.

26. U.S. Congress, Senate, Committee on Labor and Human Resources, *Hearings of Presidential Commission on National Service and National Commission on Volunteerism*, 96th Cong., 2nd sess., March 1980, p. 135.

27. Adam Yarmolinsky, "National Service Program," *Final Report of the Senior Conference on National Compulsory Service* (West Point, N.Y.: U.S. Military Academy, 1977).

28. Committee for the Study of National Service, *Youth and the Needs of the Nation*, p. 42.

29. Donald Eberly, *The Estimated Effect of a National Service Program on Public Service Manpower Needs, Youth Unemployment, College Attendance and Marriage Rates* (New York: Russell Sage Foundation, 1970).

30. Donald Eberly, *A Plan for National Service* (New York: National Service Secretariat, 1966); and Donald Eberly, "A Model for Universal Youth Service," presented at The Universal Youth Service Conference, Eleanor Roosevelt Institute, Hyde Park, N.Y.: 1976.

31. Michael Sherraden, "The Civilian Conservation Corps: Effectiveness of the Camps," Ph.D. dissertation (The University of Michigan, 1979), p. 242.

32. Barrett Potter, "The Civilian Conservation Corps in New York State: Its Social and Political Impact (1933-1942)," Ph.D. dissertation (State University of New York at Buffalo, 1973), p. 150.

33. Gallup, "Who's for National Service?" pp. 16-17.

Chapter 2
Calls for National Service*
Roger Landrum, Donald J. Eberly,
and Michael W. Sherraden

The first major call for a national service in the United States was by the social philosopher and psychologist William James. James' seminal essay, "The Moral Equivalent of War," was given as a major address at Stanford University in 1906 and first published in 1910. The essay proposed national service as a pragmatic means by which a democratic nation could maintain social cohesiveness apart from the external threat of war. In his extraordinarily vivid language, James attacked a view he considered ingrained in Western civilization from Alexander the Great through Theodore Roosevelt: that war's "dreadful hammer is the welder of men into cohesive states, and nowhere but in such states can human nature adequately develop its capacity." James wasn't any easier on pacifists, suggesting that the "duties, penalties, and sanctions pictured in the utopias they paint are all too weak and tame to substitute for war's disciplinary function." The most promising line of conciliation between militarists and pacifists, James thought, was some "moral equivalent of war."

> Men now are proud of belonging to a conquering nation, and without a murmur they lay down their persons and their wealth, if by so doing they may fight off subjugation. But who can be sure that other aspects of one's country may not, with time and education and suggestion enough, come to be regarded with similarly effective feelings of pride and shame? Why should men not someday feel that it is worth a blood-tax to belong to a collectivity superior in any ideal respect? Why should they not blush with indignant shame if the community that owns them is vile in any way whatsoever?
>
> Individuals, daily more numerous, now feel this civic passion. It is only a question of blowing on the spark till the whole population gets incandescent, and on the ruins of the old morals of military honor, until a stable system of

---

* Portions of this chapter are based on Roger Landrum, "Review of the Literature," in Committee for the Study of National Service, *Youth and the Needs of the Nation* (Washington: Potomac Institute, 1979).

morals of civic honor builds itself up. What the whole community comes to believe in grasps the individual as in a vise. The war function has grasped us so far; but constructive interests may someday seem no less imperative, and impose on the individual a hardly lighter burden.

If now—and this is my idea—there were, instead of military conscription, a conscription of the whole youthful population to form for a certain number of years a part of the army enlisted against *Nature*, the injustice would tend to be evened out, and numerous other goods to the commonwealth would follow. . . .

Such a conscription, with the state of public opinion that would have required it, and the many moral fruits it would bear, would preserve in the midst of a pacific civilization the manly virtues which the military party is so afraid of seeing disappear in peace.[1]

James argued that a permanently successful peace economy cannot be a simple pleasure economy. He proposed a conscription of the youthful population of the United States into national service to provide a new sense of "civic discipline" outside the context of war. James also believed that national service would benefit young people. They would experience "self-forgetfulness" rather than "self-seeking." No one would be "flung out of employment to degenerate because there is no immediate work for them to do." None would "remain blind, as the luxurious classes now are blind, to man's relations to the globe he lives on." The childishness would be "knocked out of them." The moral equivalent of war would cultivate in youth "toughness without callousness, healthier sympathies and soberer ideas, ideals of hardihood and discipline, and civic temper."

The logic and rhetoric of James' call for national service have an antique ring today. James was clearly thinking only of young men and the image of Ivy League undergraduates seemed to be at the center of his thinking. He didn't consider the issue of constitutional limits on involuntary servitude. His recommendation of conscription was softened only by the concepts of collectivity and social sanctions: "What the whole community comes to believe in grasps the individual as in a vise." He said nothing of cost and organization. Of course, there were half as many young people in those days, only 15 percent of them in high school, and a vastly different organization of the work force. Still, James succeeded in embedding a phrase, "the moral equivalent of war," in the national consciousness; he raised the fundamental issue of proper socialization of youth in the context of a democracy at peace; and he planted the idea of national service.

Since William James raised the issue in 1906, the idea of national service has resurfaced on many occasions, from many proponents and a variety of perspectives. This chapter reviews some of the major "calls" for national service. Three different, although somewhat overlapping, perspectives on national service are described: (1) national service as an expression of interest in the social and psychological development of young people; (2) national service which views young people as an important national resource; and (3) national service as a way of addressing disturbing social trends.

THE HUMAN DEVELOPMENT PERSPECTIVE

From the human development perspective, national service is viewed as an institution of social participation for the formative years of young adulthood, a unique form of social participation that cultivates aspects of human behavior not adequately enhanced by schooling or a conventional job. For example, it is argued that altruism or the sense of responsibility for others will be enhanced by the experience of national service. Perhaps a better appreciation of the pluralism of American society will be gained. The human development perspective is sometimes couched strictly in terms of the growth of the individual, borrowing perhaps from John Dewey's thoughts about learning through action, and sometimes expressed in terms of the shaping of better citizens—a new and more robust version of the old and feeble high school civics course.

The human development view has been presented in many contexts. This perspective is typified by Hubert Humphrey's attempt to revive the Civilian Conservation Corps in 1959.[2] Humphrey proposed a "plan to save trees, land, and boys." The "boys," or America's human resources, were one of Senator Humphrey's chief concerns. More recently, James S. Coleman and his colleagues on the Panel on Youth of The President's Science Advisory Committee concluded that for American youth the transition to adulthood is impeded by institutions that prolong dependency.[3] According to Coleman, youth were "action-rich" and "education-poor" at the turn of the century, but precisely the reverse holds for contemporary youth. As the labor of youth has become increasingly unnecessary to society, schooling has been extended as the major institution of socialization. At the same time, entry into the labor force has become increasingly problematic, and a youth culture has taken shape that is primarily inward-looking and excessively segregated from adult culture and responsibilities. The panel recommended the deliberate creation of new environments for youth that give them new responsibilities and roles.

One of these proposals was for an expansion of opportunities for public or national service. The panel took care to pinpoint the intent of this proposal as giving youth an "experience of responsibilities affecting other people." The work involved should be "interdependent, directed toward collectively-held goals . . . with persons of different backgrounds and different ages." This emphasis would complement the self-development objective of schooling. The panel also pointed out that the best examples of existing youth service programs have been notably successful, e.g., the Peace Corps, VISTA, Job Corps, Youth Conservation Corps, and the University Year for ACTION.

Another national service proposal with a human development perspective came from the Carnegie Commission on Higher Education, chaired by Clark Kerr. The Commission concluded that youth service programs "serve the national interest" and "provide valuable learning experiences."[4] The Commission recommended that national service programs be expanded and made more attractive to younger age groups, and that "the reward for service should include financial benefits that can be used in obtaining further education." They argued that "such benefits are given now for military service and should be more widely available for other types of service." The Carnegie Commission endorsed the Coleman Panel's conclusion that existing national service programs "provide too few opportunities for participation."

In *The Boundless Resource*, Willard Wirtz argued along similar lines.[5] In an analysis of the present isolation between the worlds of education and work in the lifetime of the individual, Wirtz applauded a decade of bridge building but pointed out "a new critical economic circumstance." Work-study, cooperative education, and special job opportunity programs for youth, he suggested, "run into the sobering fact that employers simply cannot provide experiential learning slots for high school and college students when employees with seniority are on the unemployment rolls." The traditional transition between youth and adulthood, Wirtz concluded, must be readjusted to a new meaning of growth. The new meaning should include a significantly larger element of "service." Wirtz proposed for high school youth at least 500 hours of work and service experience, and "further consideration of a national service opportunity—even requirement—in place of the military service so many young Americans have faced in the past."

Margaret Mead added some conceptual refinements to the view of what national service might do for the development of young people.[6] A universal youth service would be an instrument of social integration. Mead observed that "the poor and the rich, the highly technologically gifted and those with obsolescent skills, the white collar and the blue collar, are each reared in almost total ignorance of each other." Designed in such a way that units would enroll young people from all walks of life, Mead suggested that a universal national service could compensate for the increasing "fragmentation, ignorance, and lack of knowledge of their fellow citizens." Young people raised in poverty would step into a wider world, while now many such youths are "rejected and left to their own devices, or left to become the subject of inadequate and prohibitively expensive programs of re-education or rehabilitation later." National service would give these young people an early opportunity to experience the satisfaction of service performed on behalf of the nation and their fellow citizens. This opportunity and experience would provide "a paradigm for later social participation not immediately based on the standards of the marketplace."

Mead also pointed out the function national service could play in career exploration. An interval would be provided for responsible work experience that precedes further educational and vocational choices. Large numbers of youth, she observed, now go from dependency on their parents into careers chosen for them or into early marriage "as a device to reach pseudo-adult status." Through the instrument of national service, an opportunity to establish an identity and a sense of self-respect and responsibility as individuals before making career choices or establishing homes would be extraordinarily valuable, especially for many young women.

Mead was one of the few advocates of national service who explicitly recommended the inclusion of women on the same basis as men.[7] A failure to include women, she wrote, would "promote a split in the experience of men and women at a time when it is essential that they should move in step with each other, economically and politically." The "broadening educational effects" should be extended to women from isolated rural regions and from slums or ghettos. The chance to "assay their abilities" during universal national service would provide a background for appropriate career choices when women wished to enter or reenter the labor market. Marriage as the route away from the parental home would be replaced with a period of work before marriage and parenthood.

Others have elaborated on the theme of national service as an experiment in education in a broad sense. In 1967, Morris Janowitz claimed that the American educational system had been purchased at the price of complicating the process of personal development.[8] Use of the school and academic performance as the primary route to social mobility, in Janowitz's view, is particularly dangerous in a democratic society. Young people need alternatives to overcome "the boredom that comes from continuous exposure to classroom instruction." They need exposure to a wide range of adults and teachers beyond subject-matter specialists, particularly when a large proportion of faculty have achieved their positions without significant nonacademic experience. The search for personal development and individual identity in a social setting with a narrow emphasis on individual classroom performance leads all too often to various forms of rebellion and withdrawal. National service, Janowitz wrote, would provide alternative educational experiences for youth from all levels of the social strata. These experiences would develop group solidarity based on collective rather than individualistic goals. They would permit expression of public service objectives. They would give a second chance to young people from the deprived segments of our society, and they would provide the most gifted youth with vital preparation for more fully trained professional careers.

Theodore Hesburgh, in a tone similar to that of Janowitz, advanced a different point.[9] He suggested that the experience of service to others should be accepted as part of our whole educational system because "one is not a whole person without it, one will not learn well without it, and one will not relate to the world in years to come without it." Hesburgh suggested that the Peace Corps and similar volunteer programs have demonstrated that service is a "vital life experience that heightens the receptivity of persons." This is important for formal education because "the volunteer is not the same person in the system after he returns." He has been up against situations and dilemmas for which he doesn't have solutions. He is hungrier for answers. He has a much deeper sense of the challenge in the world than when he was reading books and talking in the unreal world of the campus. Hesburgh saw the central problem as creating in our society an appreciation for the experience of service as a normal part of a person's education, since service provides "a dimension that cannot be had in a classroom."

Erik Erikson also has been a proponent of national service from a developmental perspective. Erikson pointed out the necessity for a "moratorium" from the relentless pressures of deciding on a career.[10] In addition, Erikson took strong exception with those who suggested compulsory service. He predicted that a compulsory service would lead to rebellion and noncooperation. He saw as far more desirable a "volunteer army of young men and women ready for clearly necessary national as well as international service." This would require a clear "formulation of traditional and emerging values—those which give our generation the right to recruit youth, and those which would permit youth to insist on alternatives."

The most recent calls for national service have been broadly conceived, but contain prominent human development components. Among these are the reports of the Committee for the Study of National Service, *Youth and the Needs of the Nation*[11] and *National Youth Service: What's at Stake?*[12] and the Carnegie Council report, *Giving Youth a Better Chance.*[13] These reports argue, among other things, that service has been a neglected dimension in the development of youth, and that the choices currently available to youth during the transition to adulthood are limited and restrictive. National service is viewed as a more positive developmental alternative.

YOUNG PEOPLE AS A NATIONAL RESOURCE

A second perspective on national service views young people as a national resource. Young people, with their energy and flexibility, are seen as an important resource for meeting social and economic needs beyond the reach of existing institutions. The movement for civil rights, the antiwar movement, the Civilian Conservation Corps of the Depression era, and the Peace Corps are American examples of this. The youth participation efforts of Cuba, China, Israel, and other nations—although occurring in very different political and social contexts—are overseas models which represent this perspective on national service.

Perhaps the most striking American example is Franklin D. Roosevelt's Civilian Conservation Corps (1933–1942). Roosevelt initiated the CCC in part to provide jobs for young men, but his interest was also clearly on accomplishing useful work:

> Our greatest primary task is to put people to work. This is no insolvable problem if we face it wisely and courageously. It can be accomplished in part by direct recruiting by the Government itself, treating the task as we would treat the emergency of a war, but at the same time, through this employment, accomplishing greatly needed projects to stimulate and reorganize the use of our natural resources.[14]

This emphasis on the actual product of youth service has been repeated since the 1930s, although in a more muted voice than Roosevelt's. For example, Hubert Humphrey's attempt to revive a CCC-like program in the 1950s called for saving "trees and land" as well as "boys."[15] Other calls for national service that have emphasized the nation's need for the service of youth have come from Donald Eberly and the National Service Secretariat.[16] Eberly wrote in 1959 that "America should actively support a National Service which employs the instruments of peace as an alternative to military service,"[17] and went on to suggest that some young men could be of greater service to America in peaceful pursuits than in the armed forces. The National Service Secretariat, formed by Eberly and others in 1966, has produced a number of studies on national service and has consistently underscored the primacy of constructive endeavor among the several purposes of national service. Eberly has said on numerous occasions that the growth of national service should be governed by the availability of useful work.

Service may include both concrete products and social services. In 1977 Adam Yarmolinsky offered quantitative evidence of social needs.[18] He cited a demonstration youth service project in Seattle, Washington, for which 220 local, non-profit organizations identified 1,200 needed work years that could be met by nonprofessionals—the equivalent of 300,000 positions nationwide.[19] Yarmolinsky also noted that cuts in public budgets result in deterioration of public facilities such as parks and libraries; low-skill human services could permit maintenance of these facilities. A survey of needs published by the Russell Sage Foundation in 1970 specified needs for 4 million nonprofessional volunteers on a one-year, full-time basis.[20] Similar data on social needs have also been provided by Eberly in 1966 and 1976.[21] While economists would not consider this evidence rigorously demonstrative of "effective demand," and while the need for human services must be balanced against other factors such as cost, the claims of the private marketplace, and skepticism about big government and make-work, the data do at least suggest a universe of social needs of substantial magnitude. The U.S. economy has become service-oriented and this trend is very unlikely to reverse itself. Any reasonable discussion of the constructive potential of national service must take this fact into account.

The perspective that views young people as a national resource has not been in the forefront in recent years. As a nation, we seem to have largely discounted youth as productive members of society. Social programs have emphasized education, crime control, job training, and social development; but too seldom have we emphasized what young people can do for the country, and we have provided few opportunities for young people to contribute.

NATIONAL SERVICE TO ADDRESS SOCIAL PROBLEMS

A third perspective views national service as a policy option for attacking disturbing social trends among young people. This perspective dominates much of the contemporary literature on youth service. High rates of youth unemployment, high crime rates among youth, high percentages of school dropouts, drug and alcohol use among teenagers, and military manpower shortages are all trends that concern various policymaking groups. These groups weigh national service on a scale with the benefits and costs of other policy choices.

This view is represented, for example, by Coleman: "A capitalist economy or market economy has no natural place for an intermediate status between full dependency, which a person is in when he is in school, and the full productivity that he is in when he is in the labor force."[22] A range of indicators of youth dislocation are cited to document what Coleman described as a structural problem: staggering amounts of youth vandalism and violent crimes, drug and alcohol abuse, teenage pregnancy, unemployment, poor school performance, and so on. The National Commission on Resources for Youth, the National Manpower Institute, and the New York State Division for Youth have provided arguments that new policies for youth represent a compelling state interest, although they do not necessarily advocate national service as the policy answer.[23]

In the area of military policy, Senator Sam Nunn, working through the Senate Armed Services Committee, has generated several policy documents analyzing national service as a possible remedy for the problem of personnel shortages in the volunteer armed forces. The first of these studies, written by William R. King, recommended a noncoercive but large national service

system with military and nonmilitary options, backed up by universal registration and a mechanism to be used if necessary to meet military manpower
needs.[24] In short, the King Report presents national service as an alternative
to the volunteer armed forces. This study also suggests that national service
would serve plural goals, including national defense, alleviation of youth
unemployment, reductions in welfare programs, and improved citizenship.
King writes, "The national service concept has national goals and their
achievement at its roots."

The King Report was followed by a hearing before the Senate Armed
Services Subcommittee on Manpower and Personnel.[25] Nunn called for testimony and debate about national service as an alternative to the volunteer
armed forces and "the tragically high unemployment rates of our young
people." Little clear-cut agreement emerged from this hearing. Morris Janowitz, Richard Cooper, and Martin Binkin—all civilian experts on the U.S.
military—disagreed with each other about the severity of likely military
personnel shortfalls in the 1980s.[26] They also disagreed about the best reme-
dies. Janowitz argued in support of the basic King Report proposition but
from a philosophical perspective on the military. A mercenary army, he
suggested, is out of keeping with our democratic tradition of military service
as citizen service and is a danger to American society:

> We have, in our society, a unique system by which democratic institutions have
> been strengthened by the fact we have made service in the military compatible
> with political leadership and with citizenship. The hallmark of a democratic
> society is to serve in the military. That is one of the training grounds for a civil
> society in which the military knows its place, and I would like to keep that alive,
> but that has come to an end and there is no way of turning it back superficially.
> We are in a situation where we must keep alive the concept of the citizen-soldier
> in a great variety of ways and voluntary national service is the modern equiva-
> lent in such a circumstance.[27]

Thus, Janowitz testified against compulsory national service and predicted
that a voluntary system, developed carefully over a ten-year period, would
"pick up between 60 and 70 percent of the youngsters in the country."

Senator Nunn asked that national service also be considered separately
from military problems. He was especially interested in how national service
might influence youth unemployment and attitudes toward citizenship. His
most pressing question about a voluntary system was that it might continue
a situation where the wealthiest people of the nation have not served in either
military or nonmilitary programs.

Interest in national service as a policy instrument to reduce youth unemployment is widespread. William James anticipated this possible effect when
he wrote that no one would be "flung out of employment to degenerate
because there is no immediate work for them to do."[28] At a 1976 Congres-

sional Budget Office conference on youth unemployment, James Coleman outlined a typology of three institutional devices in a market economy for the transition of youth from full dependency to full productivity.[29] One is a "special competitive position for youth." The best example of this device is a lower minimum wage. The second device is the use of education as a "holding station." Coleman characterized this as the major device in American society, but one that ill-prepares young people for productive activity afterwards. The third device is "special temporary institutions which are not in the competitive market, such things as the Peace Corps, the Army, VISTA, CCC, Neighborhood Youth Corps." Coleman characterized these programs as "sheltered work shops" brought about by a war or specially devised as was the CCC in the 1930s.

Harris Wofford has suggested that a universal service program will enhance youth employability while at the same time achieve other ends: enable nonprofit organizations to improve services, enhance social integration in American society, make young people better students when they return to school, and improve the quality of civic spirit.[30] Willard Wirtz and Donald Eberly have argued along similar lines for a large system of national service, citing the observed effects of past and current youth service programs.[31] Vernon Jordan, in writing about "the endangered generation" of black youth, argued for structural changes that "go beyond inadequate piecemeal programs." In his view, the vehicle "should be a National Youth Service, open to all, but with emphasis on aggressively recruiting young people from economically disadvantaged backgrounds." Jordan recommended programs in both the public and private sectors. A national commitment to youth development, he suggests, "would enable Black youth to break the chains of poverty and discrimination that imprison so many millions of minority Americans."[32]

Clearly, one of the fascinating questions about national service is how it might operate to solve specific social problems. Would it promote social integration across racial and class barriers, as argued by James, Mead, Wofford, and Janowitz? Would it improve the civic attitudes of a new generation, as argued by virtually all advocates of national service? Would it help reduce the disturbing levels of crime, drug usage, and drifting among American youth? Would the experience provide new skills, self-discipline, and career direction for youth of all income backgrounds, as argued by Wirtz and Jordan? All of these predictions, or hopes, run through the literature of national service. If these positive effects were realized, would they cut the fiscal costs of social problems to federal, state, and local government? How would these savings compare to the costs of a national service system?

The above three perspectives on national service—human development, youth as a national resource, and concern with social problems—are obviously not mutually exclusive. Each amplifies one or another of the possibilities inherent in the idea of national service, and each can exclude or distort one or another aspect of any detailed plan of national service. A single-minded emphasis on human development, for example, might lead to a plan which would neglect broader social goals and result in make-work. On the other hand, the subordination of young people to national goals could look more like involuntary servitude than altruism or civic spirit. And targeting national service to unemployed young people or to military manpower shortages would sharply deflect any plan from universal goals. Although the perspectives are not mutually exclusive, each offers different choices and it is useful to keep these viewpoints in mind.

Many of the calls for national service described above have come from thoughtful and imaginative observers in academia or other settings which facilitate development of theories and ideas. These contributions to the discussion and debate on national service have been invaluable. On occasion, however, a call for national service comes from the more practical arena of politics. And when the call comes from the White House, the discourse is inevitably rooted in the constraints of world affairs. We turn now to calls for national service by U.S. Presidents.

PRESIDENTIAL REVIEWS OF NATIONAL SERVICE

The Civilian Conservation Corps and the National Youth Administration were dismantled after the United States entered World War II. The United States was about to put 15 million Americans, most of them young people, into uniform; and youth employment programs no longer could be justified. By the end of 1943, the CCC and the NYA had been phased out. History nearly repeated itself a quarter of a century later. By the late 1960s, the United States had 3.5 million men and women in uniform to fight an undeclared, limited war in Vietnam. The domestic War on Poverty which had been declared in 1964 was crippled but not killed by the Asian war. The effect on youth programs—Job Corps, VISTA, Youth Employment, College Work Study—was to stunt their growth. The Peace Corps, which had expanded to 15,000 by 1967, began shrinking rapidly in size. The story does not end there, however. An examination of some little publicized discussions and activities in both the Roosevelt and Johnson administrations suggests that the New Deal youth programs might have survived, and the War on Poverty youth programs might have thrived, if these programs had been cast within the context of national service. Moreover, both Roosevelt and Johnson were moving toward the national service concept when the wars intruded.

Within the Roosevelt White House, Eleanor Roosevelt was evidently the first and strongest supporter of the national service idea. As early as May 1934, she said that she "would like to see us institute a volunteer service to

the country, open to both boys and girls."[33] She believed that such a program would offer employment to the millions of young people who were out
of work, would accomplish important work in both the public and private
nonprofit sectors, and would reduce the costs of crime and vandalism
brought on by the idleness of young people. Mrs. Roosevelt suggested a
two-year enlistment and housing of volunteers in camps, but no linkage to
military service.

More politician than idealist, President Roosevelt did not come to a decision on national service until it was virtually forced on him by the impending
draft law. Franklin D. Roosevelt, Jr., and biographer Joseph P. Lash recall
President Roosevelt's emerging position on youth service:

> One of the most telling indicators of my father's views on the future of youth
> service was the very qualified support he gave a purely military draft. In June,
> 1940, after the collapse of France, when England stood alone and the armed
> forces were pressing for a draft, my father met with the Budget Director, Harold
> Smith. Smith made a note of the conversation: "The President, in confidential
> and preliminary form, outlined a plan for one year's training for the youth who
> annually came of age. He asked us to make some preliminary estimates as to the
> possible number. He has in mind that there might be as many as one million
> who would be brought into the government service for one year's training
> without compensation or at possibly $5.00 a month, this program to be merged
> with and take the place of the present CCC and NYA. Generally, this training
> might break down into possible maintenance, radio and other communication,
> training for industry, conservation work and training and government depart-
> ments. Consideration should also be given to the training of young women"
> (Smith Diary, June 17, 1940, Franklin D. Roosevelt Library).
>
> All through that summer while the Burke-Wadsworth compulsory military
> service bill was being considered by Congress, he hoped that the legislation
> could be broadened into a program of universal military and civilian training
> (Smith Diary, July 30, 1940, Morganthau Presidential Diary, August 14, 1940,
> Franklin D. Roosevelt Library). But the political situation was such that he had
> to accept the Burke-Wadsworth Bill in its narrower form. Yet fifteen months
> later, on December 6, 1941, the day before Pearl Harbor, the Budget Director
> was again with my father to talk about the budget of NYA for the coming fiscal
> year. Smith made the following note in his Diary: "In connection with the NYA
> estimate . . . he took occasion to outline his views with respect to a future youth
> training program. In general, the President has in mind that youth, as they reach
> the age of twenty-one should spend a year in the military service, in conserva-
> tion work, in the NYA type of training program, and possibly other forms of
> Federal service . . . the President told us that he had talked to Representative
> Lyndon Johnson (Texas) recently with references to a simple form of legislation
> which would authorize and direct the President to consolidate the NYA and
> CCC."[34]

On December 10, 1941, two days after the United States entered World War

II, Representative Lyndon B. Johnson introduced a bill in the House of Representatives that would have merged the NYA and the CCC into a broader effort called the Civilian Youth Administration (CYA).[35] The CYA would have been set up as a permanent entity and would have provided the framework for a continuing federal youth initiative after the war. The bill, however, was doomed by America's entry into the war.

National service did not return to the presidential agenda until 25 years later, with war again on the near horizon and with Lyndon Johnson in the White House. When President Johnson called a White House Conference on International Cooperation for December 1965, Eberly viewed it as another opportunity to submit his paper called "National Service for Peace." He had been circulating the proposal since 1958 to publishers, politicians, and friends in the hope that somebody would take the idea and run with it. Nobody did, except for an idea or two that Senator Humphrey put into his 1960 Peace Corps legislation. The most concise response had come from Eleanor Roosevelt; "I have read your proposal and I think your idea is a good one, however I fear this administration [Eisenhower's] will not consider it."

Reverend James Robinson, the founder of Operation Crossroads–Africa and a friend from mutual African interests, gave Eberly five minutes to present the idea to the 1965 Conference. There was no chance to discuss it on the floor, but the response when the session recessed was unexpected. At least 25 people, including Representative Donald Fraser (D, Minn.), sought Eberly out to applaud the idea and to ask how he was planning to carry the idea forward.

On May 7, 1966, Eberly convened a conference on national service in New York City. Some 30 persons attended, mostly friends from the educational world but also several congressional aides, a few federal government officials, two persons who had been with the CCC at Camp William James in 1940, and a reporter from *The New York Times*. The next day, the report of the conference was on the front page of *The New York Times*. Now the politicians and publishers were calling to inquire about national service. *The New York Times* editorialized on May 14:

> Nationally sound reform (of Selective Service) lies in the direction of universal national service, with limited options to serve either in the armed forces, the Peace Corps, the National Teacher Corps, or a variety of domestic urban and rural missions. Leading educators have already endorsed such a plan. It is now up to the nation's educational, manpower and military leadership to evolve a blueprint for national debate and Congressional action.[36]

The nation's leadership responded all right, but the result could not be called a blueprint. National service was the topic of both the Harvard and Yale baccalaureate sermons that year. Nathan Pusey of Harvard opposed national service; Kingman Brewster of Yale favored it. Their debate was a precursor of many to come. If one presented national service as the forced labor of unwilling youths in make-work jobs, opposition was predictable. However, if one presented national service as expanding opportunities for young people to acquire good work habits and a sense of citizenship while voluntarily engaging in constructive projects, support for the concept quickly followed.

Among other supporters of national service, Secretary of Labor Willard Wirtz recommended that all 18 year olds be registered for two years of education, employment, military service, or community service. He said that the necessity for an equitable distribution of the obligation to fight is only part of the larger need for distribution of the opportunity for all young people to learn, work, and serve. While rejecting the idea of service by compulsion, Wirtz said that "there would be insistence that [young people] use the opportunities afforded them."[37]

The biggest bombshell came from the nation's top military leader. Secretary of Defense Robert S. McNamara said in a major speech on May 18, 1966:

> It seems to me that we could move toward remedying [the draft] inequity by asking every young person in the United States to give two years of service to his country—whether in one of the military services, in the Peace Corps, or in some other voluntary developmental work at home or abroad.[38]

Many assumed that the McNamara statement was a trial balloon ordered by President Johnson. Whatever it was, it soared high for no longer than 24 hours. Because of all the clamor created by the statement, the White House was forced to comment. When it did, it came down squarely on both sides of the fence, saying in essence: Yes, we like the idea of national service. No, it is not a trial balloon.

The debate continued and, on July 2, Johnson appointed a National Advisory Commission on Selective Service with a dual mandate: to examine Selective Service and make recommendations, and to examine the national service idea. Burke Marshall was named Commission chairman and asked Morris Janowitz, Harris Wofford, and Donald Eberly to tell the Commission how national service might work. After a flurry of meetings and discussions and formation of the National Service Secretariat, an 80 page plan for national service was formulated by the Secretariat and submitted to the Commission in November. Meanwhile, President Johnson openly continued to support the national service concept. Probably his strongest statement was made in Dayton in September 1966:

> We must move toward a standard that no man has truly lived who only served himself. . . . To move in this direction, I am asking every member of my Admin-

istration to explore new ways by which our young people can serve their fellow men. I am asking a group of Governors and Mayors to meet and study ways in which city, State, and Federal governments can cooperate in developing a manpower service program that could work at every level of our society. . . . To the youth of America, I want to say: If you seek to be uncommon, if you seek to make a difference, if you seek to serve, then look around you. Your country needs you. Your Nation needs your services.

Look at yourselves and then look at our need at this very hour for more than one million medical and health workers in this Nation. Look at our need for more than a million teachers and school administrators. Look at our need for more than 700,000 welfare and home care workers; look at our need for more than two million people to help improve our cities. Almost half a million to serve in public protection of our homes and our families and our children. . . . The sign of your time is need. For while America has not ceased to be the land of opportunity to succeed, it has also become the land of opportunity to serve.[39]

Soon Johnson decided that the country could no longer support both guns and butter. He opted for guns and made no more speeches about national service. He apparently passed the word to the Marshall Commission not to recommend a national service program. When the Commission's 219 page paper was published, only three pages were devoted to national service. The Commission concluded that "the spirit which motivates interest in national service is undeniably part of our national experience today. Sensitive to that spirit, the Commission suggests that the research which must be accomplished proceed, together with public and private experimentation with pilot programs."[40]

It was apparently the Vietnam War that continued to be the major enemy of national service during the 1968 Presidential campaign. Hubert H. Humphrey, soon to be selected as the Democratic candidate for President, included in his platform: "capturing the resources of energy and commitment in our young people through a system of national service which not only distributes the burdens of military service fairly, but offers incentives and opportunities for contributing to our domestic needs."[41]

Once Humphrey became the official nominee of the Democratic party, however, national service no longer appeared as part of the Humphrey platform. Curiously, Humphrey's running-mate, Edmund S. Muskie, proposed national service in a Colorado speech in October in these words: "The national service alternative would permit us to do on a much broader and more meaningful scale the kinds of things we need to do if we are to become the kind of society our Declaration of Independence and the Constitution have promised."[42] Within days, Muskie, like Humphrey, dropped the subject of national service from his campaign rhetoric.

Similar calls for national service have come from distinguished Americans throughout the twentieth century. Why haven't these calls been answered with a full-fledged national service program, or at least with a pilot project large enough to determine whether to proceed with a nationwide effort? We think a major reason for this failure is the multipurpose nature of national service. Probably the question put most frequently to national service advocates is: What are you really trying to do, meet community needs, reduce unemployment, improve the quality of education, create a rite of passage for youth, or solve the draft dilemma? Just as scientists were skeptical early in this century that an equation as simple as $E = mc^2$ could describe a fundamental law of nature, so it seems surprising that a single program might address several major societal needs.

A second reason is more enigmatic. Why is it that the only time a president seriously considers national service appears to be when war is in the making? Is it possible that young people merit presidential attention only when their country needs them to fight a war? Does Rudyard Kipling's portrayal of the public attitude toward young soldiers now apply to young people in general?

> For it's Tommy this, an' Tommy that, an "Chuck him out, the brute"
> But it's "Saviour of 'is country" when the guns begin to shoot;[43]

Some countries have rejected this attitude. They are telling their young people that they are needed even in times of peace. Just as the United States was a leader in the development of overseas volunteer programs with the Peace Corps, other nations have taken the lead with national service. If the United States decides to move forward with national service, the nation will be well-advised to examine the experiences of these other countries. Before looking at some of these examples in chapters 4 and 5, we examine those occasions when certain elements of national service have been in place in the United States.

NOTES

    1. William James, "The Moral Equivalent of War," *International Conciliation*, No. 27 (New York: Carnegie Endowment for International Peace, 1910), pp. 16-18.
    2. Hubert H. Humphrey, "Plan to Save Trees, Land, and Boys," *Harper's Magazine* 218 (January 1959): 53-57.
    3. James. S. Coleman, *Youth: Transition to Adulthood*, Report on Youth of the President's Advisory Committee (Chicago: The University of Chicago Press, 1972). Also see National Panel on High School and Adolescent Education, *The Education of Adolescents* (Washington: U.S. Government Printing Office, 1976).
    4. Carnegie Commission on Higher Education, *Toward a Learning Society: Alternative Chan-*

nels to Life, Work, and Service (New York: McGraw-Hill, 1973). Also see Geoffrey White, *National Youth Service and Higher Education* (Boston: Sloan Commission on Government and Higher Education, October, 1978).

5. Willard Wirtz and the National Manpower Institute, *The Boundless Resource: A Prospectus for an Education/Work Policy* (Washington, D.C.: New Republic, 1975).

6. Margaret Mead, "A National Service System as a Solution to a Variety of National Problems," in *The Draft: A Handbook of Facts and Alternatives*, edited by Sol Tax (Chicago: The University of Chicago Press, 1967), pp. 99-109.

7. See also Mildred Robbins, "The Role of Women in National Service," in *National Service: A Report of a Conference*, edited by Donald J. Eberly (New York: Russell Sage Foundation, 1968). Robbins reports on a conference on the role of women in national service convened by the National Council of Women of The United States in March 1967. The conference agreed that voluntary national service, as an equal opportunity and responsibility for all men and women, would benefit the community, nation, and individual.

8. Morris Janowitz, "The Logic of National Service," in *The Draft: A Handbook of Facts and Alternatives*, edited by Sol Tax (Chicago: University of Chicago Press, 1967), pp. 73-90.

9. Rev. Theodore Hesburgh, unpublished paper for the Peace Corps (1965).

10. Erik H. Erikson, "Memorandum for the Conference on the Draft," in *The Draft: A Handbook of Facts and Alternatives*, edited by Sol Tax (Chicago: University of Chicago Press, 1967), pp. 280-83.

11. Committee for the Study of National Service, *Youth and the Needs of the Nation* (Washington: The Potomac Institute, 1979).

12. Committee for the Study of National Service, *National Youth Service: What's at Stake?* (Washington, The Potomac Institute, 1980).

13. Carnegie Council on Policy Studies in Higher Education, *Giving Youth a Better Chance: Options for Education, Work, and Service* (San Francisco: Jossey-Bass, 1979).

14. Franklin D. Roosevelt, *Inaugural Address*, 1933. Note the similarity of Roosevelt's language to William James' "Moral Equivalent of War." Roosevelt had undoubtedly read James' essay, but he never conceded that his thinking was influenced by James' proposal.

15. Humphrey, "Plan to Save Trees, Land, and Boys."

16. For example, the National Service Secretariat published in 1971 a "Ten Point Statement on Voluntary National Service," which declared: "The basic raison d'etre of a national volunteer service is the need society has for the service of youth." See also Donald J. Eberly, "A Call for National Service," *Voluntary Action Leadership* (Summer 1979), pp. 27-30.

17. Donald J. Eberly, "A National Service," *Christian Science Monitor* (April 18, 1959), p. 16.

18. Adam Yarmolinsky,"National Service Program," *Final Report of the Senior Conference on National Compulsory Service* (West Point, New York: U.S. Military Academy, 1977).

19. For a description of this 1973 ACTION-sponsored program, see *The Program For Local Service: Summary Findings* (Seattle, Washington: Control Systems Research, 1973).

20. Donald J. Eberly, *The Estimated Effect of a National Service Program on Public Service Manpower Needs, Youth Unemployment, College Attendance and Marriage Rates* (New York: Russell Sage Foundation, 1970).

21. Donald J. Eberly, *A Plan for National Service* (New York: National Service Secretariat, 1966); and "A Model for Universal Youth Service," presented at the Universal Youth Service Conference, Eleanor Roosevelt Institute, Hyde Park, New York, 1976.

22. James S. Coleman, "The School to Work Transition" in U.S. Congressional Budget Office, *The Teenage Unemployment Problem: What are the Options?* (Washington: U.S. Government Printing Office, 1976), pp. 35-40.

23. The National Commission on Resources for Youth, *Youth Participation*, Report to the Department of Health, Education and Welfare, Office of Youth Development (1975); Dennis Gallagher, *New Prospects for Youth: Worlds of Education, Work and Service*, (Washington:

National Manpower Institute, 1976); Peter B. Edelman and Martin Roysher, *Responding to Youth Unemployment: Towards a National Program of Youth Initiatives* (New York: State Division for Youth, 1976).

24. William R. King, *Achieving America's Goals: National Service or the All-Volunteer Armed Force?* (Washington: U.S. Government Printing Office, 1977).

25. U.S. Congress, Senate, Committee on Armed Services, *Hearing Before the Subcommittee on Manpower and Personnel*, 95th Congress, 1st sess., 1977.

26. Morris Janowitz is a professor of sociology at the University of Chicago; Richard V. L. Cooper is director of defense manpower studies at the Rand Corporation; and Martin Binkin is a senior fellow in foreign policy studies at the Brookings Institution.

27. See also Charles C. Moskos, "National Service and the All-Volunteer Force," *Society* (November-December 1979), pp. 70-72; and Charles Moskos and Morris Janowitz, "Making the All-Volunteer Army Work," *Bulletin of Atomic Scientists* (June 1980), pp. 6-7.

28. James, "The Moral Equivalent of War."

29. Coleman, "The School to Work Transition."

30. Harris Wofford, "Toward a Draft Without Guns," *Saturday Review* (Oct. 15, 1966); "An Action Proposal for Restless Students," *Look*, April 7, 1970; and "The Future of the Peace Corps," *The Annals of the American Academy of Political and Social Science*, (May 1966).

31. Willard Wirtz, *The Boundless Resource*; Donald J. Eberly, "A Universal Youth Service," *Social Policy* (January/February 1977); Donald J. Eberly, "National Service: Alternative Strategies," *Armed Forces and Society* (May 1977).

32. Vernon E. Jordan Jr., "Black Youth: The Endangered Generation," *Ebony* (August 1978).

33. Joseph P. Lash, *Eleanor and Franklin* (New York: The New American Library, 1973), p. 699.

34. Franklin D. Roosevelt, Jr., and Joseph P. Lash, *The Roosevelts and National Youth Service*, unpublished paper prepared for the Eleanor Roosevelt Institute (1976), pp. 5-6.

35. John A. Salmond, *The Civilian Conservation Corps, 1933-1942*: A New Deal Case Study (Durham, North Carolina: Duke University Press, 1967), p. 209.

36. "Testing for the Draft," *The New York Times* (May 14, 1966), p. 30.

37. Willard Wirtz, Remarks at the Catholic University of America (Washington, D.C., Nov. 16, 1966).

38. Robert S. McNamara, Excerpt from speech delivered before the American Society of Newspaper Editors in Montreal, *The New York Times* (May 19, 1966), p. 11.

39. Lyndon B. Johnson, "President Calls for Manpower Service Program," *National Service Newsletter*, No. 3 (October 1966), p. 1.

40. National Advisory Commission on Selective Service, *In Pursuit of Equity: Who Serves When Not All Serve?* (Washington: U.S. Government Printing Office, 1967), p. 63.

41. "Presidential Candidates and National Service," *National Service Newsletter* (June 1968), p. 4.

42. "Senator Muskie Recommends National Service Consideration," *National Service Newsletter* (Autumn 1968), p. 2.

43. Rudyard Kipling, *Barrack Room Ballads* (New York: Grosset & Dunlap, n.d.), p. 23.

Part II:
National Service Experiences in the U.S. and Other Countries

Chapter 3

National Service Precedents in The United States

Donald J. Eberly and Michael W. Sherraden

Had the nation heeded William James' call for a moral equivalent to war (see chapter 2), young men would have been conscripted to do many of the toughest nonmilitary jobs that had to be done. In the process, argued James, they would develop self-confidence and "would be better fathers and teachers of the following generation."[1] James suggested that a conscription for peaceful purposes would become a constructive way of accomplishing the youth-to-adult transition, a rite of passage which commonly occurred, said James, through participation in wars or street-corner gangs. As it happened, there has been no conscription in the United States for peaceful purposes, but in the intervening seven decades, tens of millions of young men have been drafted for military service and street-corner gangs have by no means disappeared. Still, the U.S. government has on occasion initiated voluntary nonmilitary work or service programs for young people. The programs have been started for a variety of reasons and, although a few programs have enrolled a million or more participants, most have been relatively small in size.

THE NEW DEAL

The Great Depression of the 1930s was the background against which two of the largest programs were created. Within one month of the time Franklin D. Roosevelt assumed the presidency in March 1933, his proposal for a Civilian Conservation Corps (CCC) had become law, and by midsummer the enrollment in the CCC exceeded 250,000 young men. The CCC had two main purposes: to transfer money to the poor (allotments were sent directly to the families of CCC enrollees), and to perform needed conservation work. Education and job training were, at best, secondary goals.

The CCC was generally perceived to be the most successful of Roosevelt's New Deal programs, receiving the enthusiastic endorsement of Roosevelt's

41

1936 opponent, Alfred Landon. A major reason for its acclaim was the clear evidence of CCC productivity. Reforestation projects, hiking trails, and vacation cabins were there for all to see. The CCC's contributions to preservation and renewal of natural resources and building outdoor recreation facilities were massive.

Of all the public service programs in the United States to date, the CCC most nearly approximated the moral equivalent described by William James. Organization was patterned after the military. Everyone had to pull his own weight. The physical energies of young men had ample opportunity for expression. Some 3 million young men served in the CCC during its nine-year existence.

The National Youth Administration (NYA) was bigger than the CCC but received less acclaim. By the time the NYA was created in 1935, it was one of many New Deal programs rather than one of the first, as the CCC had been. Also, the NYA was less distinctive in several respects. It was an agency within the Works Progress Administration (WPA). It enrolled 16 to 24 year olds of both sexes and had programs for students and nonstudents. NYA participants generally worked in their home towns. Over the life of the NYA, from 1935 to 1943, there were 4,800,000 participants with approximately equal numbers of males and females.

BETWEEN THE NEW DEAL AND THE WAR ON POVERTY

While not so exciting as the youth service programs of the Roosevelt period, two programs initiated between the New Deal and the War on Poverty have yielded lessons important to the consideration of national service. These programs are the GI Bill and the Peace Corps.

The GI Bill

In 1944, Congress passed a bill awarding postservice benefits to the 15 million veterans of World War II. Among the provisions of this bill was an education and training entitlement, which soon became known as the GI Bill. The magnitude of response to the GI Bill was vastly underestimated. The Army made a survey and predicted 7 percent of the veterans would be educated under the GI Bill. Earl J. McGrath, then a Dean at the University of Buffalo and later U.S. Commissioner of Education, estimated a total enrollment of 640,000 veterans.[2] In fact, the total enrollment came to 7 million persons, about 50 percent of those eligible.[3]

The GI Bill is generally acknowledged as one of the best investments ever made by the U.S. government. In returning to the tax coffers several times as much money as the $15 billion spent on education and training from 1945-

1954, it was a sound economic investment.[4] In producing what was generally conceded to be the best group of students ever found on American campuses, it was a sound investment in the quality of education as well. In greatly broadening the socioeconomic profile of persons going on to higher education, the GI Bill also was a sound investment in the cultural convergence and mixing which is essential to democracy.

A less recognized by-product of the GI Bill was its clear rebuttal of the supposed need for an educational continuum. There were predictions that the returning GIs would be a threat to American education, would require a great deal of counseling, and would not accept the authority of the educator.[5] Instead of fulfilling this dire set of predictions, the GIs demonstrated the value of an experience-rich interlude in formal education. Collectively, the returning GIs were substantial verification of the experiential learning proposals of William James and John Dewey.

The Peace Corps

The Peace Corps was created in 1961 and, at its peak in 1967, had an enrollment of 15,000 volunteers. By 1980, some 85,000 Peace Corps volunteers had served in the developing nations of Africa, Asia, and Latin America. During the two decades of its existence, most Peace Corps volunteers have been youthful college graduates. Both at home and overseas, the Peace Corps is the United States' most popular foreign aid program. It operates at a considerable distance from U.S. foreign policy concerns and has no relationship to U.S. military and intelligence activities.

The Peace Corps has yielded several valuable lessons in the field of national service. The first and most often overlooked is the manifestation of trust in young people by the government. When Congressman Henry Reuss introduced his bill for a Point Four Youth Corps, when Senator Hubert Humphrey submitted his bill for a Peace Corps, and when Candidate John F. Kennedy proposed a Peace Corps shortly before election day in 1960, the message heard by many young people was, "We trust you to serve in difficult and responsible positions."

The accomplishments of the Peace Corps volunteers disproved the predictions of those who called it a "kiddie corps" or compared it with the Children's Crusade in the Middle Ages. Where the assignments were manageable, as with teaching and agriculture, the work of the volunteers generally ranged from good to outstanding. Infrequently, most notably with the community development effort in Latin America where the assignments tended to be vague and the objectives not realistic, the record was less satisfactory.

Apart from the positive image of the United States which the Peace Corps has portrayed, probably its most lasting achievement has been the education gained by the volunteers and the way in which they intepret this education in their daily lives. Responding to a 1969 survey by the Stanford Research Institute, ex-volunteers reported learning somewhat more than they contributed during the Peace Corps experience.[6]

While the Peace Corps in practice has not always lived up to the hopes of its early advocates, it continues to stand as a small scale model of a program where government expresses its trust in young people, where young people respond positively to this trust, where they do good work under difficult circumstances, and where they return with a quality of understanding and wisdom that could be achieved in no other way. It is no accident that many former Peace Corps volunteers later choose careers with the State Department, the United Nations, the World Bank, or some other group which addresses itself to international issues.

THE WAR ON POVERTY

The United States launched two wars in August 1964—the Vietnam War with the passage of the Tonkin Gulf Resolution, and the War on Poverty with the signing of the Economic Opportunity Act. At the time, there were prospects of a budget surplus amounting to tens of billions of dollars. But the Vietnam War soon began to soak up any potential surplus and, as a consequence, the War on Poverty was kept on a short budgetary leash. Nevertheless, several of the War on Poverty programs can be described at least partially under the national service umbrella. The Office of Economic Opportunity (later renamed the Community Services Administration) originally housed these programs. All of the programs have since joined other departments or agencies.

Job Corps

Job Corps was, when the first center opened in 1965, a cornerstone of Lyndon Johnson's War on Poverty. Officials of the Office of Economic Opportunity originally thought it would be difficult to recruit underprivileged 16-21 year olds for Job Corps, a job training program away from home. Yet, within six months, they received 300,000 inquiries for only a few thousand openings.[7] Early evaluations of Job Corps, however, were not complimentary.

> Objectives appeared to be unclear. Confusion and a crisis-like atmosphere characterized these first attempts at training disadvantaged youth, and the entire program withstood a barrage of negative publicity. This inauspicious early performance and a growing realization that the nation could not simultaneously afford guns for Vietnam and butter at home, led to a scaling down of original

projections for program size. Job Corps was to have 100,000 enrollees by the end of the second year, but Congress decided to cap the program at 45,000 enrollees. President Nixon further reduced the size of the program and, to de-emphasize Job Corps' visibility, shifted program authority from OEO to the Department of Labor. As a result of these changes, Job Corps endured some very lean years during the 1970s. Program size remained at about 20,000 throughout the decade. In fiscal 1978 there were 28 Conservation Centers in operation and 36 other Centers were administered by business firms, nonprofit organizations, state and local government agencies, and labor unions.

During this period of austerity, objectives within the Job Corps program were sharpened. The urgent need for remedial education, specific job training, and connections to jobs became more clearly defined and operationalized. . . . It has also been helpful to establish specific links to employers and unions and provide adequate placement services. Cooperative arrangements between Job Corps and some labor unions have been one of the most effective approaches to youth employment in the past forty years. Under these arrangements, Job Corps training is shaped to fit union jobs and enrollees enter the union as apprentices with a foot in the door toward a promising career. . . . In addition, Job Corps has a well developed and organized network of community volunteers who assist in placement of enrollees as they leave the program.

With these changes in Job Corps, combined with more careful screening of applicants, retention of enrollees has improved and improvement in enrollee placement upon leaving the program has been dramatic. According to government statistics, the Job Corps placement rate for fiscal years 1977, 1978, and 1979 was about 93 percent. This figure includes enrollees placed in employment, military service, school, or further job training. It is all the more remarkable that this placement rate has been achieved with a disadvantaged population, 85 percent of whom had not completed high school, and 50 percent of whom were reading at or below seventh grade level when they entered the program.[8]

Following congressional recognition of Job Corps' effectiveness, appropriations were approved in 1978 to double the size of the program. By the end of fiscal year 1979, there were 95 Job Corps Centers. By 1980, the Job Corps was widely viewed as money well spent.[9] It is clear from experience with the Job Corps that the government can run an effective training and job placement program for disadvantaged young men and women.

Youth Employment Programs

Under a variety of names (e.g., Neighborhood Youth Corps, Summer Youth Employment Program), the federal government has supported up to and exceeding one million needy young people, mostly in summer jobs, each year since the War on Poverty began. These programs, in recent years, have been housed in the Department of Labor and they have been, for the most part, missed opportunities for youth participation. Eberly recalls wanting to talk about the long-range potential of national service with an official of the Hubert Humphrey presidential campaign in May 1968. Humphrey was then the Vice President and had just made a statement including national service as one of the eight major planks in his presidential campaign platform. The official said there was no time to talk about national service: "We are trying to keep our cities from blowing up, and we need the money for our summer youth program starting next month." Admittedly, this was a tense period with the assassination a month earlier of Martin Luther King, Jr., and the riots which followed. But the attitude was typical. Short-term crises and concerns not only took precedence over long-term planning; they virtually replaced a planning strategy for the future. The emphasis on short-term control has unfortunately been paramount in most youth employment programs of the 1960s and 1970s.

Another concern with targeted youth employment programs is the "label" given to participants. In these employment and work experience programs aimed at disadvantaged young people, both the enrollees and the people around them know that the young people are enrolled because of negative qualifications. This stigma is difficult to overcome. A major review of youth employment programs during the Carter administration concluded: "The evidence of seventeen years of research and evaluation indicates that whenever the hard core disadvantaged were segregated in any program, failure was almost inevitable."[10]

College Work-Study Program

The College Work-Study Program (CWSP) is currently located in the Department of Education. When initiated in 1964, CWSP was to help needy students pay their way through college and to involve those students in antipoverty efforts. However, there were no teeth in the latter objective and the result was that some 85 percent of CWSP students can be found working on campus rather than in the community. Since the employer pays only 20 percent of the CWSP student's salary, there has been pressure by college officials to keep the students on campus in such positions as secretaries, dishwashers, and library aides. With the federal government paying 80 percent of the salary, it could, by routing the money through municipal and voluntary agencies instead of college financial aid officers, have guaranteed a much stronger antipoverty effort. CWSP has grown slowly but steadily since it began in 1965, with 1980 enrollment reaching 920,000.

Volunteers in Service to America

Volunteers in Service to America (VISTA) was first publicly outlined on November 17, 1962, when President Kennedy appointed a high-level committee "to study the feasibility of a national service program patterned after the Peace Corps."[11] The guidelines then described for this new venture have held remarkably firm during the 16-year existence of VISTA. Its volunteers were to deal with the causes of poverty and work in such areas as mental hospitals, Indian reservations, migrant labor camps, and correctional institutions. It was to be a small program. The suggested enlistment term was one year. When the committee submitted its report to the President on January 14, 1963, it called for a National Service Corps that would reach a full strength of 5,000 in about three years. The Committee said that the full-time corpsmembers would, "by their example and inspiration, motivate many other citizens to give part-time service in their own communities."[12] The corpsmembers would work under the supervision of local community groups. The Corps would be open to persons 18 and over who possessed "the *highest possible personal qualifications* and requisite technical preparation."[13] Finally, the planners explored the possibility of academic credit at the university level and called for the development of standards by which experience in the Corps could be accredited.

The plans accurately describe the product. VISTA enrollment has hovered around 4,500 and has never exceeded 5,000 persons. It has served the poor, Indians, and migrants. It has generated additional resources, both human and financial, at the local level. VISTA volunteers have served under local supervision and entry qualifications have been demanding. The service role of VISTA Volunteers has been dominant in Republican administrations and the change agent role has been dominant in Democratic administrations. However, at no time has VISTA approached its potential size; the demand for VISTA Volunteers has always been many times greater than the supply.

THE 1970s: THE CONSERVATION CORPS IDEA

During the 1970s, conservation-oriented youth programs, modeled in part after the CCC of the 1930s, began to reappear. The California Conservation Corps is the major example at the state level. The two most prominent federally sponsored programs have been the Youth Conservation Corps and the Young Adult Conservation Corps. These two federal programs are described below.

Youth Conservation Corps

The Youth Conservation Corps (YCC) was initiated in 1970 as a summer residential conservation-oriented work and education program for 15-18 year olds. YCC has been targeted more broadly than many other youth employment efforts, i.e., enrollees are not necessarily disadvantaged. In fact, YCC has been criticized for not enrolling a fair proportion of urban, black, and economically disadvantaged young people.[14] The program, however,

has been very popular with enrollees and generally viewed as successful by
the public at large. The popularity of YCC should not escape us. A universally applied program, i.e., a program open to applicants regardless of economic means, has the advantage of being accepted by the Congress and the
American people without the stigma of being a "welfare" program. This is a
very old lesson in social policy, which the YCC has once again demonstrated.

Young Adult Conservation Corps

Created as part of the Youth Employment and Demonstrations Project Act
of 1977, the Young Adult Conservation Corps (YACC) has been another
programmatic descendant of the CCC. The major goals of YACC have been
carbon copies of CCC goals—jobs and conservation work. This year-round
program has been open to 16 to 23 year olds from all economic backgrounds
who are unemployed and out of school. Enrollment of mentally and physically disabled young people is encouraged.

> Of the 56,301 enrollees who entered YACC programs in FY 1979, . . . Black
> youth comprised 12 percent; American Indians 6 percent; Hispanics 7 percent;
> and other minority groups 8 percent. More than one-third were women. Thirty-
> eight percent were economically disadvantaged. Forty-two percent had not
> graduated from high school.[15]

As described in chapter 12, YCC and YACC have been economically productive. The dollar value of work performed has been approximately equal
to total program costs. These direct economic returns, combined with the
social and educational benefits of YCC and YACC have made these programs a very solid investment in America's resources, both "natural" and
human.

THE 1970s: NATIONAL SERVICE TESTS IN URBAN AREAS

ACTION, a federal agency created in 1971 to house the Peace Corps,
VISTA, and other volunteer programs, became the sponsor of a small but
significant national service experiment in Seattle in 1973-1974 and a modified national service experiment in Syracuse, New York, between 1978 and
1980.

Seattle's Program for Local Service

The smallest federally-sponsored youth service program was also the purest
test of national service. Although enrolling only 372 volunteers, the 1973-74
Program for Local Service (PLS) in Seattle, Washington, destroyed several
myths about national service and yielded valuable lessons for the future.

PLS was the creation of two men: Governor Daniel J. Evans of Washington and Joseph H. Blatchford, Jr., Director of the ACTION agency. Evans had devoted half of his keynote address to the 1968 Republican Convention to the benefits of a national service program. Blatchford had been a strong believer in the national service idea since reading William James' "Moral Equivalent of War." He was not in a position to forward the idea as Peace Corps Director from 1969 to 1971, but when ACTION was created in 1971 and he was given responsibility for the Peace Corps, VISTA, and other volunteer programs, Blatchford believed he had a launching pad for national service.

In 1972, Blatchford submitted a multi-billion dollar national service budget to the Office of Management and Budget. It never became a part of the President's budget submission to Congress, but Blatchford did obtain approval to conduct a small test project. Washington, where Evans was still governor, was the obvious site and PLS was launched there in early 1973.

Hypotheses about the test project abounded. Some said that ACTION would be made to look silly; so few young people would volunteer that most of the $1 million grant would have to be turned back. Some said that PLS would become an elitist program like the Peace Corps because the stipend being offered was somewhat less than the minimum wage, and because PLS was described as a volunteer service project. Others contended that PLS would attract only low income young people since it emphasized community service rather than societal reform, and since PLS was described as a work experience project.

The results, however, were encouraging to those who saw promise in national service. A three-state recruitment process had been planned in the event that not enough people would volunteer for the program; but more than enough 18-25 year olds did volunteer and only the first stage was utilized. PLS attracted applications from 10 percent of the youth population aware of the program.[16] PLS also identified 1,200 potential positions from 200 potential sponsors over a three-month period.

PLS volunteers covered the socioeconomic spectrum. One in ten came from households with incomes below $1,000 per year, and a similar proportion of volunteers had personal incomes greater than the amount they would receive in PLS. A few were mentally retarded; some had college degrees. One was a veteran of military service. A few had criminal records. Of every ten PLS volunteers, six were women; two were members of minority groups; seven were unemployed and looking for work; and six had attended college.

As stipulated in the experimental design, PLS was not to be a soft program. Guidelines were firmly established. Both volunteers and sponsoring agencies were expected to live up to the terms of their agreements. As it turned out, one out of every eight volunteers was released for breaking the agreement, usually for failure to report for work. One of the 137 sponsors also was released for failing to extend its day care services to more poor people, as the sponsor had agreed to do with the PLS volunteers on staff.

The two most dramatic findings relate to the two major reasons given by young people for joining PLS; namely, contributing to the community and gaining work experience. The sponsoring agencies estimated the work done by PLS Volunteers to be worth $2,150,000, double the $1,086,000 federal grant which funded the program.[16] And the unemployment rate among persons in PLS fell from 70 percent at time of application to 18 percent six months after leaving PLS.[18]

Youth Community Service in Syracuse

ACTION conducted a modified national service test project in Syracuse, New York, from 1978 to 1980. Youth Community Service (YCS), with approximately 2,000 volunteers ages 16 to 21 and a budget of $10 million was somewhat larger than the Program for Local Service in Seattle. However, some of YCS's value as a national service experiment was diminished when the Labor Department, which provided the funds, insisted that incoming volunteers be out of school, unemployed, and looking for work. The result was predictable. Whereas Seattle residents viewed PLS as a constructive community service program for young people, people in the Syracuse area perceived YCS as a "jobs for needy youth" program.

Nevertheless, the YCS experience is useful in considering a future national service. Most important, the experience of YCS suggests that the National Service Secretariat's estimate of a need for more than a million young people in national service is close to the mark. In just under two years, the YCS project developed 2,456 positions.[18] If the same proportion of positions were developed nationally, there would be some 1,100,000. In the process of developing positions for young people, it became clear, as it had in Seattle, that the real prospect of engaging young people in a service program led directly to the creation of positions that would not have been revealed in a theoretical survey.

CONCLUSION

The national service precedents described above are by no means all of the national or community service programs which have taken place in the United States. These are only the major efforts at the federal level. Literally thousands of other projects have taken place at the state and local levels over the years. To take one small example, in some rural areas of the United States it was customary, in former years, for each young man in the area to devote a week or two's labor during the summer to maintain local roads, drainage ditches, etc. This commitment was completely taken for granted and uncompensated; it was a community service. Altogether, there is a very rich tradition of cooperative community and national service in the United States. It is against this background, and drawing on these values and experiences, that a national service program would develop and grow. Moreover, there are a wide variety of national service experiences in other countries from which valuable lessons can be drawn. In the next two chapters, Irene Pinkau and Roger Landrum describe major national service programs in other countries.

NOTES

1. William James, "The Moral Equivalent of War," *International Conciliation*, no. 27 (New York: Carnegie Endowment for International Peace, 1910).

2. Frank Newman, "Proposal for a Community Service GI Bill," *Congressional Record*, entered by Senator Jacob Javits (April 12, 1973), p. S7244.

3. Sar A. Levitan and Karen Cleary, *Old Wars Remain Unfinished* (Baltimore: The Johns Hopkins University Press, 1973), p. 125.

4. There appears to be no full-scale analysis, generally acceptable to economists, on the rate of return on the GI Bill. Albert E. Smigel has estimated that the GI Bill from 1945 to 1973 yielded a 16-fold return solely in terms of increased federal tax payments. Smigel's analysis does not discount the future value of these returns, but he suggests that this amount is more than compensated for by the economic returns of the GI Bill in addition to federal tax payments. An official of the Veterans Administration reported that the VA has not made a study of the GI Bill as an investment because it might appear that the VA was trying to make a case for a "universal GI Bill" (Telephone conversations with Donald Eberly, 1976).

5. Newman, "Proposal for a Community Service GI Bill," p. S7244.

6. Terrence Cullinan, *Attitudes of Returning Peace Corps Volunteers Concerning Impact of Peace Corps Interlude on Subsequent Academic Work* (Menlo Park, California: Stanford Research Institute, 1969), p. 3.

7. Christopher Weeks, *Job Corps* (Boston: Little, Brown, 1967), p. 191.

8. Michael W. Sherraden, "Job Corps" in *Government Agencies*, edited by Donald R. Whitnah (Westport, Connecticut: Greenwood Press, forthcoming).

9. See, for example, Mathematica Policy Research, Inc., *Evaluation of the Economic Impact of the Job Corps Program; Second Follow-up Report* (Princeton, New Jersey: Mathematica, 1980).

10. Garth Mangum and John Walsh, *Employment and Training Programs for Youth: What Works Best for Whom?* (Washington: U.S. Government Printing Office, 1978), p. 58.

11. The President's Study Group on a National Service Program, *Information on a Proposed National Service Program* (Washington: The President's Study Group, 1963), p. I-1.

12. Ibid., p. I-4.

13. Ibid., VII-1.

14. Mangum and Walsh, *Employment and Training Programs for Youth*, p. 60.

15. Human Environment Center, *Youth-Conservation Employment* (Washington: Human Environment Center, 1980), citing U.S. Department of Labor, *Joint Annual Report to the President and Congress, Young Adult Conservation Corps* (Washington: U.S. Department of Labor, 1979, mimeographed).

16. Control Systems Research, *A Survey of Public Awareness of, and Reaction to, the Program for Local Service Among Potential Participants* (Arlington, Virginia: Control Systems Research, 1973).

17. Control Systems Research, *The Program for Local Service: Special Report* (Seattle, Washington: Control Systems Research, 1973), pp. 4-12.

18. Kappa Systems, Inc., *The Impact of Participation in the Program for Local Service Upon the Participant* (Arlington, Virginia: Kappa Systems, Inc., 1975), sections 2 and 4.

19. Youth Community Service, *Report to the Community* (Syracuse, New York: Youth Community Service, 1980), p. 2.

Chapter 4

National Service in Kenya, Nigeria and Indonesia

Irene Pinkau

National service is not a new idea. More than 6,000 years ago people in Egypt joined a cooperative national labor scheme to build dikes and canals to control the Nile. For centuries, China carried out rural public works programs to improve the agricultural infrastructure through irrigation, drainage, and terracing.[1]

Today, the majority of the close to 160 nations on this globe has some form of national service devoted to civilian and developmental needs. In a broader sense, national service engages citizens—by voluntary or obligatory recruitment—in civilian and/or military service for a certain period of time. Apart from the strictly military service, which is not the focus here, the emphasis of national service worldwide is on development work. Only a smaller proportion of cases links civilian service and military draft and provides options for either route (for example, in the Federal Republic of Germany, a case which is discussed in chapter 5). A third variation of ties between civilian and military service exists when certain military and disciplinary training components are provided before development work assignments. Such training readies participants in civilian national service as a military stand-by force (for example, Iran's four development corps under the late Shah), or leads them into careers in the military or police forces after completion of service (such as the National Youth Development Corps of Malaysia). Finally, a fourth variation of linkage between civilian and military service embodies national programs engaged in development work and organized in camps characterized by a paramilitary organizational structure; participants can be employed in cases of national emergencies and civilian unrest (such as Kenya's National Youth Service and the former Zambian National Youth Service). In these cases, where certain linkages between military and civilian service exist, the civilian service can be and has been used to support a certain form of government or ruling party (for example, in the case of Zambia). Thus, civilian national service has on occasion been used as a political instrument. Its overwhelming emphasis, however, has been on the needs of the citizenry and the development of the country.

Inevitably, there are not one but several causes which spark the establishment of a national development service. These include 1) lack of education, 2) youth unemployment, 3) cultural and status gaps between diverse population groups (nation building), 4) demands to implant social obligation in privileged and higher educated citizens, and 5) a need to direct the education system to better serve communities in providing social and economic services. National service has always derived from needs of individuals—both participants and service clients—as well as needs of the local community and the nation–state. At a time of increasing global interconnectedness, national service builds not only nations but the world community. It promotes devotion to work for the benefit of others and removes the barriers of "we vs. they" perceptions among peoples of diverse backgrounds. In questioning the causes for their establishment in a comprehensive evaluation of 30 volunteer development services in 15 countries, four major categories of national development service have been identified. These categories are 1) training and employment programs, 2) study-services, 3) social and technical development services, and 4) foreign volunteer services.[2] In each category, of course, there are many variations among services; many different combinations of programs under one national service roof are possible.

TRAINING AND EMPLOYMENT PROGRAMS: THE CASE OF THE KENYA NATIONAL YOUTH SERVICE

Kenya's National Youth Service (KNYS) is an example of a training and employment approach to national service. Such programs are created to compensate for lack of access to education, inadequate learning, high drop-out rates, and high rates of unemployment and underemployment among youth. They are also sometimes sparked by a need to bridge the division among ethnic groups and converge their different cultural backgrounds into a sense of national community (but not melting pot). Training and employment schemes primarily involve the less educated, or illiterate, and unemployed youth in a combination of literacy, civic, and technical skill training and in work programs for a duration of six months to two years. Work includes either large-scale public construction and conservation programs or small-scale community based agriculture, craftsmanship, small-scale industry, and delivery of local services (health, nutrition, and community development). These programs are most effective when their training is accredited by the education system and/or technical training boards and their work programs are formally linked with the employment system, providing participants with access to both continuing education and long-range employment opportunities. Other examples of training and employment schemes include 4-D Clubs in Benin, Botswana Brigades, Cost Rica's National Youth Movement, and Malaysia's Young Pioneers. Most have community–based work programs that provide more locally integrated on-the-job training. In the case of Malaysia, the business community directs work assignments on behalf of the governmental program.

The Kenya National Youth Service was established on September 1, 1964, by the National Youth Service Act. Created only nine months after winning independence, KNYS is a voluntary, two year, full-time service for youth aged 16-30 years. The program is under the supervision of the Ministry of Labour.

Conditions Which Led to the Creation of KNYS

Seven major conditions sparked the creation of KNYS in Kenya:

1. National independence and the need to move from a multitribal society to a united nation;
2. Presence of militant youth without a cause; these young people had been involved in liberation movements and needed to be assimilated into normal working life (early on this was a pressing issue which, over time, has diminished);
3. Lack of education and training among young people and the need for preparation for a useful role in the community;
4. Unemployment, especially among youth;
5. Great needs for public works construction, especially in remote rural areas;
6. Needs for pools of trained workers in various skilled tasks; and
7. A need for an organized and trained labor force available in case of national emergencies (this provision of the Act has, so far, not been implemented).

Recruitment Criteria and Participants

Candidates for KNYS must be Kenyan citizens, unemployed, healthy, and without dependents. There are no educational requirements. Applications are directed to District Committees and equal quotas are allocated to each Province to ensure national representation among participants. In 1974, there were about 50 applicants per service vacancy. Major motivation to apply for service has been hope for later employment and access to education. Moving out of the village and from under the control of parents and wider family has also been a motivating factor. Also, Kenyans are proud of their national service and the participation of their youth in national development. On national holidays, KNYS often participates; uniformed members carry shovels in parades and other official events.

Since 1964, approximately 52,500 volunteers have participated in KNYS and the service is currently at an annual strength of 5,000 young men and women. The law provides for up to 7,000 participants annually. In the early years, about 25 percent of the volunteers had no schooling, 25 percent up to five years of primary school, and 45 percent up to eight years of education. Today, most participants have a minimum of seven years of schooling and the number of high school and college students interested in service is on the rise. After completion of service, at least 50 percent of the participants find immediate employment, about one-third in the industrial sector, while two-thirds remain in rural areas in agriculture, small trade, and informal services.

The Training and Work Program

There are six phases of training and work which alternate over the two year service period. Table 4.1 summarizes these six phases.

By design, work projects are not community based but focus on large-scale public works in remote areas and on advancement of agriculture. According to G. W. Griffin, Director of KNYS:

The Service is playing the major role in the Bura Irrigation and Settlement Scheme on the River Tana . . . the main canal, subsidiary canals, feeder roads, an air field and we are doing land planning. We are also heavily involved in the construction to bitumen standard of the trunk road to the North–Eastern Province. . . . We continue to maintain our various farms and, in particular, are transforming the 10,000 acre Yatta Farm. . . . Huge areas are being cleared and irrigated and a great deal of coffee is being grown (our own coffee factory is under construction). There is also cultivation of subsistence crops . . . citrus fruit . . . and experimental work with crops new to Kenya. Because of our growing agricultural expertise we have been called upon to set up demonstration farms in backward areas. . . . We continue to maintain one of the largest fleets of trucks in the country and have been heavily committed to the emergency movement of grain during the recent period of population feeding problems in Kenya.[3]

Vocational training also has been diversified and reflects the improved educational background of new recruits, including: Basic Vocational Training (550 trainees); Advanced Engineering School (76 trainees); Advanced Automotive School (59 trainees); Secretarial School (79 trainees; increase to 200 planned); Upholstery School (15 trainees; increase to 200 planned); Driving School (75 trainees); Tailoring School (226 trainees); and Rural Craft Training Centre (128 trainees). A School for Plant Operators, Mechanics, and Road Foremen is scheduled to open soon. An Agricultural College for 400 students is in the planning stage. In 1973 (the latest figures available), approx-

Table 4.1. Training and Work Phases of Kenya's National Youth Service

Training

Type of Training	Duration	Major Topics
Phase 1 Basic Training	months 1 and 2	Basic training, which includes discipline (no weapons), literacy, English, and civics
Phase 3 Centralized full-time education	months 9 to 12	Basic science up to lower secondary level
Phase 5 Centralized full-time education	months 17 to 20	Vocational training in basic agriculture, masonry, carpentry, etc.; and continuing education for government labor qualifications

Work Projects

Type of Work	Duration	Project Description
Phase 2 Project or farm work	months 3 to 8	Major projects requiring at least 100 men for completion and not competing with
Phase 4 Project or farm work or vocational work	months 13 to 16	local self-help schemes and community development, e.g., road building, bush clearing to combat tsetse fly, general earth works for river embankments, etc.; farm work includes sheep and cattle raising, and mixed farming
Phase 6 General duties in service	months 21 to 24	Accounting, clerical duties, health work, and day to day running of service instead of using hired personnel

imately 85 percent of volunteers graduated after vocational training with a Grade III Trade Test, the recognized worker qualification for industrial employment. A small group continued and completed the Grade II Trade Test.

Costs and Achievements

In 1973, the average cost per volunteer year was US $302, including administrative overhead, training facilities, and construction equipment for work programs. Earnings through work projects are billed to the respective governmental departments and public corporations. Work income is paid back to the Treasury as an appropriation-in-aid against KNYS expenses. Currently, KNYS is consolidating its facilities from tents and temporary structures to permanent barracks, dining halls, workshops, and staff housing.

The achievements of KNYS are seen in various areas. The accreditation of its training and the acceptance of service graduates by the employment system are foremost indicators of its effectiveness. KNYS has removed, for the participants, the dead end street of lack of education and no hope for employment. Another important achievement is the flexibility displayed in adapting training programs to the changing needs of Kenyan youth.

The continued convergence of Kenya's different cultures in joint work and learning, under equal conditions, must also be stressed as a major achievement, while in other sectors of the society ethnic divisions are by no means diminished.

The continued demand by Kenyan youth to gain a place in the service is, of course, due largely to their economic distress and their hope for later continued education or employment. This is *not* a negative motivation for voluntary service (as some might assume from a "purist" view of voluntarism which, in fact, requires a person to be economically secure to give voluntary service to society). Employment not only ensures economic survival of the individual but it is an essential expression of human dignity and a contribution to society; it is the linkage that establishes kinship with the immediate community and the nation. Therefore, those who now volunteer to work hard for two years to gain a dignified role in society are an invaluable resource for any nation, a resource that should be respected and cherished.

Finally, that the Kenyan National Youth Service still enjoys the support and pride of the public after 17 years is an indication not only that needs still exist but also that the Service has been able to meet the expectations of its citizens.

STUDY-SERVICES: THE CASE OF THE NATIONAL YOUTH SERVICE CORPS OF NIGERIA

In general, study–services have been sparked by the need to make higher education more relevant to the needs of the community and the development of the nation, "to strengthen what might be called the learning capacity of the nation," in the words of K. Soedjatmoko, who became the Rector of the United Nations University in 1980.[4] In order to provide students with opportunities for experiential learning in real life situations (not just technical praxis), students are assigned to development projects, often in remote communities, to serve ordinary citizens in health and nutrition, primary and adult education, agricultural extension and marketing, building of the local infrastructure, and community development. Preparatory training and the work assignment are in most cases integral parts of the curriculum. Students serve for three months to one year, full time or part time, with long-term commitments to projects. The work provides intercultural encounters and problem–solving experiences outside the academic enclave and helps consensus–forming processes among peoples of diverse backgrounds and, thereby, builds new value preferences that go beyond academic disciplines and address the social issues of the community. Thus, study-services link educational institutions with the community and bridge gaps between ethnic and

cultural groups, the educated and uneducated, and urban and rural populations. Study-services provide management, administrative, and teaching
skills; stimulate creativity; and create an environment of social learning
which sensitizes those who will be the future leaders of a nation to a public
obligation.

In many developing countries, study-services are obligatory and regarded
as any other compulsory course in the curriculum. Study-services are most
effective when work assignments are conducted in a block of time after some
period of classroom study. For undergraduates, the time after completion of
the second year or during the third year is usually best. Also, the measure-
ment of both the students' competence at work and their theoretical reflection about the service experience are indications that the program is effectively integrated into educational institutions.

Examples of study-services include *Kuliah Kerdja Njata* in Indonesia
(compulsory); National Development Service in Nepal (compulsory); Graduate Volunteer Program, Thammasat University, Thailand (voluntary); university services in Morocco, Ghana, and Tanzania (compulsory); and university services in Colombia, Costa Rica, and Brazil (voluntary). The only
example of a voluntary and accredited study-service in Europe is the Community Service Volunteers' study-service for high school and college students in the United Kingdom. In the United States, the early work-study
programs at Antioch, Goddard, and Sarah Lawrence paved the way; today,
the National Center for Service–Learning of ACTION supports a broad
diversity of study-services throughout the country, even though the U.S.
program has not yet achieved proportions of outreach and acceptance that
one might speak of as a national service.

Background of the National Youth Service Corps of Nigeria

The National Youth Service Corps of Nigeria (NYSC) is a study-service that
bridges the gap between education and employment systems. The idea for a
national service by students originated in 1969 in the Committee of Vice
Chancellors of Nigerian Universities. The Committee recommended that
students' academic education should become relevant to the development of
the nation, that cultural gaps among the 250 tribes should be bridged, and as
a 1970 consultant report suggested, faculty should participate in the service
in various functions to truly integrate service-learning into the educational
institutions. The discussion of these proposals ran into two main difficulties:
academia could not agree on the extent to which work-service assignments
should actually be integrated into the curricula and given credit, and some
government authorities felt that there was a greater need to involve instead
uneducated and unemployed youth in a training and employment scheme.

In 1972, the Head of State cut the "Gordian Knot" and decreed the establishment of NYSC for all university students immediately following their first degree. This compulsory national service scheme was formally created on May 22, 1973, and amended on September 19, 1974, to cover also all Nigerian students graduating at foreign universities with the one year full-time service obligation. Enforcement of these provisions is secured by a discharge certificate after completion of service and the legal obligation of any prospective Nigerian employer to demand and obtain the discharge certificate before an employment agreement is finalized.

Objectives and Organization

The motto of NYSC is "Service and Humility" and the objectives reflect the problems Nigeria hopes to solve with this service program:

1. To inculcate discipline in Nigerian youths by instilling in them a tradition of industry at work and of patriotic and loyal service to the nation in any situation they may find themselves;
2. To raise their moral tone by giving them the opportunity to learn about higher ideals of national achievement and social and cultural improvement;
3. To develop in them attitudes of mind, acquired through shared experience and suitable training, which will make them more amenable to mobilization in the national interest;
4. To develop common ties among them and promote national unity by ensuring that
   a) As far as possible, youths are assigned to jobs in States other than their States of origin;
   b) Each group assigned to work together is as representative of the country as possible;
   c) Youths are exposed to the modes of living of the people in different parts of the country with a view to removing prejudices, eliminating ignorance, and confirming at first hand the many similarities among Nigerians of all ethnic groups;
5. To encourage members of the service corps to seek, at the end of their corps service, career employment all over the country, thus promoting the free movement of labor;
6. To induce employers, partly through their experience with members of the service corps, to employ more readily qualified Nigerians irrespective of their States of origin; and
7. To enable Nigerian youths to acquire the spirit of self-reliance.[5]

NYSC is governed by a Directorate consisting of the Chairperson; five persons representing the universities of Nigeria; one member of the armed forces; one member of the Nigeria Police Force; a representative of the Nigerian Employers' Consultative Association; the Director, who is appointed by the Head of the Federal Military Government; one representative of the Cabinet Office; one representative of the Federal Ministry of Education; one representative of the Federal Ministry of Labour, Youth and Sports; two representatives each of polytechnics or equivalent institutions, and of advanced teacher training colleges; and three other persons, at least one of whom is to be a woman. State Committees in each of the 19 States are charged with management and field supervision. Members are appointed by the Governor, and Chief Inspectors coordinate training and work projects in each state.

Participants and Orientation

In 1979-80, 18,000 graduates participated, of which 77 percent were men, 23 percent were women, and approximately 15 percent were trained in other countries. Final year students at all institutions of higher education are recruited by a call-up and are obligated to serve if under 30 years of age. Exemption from service can be granted to individuals or groups by an order of the Directorate published in the Gazette, provided the order has received prior approval by the Federal Executive Council. Refusal to serve is a federal offense and liable to a fine or 12 months imprisonment or both.

General orientation is conducted for four weeks. The curriculum includes cultural training, language, skills for work assignments, physical training, drills, and leadership and initiative training at Man O' War Bay School, an Outward Bound School established with the assistance of the United Kingdom before independence. An additional three weeks of professional orientation is provided for medical doctors (2.8 percent of corps members) in the six medical schools to prepare them for work with mobile health units, service in remote areas, and specific medical assignments.

Work Assignments

Work assignments, to the extent possible, are not in the home state of corps members in order to provide intercultural experience and promote understanding between the 250 ethnic groups that make up Nigerian society. This policy has been successful. In 1974, 62 percent of the corps members served in states they had never visited before. This average was higher for the less accessible northwestern states (83.2 percent) and southeastern states (91.3 percent). Considering that NYSC was initiated in part to overcome the rift between ethnic groups after the Biafran War, this is an important feature of the service.

Work assignments have been approximately 93 percent within the public sector, including post primary education (65 percent), health (5.5 percent), public administration (2.5 percent), cooperatives (6 percent), agriculture (3 percent), and banks (1 percent). About 7 percent of the work assignments focus on the private sector; these include farming, small scale industry, business, and charitable organizations.

As secondary work assignments, corps members are required to spend four weeks in community development work side by side with local citizens. The total number of local projects executed in 1979-80 was 532. These were primarily local construction projects such as classrooms, dispensaries, maternity centers, farm to market roads, small dams, bridges, and culverts. In addition, voluntary community development is encouraged and has included remedial classes for school dropouts, evening classes for workers to prepare them for trade tests, adult literacy classes, clean-up campaigns, drama and sports, development of school farms, and health education.

Costs and Achievements

The 1973-74 budget (for 2,271 corps members) was N 6 million (US $9.2 million). Costs per NYSC corps members per year in 1973-74 amounted to $4,065 including administrative overhead. The monthly allowance for board, lodging, and incidental expenses per corps member totaled $185 (in 1975 it had increased to $230). This was high compared to other services. The reason was that corps members were university graduates about to enter employment and their allowance should approach an equivalent wage level. This reasoning and the level of allowance is somewhat contrary to the service concept. As a rule, national service makes a strict distinction between the stipends provided for participants and wages or minimum wages of the employment system. Allowances are determined by subsistence levels and sometimes provision of room and board free of charge. Such remuneration, of course, is given so that even the poorest citizens are able to participate in the service. Consideration of wages, however, has no place in national service because wages are determined by the formal employment system. Remuneration in national service should be clearly distinct from the labor conditions governing such employment. Most advocates of national service believe that these two types of remuneration should not be confused—not even in the terminology used to describe the payments given to participants.

Achievements of NYSC can be identified in these areas: 1) That NYSC reached all university graduates in Nigeria is no special accomplishment for an obligatory service, but that NYSC has reached a large proportion of Nigerian foreign graduates is a notable achievement. NYSC keeps regular contact with Nigerian students in senior semesters at universities in foreign countries and the Director of the service regularly visits the various regions.

Most graduates return voluntarily to Nigeria to take up their service obligation and consequently no "brain drain" has resulted. Of course, students do not want to forego later employment in Nigeria, a provision which prods them to accept the service commitment. 2) NYSC has achieved a cultural mix both within its groups and vis-à-vis the communities it serves. This mix is important for a war-torn country with deep ethnic and religious divisions. That intercultural cooperation takes place day-in and day-out and that participants jointly tackle the small problems of life without rejection of the program or revolt by citizens indicates acceptance of the service obligation. (3) This acceptance may have been stimulated by satisfaction with work assignments. Experiences in other programs have indicated that voluntary services can fail when the volunteer is not needed on the job, does not have a full work load and a work responsibility compatible with his or her qualifications. By the same token, obligatory services succeed and participants gain a positive attitude toward their service when such work conditions are met. Therefore, it can be assumed that the majority of NYSC work assignments achieve a high level of satisfaction and performance.

SOCIAL AND TECHNICAL DEVELOPMENT SERVICES: THE CASE OF BADAN URUSAN TENAGA KERDJA SUKARELA INDONESIA (BUTSI)

Indonesia's *Badan Urusan Tenaga Kerdja Sukarela* (*BUTSI*) is an example of social and technical development services. This approach to national service is sparked by community needs for specific services and by individual citizen desires to participate in society. Service needs include: care of the sick, disabled, elderly and children; economic assistance to small businesses; services to generate local employment; community development and education; protection of the environment; support for public transportation; and integration of refugees.

Social and technical development services are more diverse than other types of national service described above and involve primarily educated, life experienced seniors and professionals. Age of volunteers ranges from 15 up to 85 years and over. While most social and technical development services are small, local, and private, the national service programs are often full time and for periods of one or two years. Other examples of social and technical development services include: *Arsa Pattana* in Thailand, Community Service Volunteers in the United Kingdom, Voluntary Social Services in the Federal Republic of Germany, National Youth Movement in Costa Rica, and VISTA and the Older American Programs in the United States.

Formally established in 1968 by the Ministry of Manpower, *BUTSI* is a Board for Volunteer Service which coordinates and manages a two year, full-time service of graduates in Indonesia; gives direction to all activities in Indonesia related to volunteer manpower, including foreigners; supervises governmental policies in the field; and fosters cooperation between Indonesian volunteers and those in other countries (overseas assignments).

Conditions Which Led to the Creation of *BUTSI*

BUTSI was created to address a combination of conditions which demanded attention in Indonesia at the end of the 1960s. These included:

1. Increasing numbers of unemployed university graduates in urban centers with an oversupply in "prestige fields" such as law, education, liberal arts, and social sciences, and an accompanying lack of engineers, agriculturalists, planners, and managers;
2. The general view on the part of the public that "good" university graduates are employed in urban centers and only the failures agree to rural employment, resulting in the graduates' refusal to seek rural employment and provide needed professional services;
3. The need for services in remote areas; 83 percent of the population live on the more than 30,000 populated islands in about 56,000 villages administered by the village head in the traditional form of local government; Indonesia has a long tradition of local voluntary action and mutual help (*gotong royong*) and, therefore, villagers were prepared to receive volunteers from the city; and
4. The international climate in the mid-1960s was favorable to the establishment of volunteer services and the International Secretariat for Volunteer Service succeeded in rendering assistance in the planning stages and pilot projects.

Volunteer Recruitment, Selection, and Training

In 1977, a total of 2,666 volunteers participated in the two year, full-time service. Their ages ranged from 22 to over 30 years, with the majority in the 25-30 age bracket. It is not known how many women participated at that time but, in the early stages in 1973, 20 percent of the volunteers were women.

Volunteer recruitment has used mass media, leaflets, and posters at universities to motivate application. Most important, however, have been the successes and public visibility of the first batches of volunteers in pilot projects. They have given *BUTSI* a positive beginning in the mind of the public. Criteria for eligibility include: 1) a university degree or sufficient level of training (in case of dropouts); 2) unmarried status (in case of married graduates, both spouses are treated as single volunteers and assigned to projects in the same village); 3) willingness to work in any rural area in Indonesia; 4) willingness to live for two years in rural areas on low living allowances; 5) agreement that *BUTSI* has no obligation to provide employment after completion of service; and 6) agreement to pay back to *BUTSI* all money received as a volunteer if there is an early departure from the two years service.

Volunteer selection from the pool of applicants is conducted by three separate teams. One team is for health examinations; another for professional qualifications; and a third for personality qualifications. In 1974, out of 1,950 applicants, 770 volunteers entered training.

Volunteer training lasts eight weeks and has three sections. There is a general introduction lasting one week at the provincial capitals to brief the volunteers on development programs in the province, to give details on the assigned village, and to introduce the village chief and future volunteer. The chief has a say in the final selection and placement of the volunteer. The second phase of training, village observation, lasts three weeks and includes a survey of the village of assignment and development of preliminary plans for the volunteer's tasks. Theoretical and practical training at provincial capitals lasts four weeks and includes technical skill training, methodology of project implementation, and planning of the assignment.

Work Programs

Work programs follow these guidelines: one volunteer is assigned to one village and he or she is expected to live in the house of the village chief and pay for accommodations from the allowances paid by *BUTSI*; one team of four to five volunteers works in one sub-district; the village should not be located near a large city and must have a clear need to development assistance; if possible, the village should participate in government sponsored development programs such as applied nutrition and cooperative development; and there will be no second assignment to the same village once the volunteer has completed his or her term of service.

Volunteer activities include erosion control, reforestation, improvement of cultivation techniques, introduction of new or improved cash and food crops, improvement of existing animal and poultry husbandry and the introduction of new species, encouragement of cottage industries, and other contributions to production; adult education literacy teaching, nutrition education, health education, home economics education, improvement of village administration, preparation for transmigration, youth leadership training, encouragement of local cultural and social activities, cooperative movements and other educational activities; and rehabilitation or construction of roads, bridges, irrigation canals, drinking water supplies, school buildings, community sanitary facilities, markets, and other physical facilities.

Costs and Achievements

The 1973 annual budget for *BUTSI* amounted to US $200,500. At that time, there were 500 volunteers. Including administrative overhead, the cost per volunteer per year was US $401.

In 1977, *BUTSI* volunteers were assigned to villages in 19 of the 26 provinces of Indonesia. They were successful as liaisons between villagers and district officials in drawing down to the village level the various development programs administered by different governmental departments and introduced by international organizations, for example, UNICEF's village nutrition program.

"Client training" has been another successful *BUTSI* feature. Client training refers to the preparation of volunteer supervisors and village chiefs on how to best work with volunteers. *BUTSI* borrowed this approach from the Community Service Volunteers, which introduced it first in the United Kingdom.

Since inception, *BUTSI* has become a regular part in the budget of the National Development Plan and its participants have become a much preferred pool for recruitment of junior civil servants, gradually replacing the old reward system which operated by class and political affiliation. *BUTSI*'s success also has sparked the creation of the Indonesian study-service *Kuliah Kerdja Nyata*, now a mandatory part of the academic curriculum. This is an example of mobilization of new norms in another sector of Indonesian society.

FOREIGN VOLUNTEER SERVICES

Foreign volunteer services is the fourth and last major category considered under national development service. These services are distinctly different because they respond to demands and needs of foreign nations, generally problems of underdevelopment and poverty in Third World countries. Foreign volunteer services respond by supplying skilled manpower to projects where no qualified national labor is available. In addition, these services respond to the need to learn more about peoples of other cultures and nations, increase mutual understanding, and establish international relations and friendship among ordinary citizens around the world. Most volunteers have completed their education and often some professional training. The minimum age is usually 21 years and the current average age reaches 28 years. Volunteers are assigned for periods of two years with extensions possible.

Examples of foreign volunteer services include the Peace Corps in the United States, *Stichting Nederlandse Vrijwilliger* in The Netherlands, *Mellem-*

folkelight Samvirke in Denmark, *Deutscher Entwicklungsdienst* in Germany, and Canadian University Service Overseas. In a few instances (Germany, the Netherlands, and France, for example), overseas development service is accepted as alternative service to the military draft. Draftees must commit themselves for overseas service at the time of call-up (normally at the age of 18); must undergo preselection by the respective foreign volunteer service; and complete their technical education, area studies, and language training before they are assigned overseas (about at the age of 25). This is a cumbersome process with many uncertainties, and only a small proportion of those opting for civilian service are accepted for overseas assignments. Furthermore, the linkage of a volunteer development service with the military draft has created a negative image of the program in the eyes of the nationals accepting foreign volunteers.[6] The nationals often have felt that avoiding military service is the main reason why Europeans choose to work abroad. Creating the impression of being the "dumping ground" for draft evaders is, of course, counterproductive for any foreign volunteer service. Therefore, if national civilian service is linked to a military draft, the exclusion of foreign volunteer services from the national program is strongly recommended. If, however, the national service concept is solely devoted to civilian service and development, then overseas programs should be included and, in fact, the inclusion of foreigners in domestic service (for example, the many foreign students in the United States) should be considered as part of the national service scheme. This would provide reciprocity of service to the overseas program and strengthen the ties of the worldwide movement of national service.

DISCUSSION

Local Voluntary Action Is a Worldwide Tradition

Voluntary action among neighbors within the confines of the local community is part of human nature and exists in all cultures. It is mutual self-help to survive and maintain life. This kind of voluntary action is built on reciprocity: If I help you, you will help me. Examples include the many voluntary arrangements in pioneer times, such as joint barn raising in the United States, to the *gotong royong* self-help system in villages in Indonesia, and the *Mwethga* (cooperative work groups) and *Ielo* (resource policy groups) in East and Central African villages.[7] Voluntary action that goes beyond mutual self–help and beyond the community is different—it can be mobilized only if the moral obligation is overwhelming, such as in the case of national emergencies, natural disasters, war, or other compelling reasons.

Voluntary National Service Requires a Mix of Compelling Reasons

For any individual, various compelling reasons must exist that would lead him or her to join a national service voluntarily. These might include:

- A high rate of unemployment and the hope for a job after completion of service;
- Credit for service at an educational institution;
- A way to get out of the home, escape an undesirable social environment, or cut ties to parents;
- A way to solve a personal problem;
- A way to meet other people; or
- An opportunity to do something worthwhile.

These are all realistic reasons and they should be taken seriously and welcomed as legitimate. The "purist" motivation of voluntary action to do good and show empathy toward others without any personal reward may be found here and there, but it requires a rich person to sustain it, generally one who is economically independent.

Voluntary Versus Obligatory Service: A Question of Value Mobilization

The question of voluntary versus obligatory national service relates to moral values for service and how those values are mobilized in the individual. Voluntary commitment, of course, is normative mobilization before the application for service is forwarded. On the other hand, for those who join because of legal obligation, the question is whether they will gain new values after their compulsory recruitment through practical work and service experience. This is, of course, the outcome hoped for by proponents of compulsory service. A study by Irene Sie in the Philippines supports this notion.[8] She reports that two student groups in study-service assignments, one voluntary and the other compulsory, performed equally well on the job and had equally positive attitudes toward their work in communities—provided that the work was useful and participants felt that they were needed. This is also the experience of many volunteer services in the United States and elsewhere. Voluntary commitment does not lead to learning, better understanding among cultures, and tolerance if the work assignment does not genuinely contribute to the community and if volunteers do not have a full work load and a full measure of responsibility. When there is no genuine contribution, old prejudices are reinforced, intolerance prevails, and the values mobilized earlier to serve the needs of others are questioned. At the same time, compulsory recruits placed in full workload assignments gain, retroactively, a service commitment very similar to that of volunteers. In sum, the design of the work assignment may, in the final analysis, be more important for a national civilian service than the question of voluntary or compulsory recruitment.

Historical Perspective and Culture Will Shape National Service

National civilian service is inevitably intertwined in the history of a nation. While national service may be sparked by specific social, economic, and political events, it is shaped finally by what is historically and culturally possible in a given political system at a given time. For example, Anglo-Saxon nations, wherein a philosophy of voluntarism is a centerpiece of democracy, will have difficulty in accepting a national compulsory service. In continental Europe, which has a background of absolutism, compulsory military service is much more of a tradition. For example, it was a relatively small step for West Germany and France to open the military draft to alternative civilian service. In Third World countries, most of which have won independence during the past 40 years, the issue of nation building as both a socioeconomic and a cultural process is of dominating importance and demands a different set of priorities in deciding the question of voluntary versus obligatory national service. Furthermore, in Islamic countries, different approaches are used in educational processes; drill and discipline training are normal features and a well structured control hierarchy reflects the accustomed social order. Thus, national service as a disciplined force is part of the Islamic cultural tradition.

Cultural Convergence as a Key Feature of National Service

Civilian service cannot be truly national if it does not involve a cross-section of its citizenry—the educated and the uneducated, the urban and rural, Anglo-Saxons, Native Indians, Africans, Hispanics, Asians, and the many others. The "compelling reasons" stated earlier may help to ensure this multicultural make-up. People may participate in national service for many different reasons, and it is important for the program to recognize and respond positively to all of these motivating factors.

Second, cultural convergence requires service in another community. Service in one's own neighborhood and community does not necessarily result in new perspectives—the old life styles, alliances, and dependencies remain the same. A move to another community opens new relationships, new challenges, and new skills in consensus forming in different local cultures and different sets of circumstances. For the United States, cultural convergence is an essential feature if a national civilian service is to achieve its goals.

NOTES

1. Erik P. Eckholm, "Generating Employment and Output through Rural Public Works," *International Development Review* no. 4 (1973).

2. Irene Pinkau, *Service for Development*, three volumes (Dayton, Ohio: Charles F. Kettering Foundation, 1978).

3. G. W. Griffin, correspondence to Irene Pinkau, March 19, 1981.

4. K. Soedjatmoko, "Some Thoughts on Higher Education," Occasional Paper no. 15 (New York: International Council for Educational Development, 1975).

5. Government of Nigeria, Decree no. 24, establishing the Nigerian National Youth Service Corps (May 22, 1973).

6. Pinkau, *Service for Development*.

7. Philip M. Mbithi, *Localizing Youth Volunteer Development Service in Kenya* (Nairobi University: Institute for Development Studies, 1971).

8. Irene Sie, *Volunteer and Obligatory Service of University Students in a Domestic Development Service Programme: A Comparative Study* (Manila: The Philippines School of Social Work, 1975).

Chapter 5

National Service in West Germany and France*

Roger Landrum

WEST GERMANY

From the ashes of the Nazi experience has emerged a system of national service in West Germany that is probably the most interesting and unusual expression of the concept among Western industrial democracies. National service is compulsory for all male youth in the Federal Republic of Germany. This is not unusual. France, Italy, Switzerland, Belgium, The Netherlands, Norway, Sweden, and Denmark all require a period of service from young men as an obligation of citizenship. Great Britain, Canada, and the United States are unusual in relying on volunteerism. Nor is it unusual that the majority of West German youth serve in the armed forces. The dominant focus of national service in France and other European democracies is on national defense, following long-standing tradition.

The West German system is set apart by other features. A range of needs beyond national defense are addressed; relatively large numbers of young people meet the service obligation in civilian programs. Many of the other European systems are exclusively military. Both the military and civilian services are administered in such a way that participants consider the experience useful to the country and valuable to themselves. In contrast, the service experience in France is often considered a waste of time. The right not to bear arms, and thus to serve the country in other capacities, has constitutional status in West Germany. In other countries, conscientious objection is either forbidden or conscientious objectors are treated as social outcasts with their period of nonmilitary service designed as punishment. The balance, fairness, and social usefulness of the West German system set it apart. It may well be a model of future trends for national service in other democracies.

* Research was conducted with a grant from The German Marshall Fund Of The United States.

The West German system of national service consists of four parts: the armed forces, the overseas development service, the Technical Aid Service, and the Civilian Service. The largest by far is the armed forces (*Bundeswehr*). All male youth must register and be classified at age 18. About 232,000 young men are inducted annually into the military services to serve as short-term soldiers. This is roughly 65 percent of each cohort. They serve for a period of 15 months at an average age of 20.9, and account for slightly less than 50 percent of total military manpower. Pay is low since the 15 months are viewed as a contribution to the country. However, civilian jobs and any dependents are carefully protected and conscripts, along with other soldiers, are represented by a union.

The basic perspective on military service is reflected in a recent government document:

> Compulsory military service is not an end in itself, but rather a civic duty essential for the preservation of the Community. State and Society do not place any unreasonable demands upon young men by calling them up for 15 months of basic military service. Young people must realize that they have to accept responsibilities in return for the many rights guaranteed to them by the Community. Conscripts serve in the armed forces in order to safeguard our future— they do it in their own interests and in the interests of our country.[1]

The geographical proximity of the Soviet Union and its satellites, and a forward position in the North Atlantic Treaty Alliance, bring home the obligations of military defense with a special force in West Germany. By all accounts, conscripts are an essential part of the *Bundeswehr* and serve effectively, accounting for over 50 percent of manpower in the Army, 31 percent in the Air Force, and 24 percent in the Navy.

A second component of national service is a group of programs known collectively as overseas development service, roughly equivalent to the U.S. Peace Corps. This form of service, like 15 months in the armed forces, meets the compulsory service obligation. In legal terms, it is defined as "alternative service." To qualify, one must precontract before registration at age 18. The period of service is likely to come years later after extensive educational preparation. The average age of those serving overseas is 29. They are a highly select group who serve for a period of at least 24 months in projects in the Third World.

Each year, about 35,000 youth contact the Federal Ministry of Economic Cooperation to inquire about overseas development service. Only some 3,000 qualify, with about 1,200 entering overseas service annually. Five private organizations administer the projects. The largest, the German Volunteer Service (*Deutscher Entwicklungsdienst*), was launched in 1963 as part of the honors for President Kennedy's state visit. From 1963 until 1981, over

20,000 had served in this branch of national service. In addition to meeting needs in developing countries and improving North-South relations—a core objective of West Germany's foreign policy—these 20,000 are viewed as an invaluable supply of knowledge about the Third World and future leaders in North-South relations. This branch of service is given high visibility and broad public support. The experience is considered highly desirable by West German youth.

The third component of national service is the Technical Aid Service (*Technisches Hilfswerk*). It is organized by the Federal Government to provide swift assistance for major disasters or public emergencies related to transportation or floods. Service in the Technical Aid is legally defined as alternative service and meets the service obligation. About 17,000 young men of draftable age are permitted to take this option each year. Of 50,000 total manpower in the Technical Aid, about 65 percent entered with alternative service status.

To meet the service obligation, a minimum of one day a week is required, without pay, over a period of 10 years. Arrangements are made with employers for emergency leave. Qualifying requires a six-month trial period with a local unit. If standards of discipline are not maintained, the applicant reverts to military draft status. The Technical Aid is attractive to some young men for several reasons. One can enter the work force after schooling without an interruption of 15 or more months of full-time service. The work is adventurous and involves training in the use of elaborate equipment in mobile units. A high state of readiness is maintained by regular unit exercises.

The Technical Aid is administratively decentralized with 600 local units reporting to 100 area headquarters throughout the West German states. The units turn out when called by area headquarters to deal with floods, multiple-collision highway accidents, and even earthquake destruction in nearby countries. The Technical Aid permits the federal government to meet a range of emergency needs of the civilian population at a low cost to the federal treasury.

The fourth component of the system is the Civilian Service (*Zivildienst*). It is made up entirely of young men who refuse to bear arms as a matter of conscience. The authors of the West German constitution were understandably sensitive to appropriate limits on the state's powers of compulsion over citizens in military matters. Since 1956, the apparent conflict between compulsory military service and the constitutional right to object to military service on the basis of conscience—extending beyond religious to ethical and political beliefs—has been resolved by granting preference to the freedom of conscience of the individual.

In 1980, about 10 percent of the cohort of 18 year olds declared themselves conscientious objectors, with a roughly 80 percent acceptance rate by local boards. Approval results in enrollment in the Civilian Service. Some 30,000 youth were enrolled in 1980, working for a period of 16 months in programs addressed to a wide range of domestic social needs approved by the Federal Commissioner of Civilian Service. These young men usually serve through local, private, cooperating organizations. Since the constitution protects the equivalency of their service, they are paid the same wages as soldiers and entitled to all other benefits provided to soldiers.

The largest concentration of youth in the Civilian Service—some 10,000—work with centers providing services to the elderly. They are part of a major national effort to minimize institutionalization. Another large concentration is in health work, serving with local organizations of the German Hospital Association and the German Red Cross. Others work in schools, museums, the Youth Hostel Association, the Technical Aid Service, and the German Volunteer Service. Care is taken by the Federal Commissioner of Civilian Service to ensure that the programs are well-organized, represent a discernible contribution to national goals, and are sufficiently strenuous to appear no less of an obligation than the military services.

Finally, some 20 percent of male youth are excused from obligatory service for physical or social reasons. These may include mental or physical impairments, criminal convictions, election to federal or state offices, training for a religious profession, recent immigration from East Germany, Nazi persecution or severe family losses during the war, great personal or family hardship, and so on.

Each age cohort of 18-year-old males is composed of roughly 450,000 individuals, in a national population of approximately 62 million. Overall, about 80 percent complete some form of national service, with 65 percent serving in the armed forces, 10 percent in the Civilian Service, and the remaining 25 percent either serving in overseas development service and Technical Aid or exempted from service. Eight of ten young men entering the work force in West Germany will carry with them into the professions,

Table 5.1. Approximate National Service Distribution in West Germany, 1979

	Military Services	Civilian Service	Development Services	Technical Aid Service
Number	232,000	30,000	1,200	17,000
Average Age	20.9	21.5	29.0	?
Federal Auspice	Defense	Labor	Economic Cooperation	Interior
Service Period	15 months	16 months	24-36 months	10 years, part time

Source: Federal government documents and interviews with federal officials.

trades, or civil service what they have learned in national service. The nation obtains their service to national defense, North-South relations, civilian emergencies, and domestic social problems. It also obtains the sense of national community and purpose which is nurtured by the experience of national service.

How the West German System Took Shape

The West German system in operation today evolved gradually over the last 20 years from the interplay of a combination of forces. These forces have included perceived needs for the services of youth, legislation, assertion by youth of their constitutional right not to bear arms, and the leadership of several visionary individuals.

After World War II, the new constitution of West Germany left open the issue of whether a conscript or volunteer armed forces would be maintained for national defense. In 1956, the Parliament (*Bundestag*) took the first step in creating the present system by approving a National Military Service Act setting forth rules of compulsory military service. Since that time, the highly respected West German armed forces have relied on a stable supply of conscripts. Although all males must register for military service at age 18, not all have been needed and the Act effectively functioned as a selective draft.

To extend the service obligation and to meet other goals, one foreign and one domestic, the government later established overseas development service and the Technical Aid. In all three branches of service, young men proved to be valuable manpower in serving the defined goals at low cost to the federal government.

For about 10 years following adoption of military conscription, few West German youth invoked their right of conscientious objection. However, with the spreading moral ferment and social criticism among youth in the 1960s, the number of declarations of conscientious objection had grown to 5,963 by 1967, with 4,739 approvals by local boards. By 1970, the number had climbed to 19,363 and many were escaping any service obligation due to the absence of a system of equivalent service. This represented a troublesome political problem and the government was forced to act.

Chancellor Willy Brandt appointed a Federal Commissioner to produce a plan which would insure that conscientious objectors met a service obligation equivalent to military service, and that such service was a significant contribution to society. This led to the next step in the creation of the present system, the *Zivildienst*.

Like other branches of service, the *Zivildienst* has become an established part of the compulsory service system. The large majority of conscientious objectors have met their service obligation with considerable skill. Their visibility in local organizations, particularly in work with the elderly, has sharply improved public acceptance of a constitutionally protected and legislatively mandated program. By 1976, the number of conscientious objectors had risen to 40,618, or about 10 percent of the youth of conscription age (see table 5.2).

There is still considerable controversy and fascination with this segment of the youth population. Their refusal of military service, and especially their freely voiced criticisms of German society and even the institutions with which they serve, creates a certain ambivalence among their peers and the German public. They are frequently characterized as "political radicals," "narcissistic," and "rebelling against their fathers," even while the service they give is widely recognized as useful to society. Others defend not only the merits of the Civilian Service but also the moral values of the youth who, along with the constitution, have given it life. The Federal Commissioner of Civilian Service, Hans Iven, suggests that society and its institutions have much to learn from their "spiritual vividness."

Will the West German System Last?

The alternative services and especially the Civilian Service exist in a practical equilibrium with the National Military Service Act. As one high official of the German Protestant Church observes, "If there were no military conscription, there would be no conscientious objectors; if there were no conscientious objectors, there would be no Civilian Service." This and military manpower quotas raise some interesting questions about the future of the system.

Table 5.2. West German Conscientious Objectors: Applications, Decisions, and Approvals

Year	Total Applications	Decisions	Approvals
1967	5,963	5,433	4,739
1970	19,363	11,864	9,521
1971	27,657	14,444	11,033
1972	33,792	18,431	13,132
1973	35,192	25,087	16,649
1974	34,150	27,330	18,621
1975	32,565	26,508	18,496
1976	40,618	22,366	16,505
1977	69,969	26,745	18,474
1978	39,698	25,128	17,525
1979	45,454	38,775	30,725

Source: Office of the Commissioner of Civilian Service, Federal Republic of West Germany.

Will the Civilian Service continue to expand? This depends in part on whether the number of conscientious objectors grows, diminishes, or holds steady. Some predict that the number of conscientious objectors will begin to diminish with a waning of moral ferment and social criticism among West German youth, resulting in a withering away of the Civilian Service. On the other hand, the Federal Commissioner, who has planned for 44,000 placements, estimates that the numbers will stabilize at about 10 percent of the youth population.

Led by the Social Democrats, the *Bundestag* passed a law in the late 1970s permitting young people to achieve conscientious objector status without examination by local boards. This resulted from two concerns. There was a backlog of 70,000 young people awaiting decisions by the local boards, and there was also skepticism that boards could justly "read the heart" of someone who refused to bear arms. The Supreme Court invalidated the law, by a split decision, on the grounds that such examination is necessary to preserve the equivalency between military and civilian service. The law is being revised for a second round.

Another key factor looms on the horizon. The youth population in West Germany is shrinking (see table 5.3). If military manpower quotas are threatened, this raises the prospect of cutting back either on military service exemptions, on the alternative services, or making the process of examining conscientious objectors more severe and restrictive.

There is no way to forecast the outcome of these issues and questions about the system of national service that has evolved in West Germany. The nonmilitary dimensions of the system may expand or wither away with the interplay of political forces in the 1980s. The political culture of a nation is not static and it is decisive in shaping the way the concept of national service

Table 5.3.   Annual Size of Cohort of 18-Year-Old Males in West Germany

1975	417,100
1980	487,100
1981	488,500
1982	505,700
1983	509,800
1984	497,300
1985	493,600
1986	477,500
1987	456,800
1988	420,700
1989	366,900
1990	346,200

Source: Office of the Commissioner of Civilian Service, Federal Republic of West Germany.

is operationalized. For now, the West Germans have created a unique and delicately balanced system of compulsory service that other democratic nations should find worth observing.

FRANCE

The admirable features of the West German system can be seen more clearly in comparison to the French system. The formal system of national service in France is similar. Service is mandatory for males. Indeed, compulsory military service has been continuous in France since the revolution of 1792. A *levée en masse* was declared in 1793, and codified into law in 1798. The basic tradition was restated by former President Giscard in 1979: "The truth is that entrusting a professional army with defense makes people lose interest in their defense, whereas defense is an element of collective life that has to be ensured by the population itself."[2]

In 1965, observing the flow of American Peace Corps volunteers into French–speaking African nations, Charles de Gaulle convinced the French parliament to considerably alter the system of compulsory service. Conscription legislation was revised to establish four branches of a "Service National." Military service remained the dominant branch, with some 280,000 drafted into the military services or national police force (*gendarmerie*) each year. A centerpiece of the new legislation was twin branches of overseas development service, one for French-speaking nations in Africa and one for France's overseas territories. About 4,500 enter these services each year. A fourth branch puts conscripts to work on natural disasters, protection of the civilian population, and domestic economic development. About 25 percent of male youth are exempted from compulsory service for medical or social reasons.

The French system differs from the West German system in two respects. One is the matter of conscientious objection, which is a legal and not a constitutional right in France. When de Gaulle returned to power in 1958, he stated that treatment of conscientious objectors as delinquents was absurd and undignified for a civilized nation. In 1963, after much political dispute, a new law was passed with results that still contrast starkly with the German approach. Conscientious objectors must pass examination by tribunal and, if approved, serve twice the period of military service. Of about 3,000 applications each year, only about 1,000 are approved. The service period, which is not organized as a civilian service, is designed as hard labor. Some young people describe it as "preventive detention." The law defines the use of propaganda which tends to incite conscientious objection as punishable by six months to two years imprisonment plus a fine. It is also said that the government and many private organizations will not hire those who have been conscientious objectors. They are still treated as social outcasts. Those who are denied conscientious objector status and still refuse military service, or those who attempt to evade the system of national service, are classified as "condemned" and imprisoned. Some 700 condemned are now serving prison terms.

The French system also differs from the West German system in quality of implementation. Military conscripts are called *pietaille* (foot sloggers) by the public, and they spend 12 months in military exercises that many consider meaningless and conducted in a repressive and right-wing atmosphere. Public demonstrations by conscript soldiers have broken out in small towns. Military service can be deferred until age 22, in what is called the *a la carte* draft. Draftees cannot be sent into combat outside Western Europe without parliamentary approval; while an External Action Force of professional soldiers, known as the President's Centurions, enables France to take military action without endangering the lives of draftees. Neither the military bureaucracy nor the conscripts seem to take the period of compulsory military service very seriously. The specific charge is that the military hierarchy sees little value in the conscript units and has let the training activities degenerate into meaningless exercises.

Legislative reforms have cut back on abuse of exemptions and deferments by the well-positioned, but it is still widely believed that sons of the privileged are streamed into the overseas development services, rather than military service, and often assigned to French schools near choice diplomatic missions rather than to posts in developing countries.

In general, there is an atmosphere of resentment about the system of national service among many participants and of cynicism by the public. Only the overseas development branches are well-administered and viewed by French youth as an experience to be valued. In comparison to the West German system, the goals and tone of the French system are slack. While this may, in part, be a reflection of differences in national character, since the systems are similar in structure except in the provisions for conscientious objectors, it also points out the potential gap between the expressed intent of a system of national service and its actual implementation.

The paradox of the situation in France is that despite widespread public dissatisfaction and cynicism about the system of national service, there is also massive public support for compulsory national service. In part, this results from the tradition of citizen responsibility for national defense; in part, it comes from the view that an experience of discipline and class equality ought to be a required element of growing up French. Leftists support conscription as a form of public "voice" in the military and point out that the refusal of draftees to obey their officers undercut an uprising of generals against deGaulle over the conclusion of the Algerian war. Even young people who demonstrate against the treatment of military conscripts and conscientious objectors support the basic concept of national service. Reform may follow the Socialist victory in the 1981 elections. Michel Rocard, a Socialist Party leader, called for reforms of the system prior to the election.

IMPLICATIONS FOR THE UNITED STATES

Americans seldom look abroad for guidance on our institutions or domestic policies, and compulsory service is much less of a tradition in the United States. However, certain trends suggest that a return to a military draft is far from unlikely in the future. The United States is also unlikely to have a selective military service without substantial numbers of young people who refuse to bear arms as a matter of religious, ethical, or political conscience. It would be tragic to force them into exile or prison, or even subject them to questionable examinations, social abuse, or chaotic placements when they could usefully serve the country in a variety of alternative services without violating their consciences. If we do return to a military draft, we would do well to consider the West German view of conscientious objection as a fundamental democratic right and the West German model of civilian service as a positive utilization of the skills and moral commitments of young people.

If the United States should turn to a larger form of national service, it is certainly not beyond our capacities to shape an effective system of multiple services. Some could enter the armed forces and others could enter an array of nonmilitary programs: the Peace Corps, conservation work, services to the elderly, and so on. Women as well as men could serve. We have our own program models to draw upon, and we could borrow from the best features of the European models while avoiding their weaknesses.

NOTES

1. Federal Republic of Germany, Ministry of Defense, *The Security of the Federal Republic of Germany and the Development of the Federal Armed Forces* (1979).
2. Giscard d'Estaing, quoted in *France* (November 1979).

Part III:
Proposals for National Service in the United States

Chapter 6

Alternative Models of National Service

Donald J. Eberly and Michael W. Sherraden

It is evident from the preceding chapters that a variety of national service concepts have been advocated and tested in the United States, and many have been put into place overseas. Compared with the number of national service advocates and the ideas they espouse, the number of national service models is relatively small. This chapter reviews specific national service proposals and describes ways of putting the national service concept into effect. The models outlined in this chapter are presented chronologically and are representative of the variety of national service proposals.

1965-1970: MODELS FOR NATIONAL SERVICE

By 1966, the draft had been in effect almost continuously for 25 years and the United States was escalating its participation in the Vietnam war. With the 1966 National Service Conference, the McNamara speech which supported national service, and the appointment by President Johnson of the National Advisory Commission on Selective Service, the question most often faced by Eberly as Executive Director of the National Service Secretariat was no longer "Why national service?," but "How is it going to be done?" Eberly concluded that civilian youth service would have to be linked in some way to the military draft then in effect, but he did not want the civilian service program to depend on the draft. If it did, it would inevitably be military-oriented and would disappear when the draft disappeared.

This problem was posed to Radcliffe President Mary I. Bunting, who suggested setting up a national foundation. A National Foundation for Volunteer Service then became a cornerstone of the plan Eberly submitted to the National Advisory Commission on Selective Service.[1] The Foundation would be a federally funded agency similar to the Corporation for Public Broadcasting. Grants from the Foundation for the local operation of youth service projects would be much further removed from political pressures than grants from federal departments.

The second cornerstone was called the "option plan." Under this plan, a young man registering for the draft "would have the option of declaring his intent to enter either military or nonmilitary service and would have some freedom as to when he would enter that service. Those who selected neither option and did not register as conscientious objectors would have their names placed in the lottery or selective draft pool."[2] If military manpower requirements exceeded the number of volunteers for military service, persons would be drafted first from those in the pool; when the pool was emptied, they would come from persons who had opted for service but not yet entered service. Persons who had completed nonmilitary service, like those who had completed military service, would be at the very end of the draft queue and unlikely to be called for another period of service.

In Eberly's 1966 plan, young men would be informed of their options when they registered for service at the age of 18. Information on nonmilitary activities would be prepared by the National Foundation for Volunteer Service and distributed to all National Service Boards, which would replace the local Selective Service Boards then in existence.

Universal opportunity was the third cornerstone of Eberly's plan. Except for minimal mental and physical criteria that would have permitted nine out of ten young people to enter civilian service (military standards at the time were admitting only six out of ten), the only criteria for entry was willingness to serve. If a young person wanted to serve, a job would be found. If a participant was not capable of performing the job he was in but was still willing to serve, he would receive training or be offered another position.

The fourth cornerstone was a gradual build-up of national service. Eberly wanted to build a firm foundation for national service and saw a rapid expansion of national service as detrimental to its chances of long-term success. The option plan with its guarantee of service opportunities would not become fully effective until a sufficient number of useful tasks was identified, until the number of trainers and supervisory personnel was adequate to administer the nonmilitary activities, and until the logistical machinery and financial support were sufficient to meet the demands of an expanded program of national service.

Eberly also recommended National Service Summer Camps for 16-18 year olds to familiarize participants with their national service options, to give them a crosscultural experience, and to provide some kind of community service or conservation work.

Young men who opted for nonmilitary service could apply directly to an approved agency or could first enroll in a National Service Placement Center. These centers would be sponsored by educational, fraternal, religious, business, labor, and other community groups. The centers could provide specialized training, as in the Job Corps, and match participants with suitable positions.

At the conclusion of the service period, the participant would be offered counseling on employment and educational opportunities, and receive an education or training entitlement along the lines of the GI Bill for World War II veterans.

The Eberly plan was not the only national service model circulating in 1966 and 1967. Morris Janowitz, founder of the Inter-University Seminar on Armed Forces and Society, produced a fairly similar design from a very different rationale.

Janowitz was especially concerned with the representativeness of the armed forces. He was critical of the educational deferments widely available at the time on the grounds that such deferments discriminated against persons not in college by increasing their chances of being drafted. The same system had a damaging effect on higher education, Janowitz maintained, because of pressure to admit students to "post-graduate study as a basis of avoiding military service."[3]

Janowitz pointed to the educational value of national service and confronted those who said young people were not well enough trained to tackle important societal tasks by arguing that in some cases young people would perform them better than careerists. "We are dealing . . . with the inescapable fact that many operational tasks are better performed by persons who do not have trained incapacities. One way of organizing these work situations is to have persons perform them for short periods of time without having to confront the issue of a career in that particular vocation."[4] Young people serving short–term stints in nursing homes and day-care centers presumably would not be subject to the "burn-out" syndrome that hardens and discourages many long-term subprofessionals in such jobs.

While the Janowitz and Eberly models were generally similar, Janowitz offered a different option to 18 year old men. A person who did not volunteer for military service nor apply for Conscientious Objector status would "declare himself subject to selective service and indicate what type of alternative volunteer national service he prefers in the event he is not selected for military service."[5] Where Eberly would permit a young man to choose civilian service before being exposed to the lottery, Janowitz would not.

With his colleague, Charles C. Moskos, Jr., Janowitz later added another dimension to his national service model. Moskos and Janowitz recommended that participation in a voluntary national service program, in which military service would be an option together with various types of civilian service, be made a prerequisite for future federal employment. Using survey data, they argued that this provision would substantially increase the number of middle-class young men entering the armed forces, thus increasing their representativeness.[6]

While Eberly and Janowitz were putting forward option plans for national service, Edward F. Hall was formulating a plan for compulsory service.

Hall's proposal for compulsory national service was based on the assumption that without "the element of compulsion, those who would benefit most from the program would be the least likely to be involved. The appeal of such service, however advertised, would not reach them. This untapped segment of our youth would be those who have been most deprived and underprivileged."[7] Within his mandatory system of national service, Hall envisioned a wide freedom of choice. National service participants could choose to serve overseas with the Peace Corps or with other public or private agencies. Domestic service opportunities would be available in such fields as teaching, public health, community development, public works, agriculture, and vocational training. For the grossly disadvantaged, Hall said, "their own schooling toward the acquisition of self-confidence and employable skills should be credited as national service."[8]

Under Hall's plan, all young men would be inducted into national service within a year of reaching 18 or completing high school. They would be sent to three-month orientation and training centers, each accommodating some 10,000 trainees. A major reason for setting up centers of this size would be the creation of melting pots, a mix of young men with "all gradations of mental and physical ability, social and educational status, ethnic background, ideology and environment."[9] Each inductee at these centers would be responsible for "application to academic work, adherence to an assigned schedule, performance of housekeeping duties, respect for authority and cleanliness."[10] After several weeks, each serviceman would make a tentative choice of a national service assignment. If his choice was approved, his academic and training assignments would be narrowed to permit him to concentrate on the selected option. If it was not approved, he would be advised of options more suitable for him. If extended schooling were needed before the young man could begin service, he would be able to return to school after this preliminary training period so long as he made a firm commitment regarding when and where his service would be undertaken. With that contract, he would be permitted to study for four years or more.

The most idealistic plan for national service in 1966 was put forward by Harris Wofford.[11] He suggested a federal initiative to stimulate volunteering, an initiative that would include: (1) *Volunteer service fellowships* to provide living allowances and subsequent educational aid to volunteers 16 and over who would work in service programs at home and overseas. (2) *Volunteer service summers* that would be the equivalent of Eberly's National Service Summer Camps for persons leaving high school. (3) *A national volunteer registry* which would invite everyone in high school to enter his or her name on a roster which would be used for recruitment by volunteer service programs. (4) *Local voluntary service boards* to provide information on service opportunities at home and abroad. (5) *Academic credit for volunteer service*; educational institutions would be encouraged to award academic credit for service experiences, and to give weight to a period of service, and possibly even require it, as a criterion for admission.

The boldest and most controversial part of Wofford's plan was its relationship to military service. He suggested that his plan could lead in a few years to nearly 200,000 full-time volunteers serving in the several parts of his plan. If that happened, Wofford said:

> Those drafted into the army would soon be the minority. Then, instead of talking about exemptions for Peace Corps Volunteers, we would find the problem turned upside down. It could be said that those drafted for military service were exempt from the system of universal voluntary service. In fact, if practically all young Americans came to feel the obligation to volunteer for some kind of service, the draft might be put out of business altogether. All the calculations of the high cost of putting the military on an entirely volunteer basis leave out the possibility of universal voluntary service.[12]

As visionary as Wofford's model was, it had a practical aspect reminiscent of the Franklin Roosevelt-Lyndon Johnson approach of 1940. Most of Wofford's volunteers would have entered the Peace Corps, VISTA, and the Job Corps. The emphasis would have been placed on expanding already existing programs rather than creating new ones.

1969-1980 CONGRESSIONAL INITIATIVES

During the period 1969-1980, four different national service proposals were submitted to Congress by Senator Mark Hatfield (R-Oregon), and Representatives Jonathan Bingham (D-New York), Paul N. McCloskey (R-California), and John Cavanaugh (D–Nebraska). While none of these proposals survived the legislative process, they spanned the full range of key issues from voluntary to compulsory, from limited to universal service opportunities, from a strong military service linkage to none, and from federal service only to both private and public service opportunities. These national service proposals are presented below, and then compared and contrasted toward the end of the chapter. Also discussed are the 1979-80 initiatives of Senators Paul E. Tsongas (D-Massachusetts) and Alan Cranston (D-California) and of Representatives Leon Panetta (D-California) and Patricia Schroeder (D-Colorado).

The Hatfield Plan of 1969

Senator Hatfield was first off the mark with his Youth Power Act of 1969. He had heard Eberly describe his plan for a National Foundation for Volunteer Service and asked him to put it into legislative form. A strong proponent of the All-Volunteer Force, Hatfield stipulated that there be no linkage with military service. Apart from this caveat, he gave Eberly carte blanche and the services of a professional bill writer. The purpose of Hatfield's bill was "to supplement and increase, not to replace, the service and learning opportunities currently available to our young people. The goal is to provide enough opportunities so that no young person is denied a chance to serve and to learn."

The operating arm of the Hatfield bill would have been a National Youth Service Foundation. Fifteen of its 21 trustees would have been appointed by the President. The other members would have been the directors of VISTA, the Peace Corps, the Teacher Corps, the Job Corps, the Neighborhood Youth Corps, and the National Youth Service Foundation. The Foundation would have been authorized to fund public or private nonprofit agencies for the support of service-learning activities by 17 to 27 year olds. For this purpose, the Foundation would have been authorized to spend $150 million in the first year, $500 million in the second year, and $900 million in the third year.

Hatfield would also have created a National Youth Service Council to coordinate the youth service and learning programs of the federal government. In addition to the ex-officio members of the Foundation, the Council would have been composed of the Secretaries of Agriculture; Interior; Labor; Housing and Urban Development; Health, Education and Welfare; the Chairman of the Civil Service Commission; the Commissioner of Education; and the Director of the Office of Economic Opportunity.

In introducing his bill to the Congress, Hatfield recognized the energy of young people and the importance of offering them constructive ways to express their energy:

> I wish to stress the positive objective of the bill. We are passing through a time when the temptation is great to adopt measures designed to repress the energies of young people in the cities and on the campuses. But we have to recognize that energy per se is neither moral nor immoral. It is amoral. It can be used to shape a sword or a plowshare. By providing constructive ways for all young people to use their energies and talents, they will have a chance for a better life and a chance to relate to and serve their society—as well as to help peacefully improve it where necessary.[13]

The Bingham Plan of 1970

One year later, Representative Bingham submitted his bill entitled the National Service Act of 1970. It had a strong linkage with military service and required that employers pay the prevailing wage of national servicemen to the National Service Agency which would, in turn, pay subsistence wages to those in the service. The bill, drafted largely by Bingham's son Timothy and his colleagues at Yale University, is summarized below:

Each male citizen of the United States will have to register with a local placement center of the National Service Agency at age 17. During the interval between 17 and 18, the registrant will receive counseling from trained personnel at the placement center on the three options: first, enlistment in the military; second, enrollment in the civilian service for a period of time "equivalent" to two years in the Armed Forces; or third, the option to register for a military lottery similar to the one now in effect.

A registrant who elects civilian service will attempt to find a job with an employer who has previously "qualified" the job for participation in the civilian service program. Local placement centers will maintain lists of qualified job categories as well as specific qualified jobs which exist throughout the Nation. Each local placement center, therefore, will be able to direct interested registrants to civilian service job opportunities anywhere in the United States.

Jobs will qualify for participation in the civilian service system if the Director and those to whom he delegates the task find that the occupation fits within both standards outlined in the statute as well as standards promulgated by regulation. . . .

In order to qualify, employers will have to (a) meet requirements detailed by regulations promulgated by the Director, on the type of job and the amount of job training and supervision available; and (b) indicate, to the extent possible, how they intend to insure that participation of civilian service registrants in the occupation will not interfere unreasonably with the regular labor force in that area.

Qualified employers will have to pay the going rate for the type of work that the registrant does. This salary, however, will be paid to the National Service Agency which, in turn, will return to the registrant an amount determined by the Director for "subsistence." This amount will vary depending on the cost of living in the area, and the number of dependents the registrant has to support. The difference between the subsistence allowance and the wages paid will go to the National Service Agency to offset the cost of administering the civilian service program. . . .

The local placement center will provide to registrants who are employed in the geographical area assistance in finding housing, recreation, and health care. Local government and community organizations will also be asked to take some responsibility for the welfare of civilian service workers in the area—for example, housing in YMCAs or housing in local homes, police assistance in physical training, a lecture series, and so forth.

A registrant unable to find a qualified job on his own initiative will enter the National Service Corps. The Corps will directly operate federal programs in areas of social need such as reforestation and mass-produced housing for the poor. For example, the Corps might well operate an "environmental task force" as recommended recently by Secretary of the Interior Hickel (*New York Times*, March 6, 1970, 13:1). The Corps will also operate educational and training programs especially for registrants from deprived backgrounds. These programs will enable the registrant (a) to do useful and semiskilled work for the remainder of his civilian service tour, and (b) to find skilled jobs following the completion of his service.[14]

The McCloskey Plan of 1979

In 1979, Representative McCloskey, who had for a long time been making speeches about national service, introduced the National Service Act. His bill was based in large measure on Eberly's 1966 plan, and utilized both the option plan for choosing a preferred form of service and the creation of a national foundation to administer and fund civilian service. A summary follows:

1. The Selective Service System will be replaced by the National Service System and all persons, men and women, will be required to register within 10 days after their 17th birthday.
2. Information on service opportunities will be made available to all persons between their 17th and 18th birthdays.
3. All registrants will have the option of serving in a civilian capacity for one year or in the military service for two years or more, and will be allowed to defer such service until the age of 23.
4. At the age of 18, persons will have the right to elect:
   (a) Two years of military service, which will entitle them to four years of educational and training benefits paid at the base monthly rate provided to Vietnam-era veterans, but adjusted to account for cost-of-living increases since that time;
   (b) Six months of active duty, followed by five and one-half years of Reserve obligation;
   (c) One year of service in a civilian capacity; or
   (d) None of the above, in which case they will be placed in a military lottery pool for six years of draft liability. If military manpower requirements are not filled during this period, these individuals might be required to serve two years of active duty and would also incur a four-year Reserve obligation. They would be entitled to two years of educational and training benefits.
5. If voluntary enlistments are not adequate, then and then only would one be subject to possible conscription.
6. The Civilian Service Corps will be operated by a National Youth Service Foundation. (See description of the foundation in chapter 8.)[15]

McCloskey also proposed that military pay for junior enlisted personnel (those with less than two years of service) be reduced to a subsistence level, and that the Civilian Service Program be phased in gradually over a three-year period.

The Cavanaugh Plan of 1979

A few weeks later, Representative Cavanaugh introduced the Public Service System Act with several distinct features. Alone among these bills, young people could be compelled to enter civilian service. All civilian service would be performed within federal agencies, and most federal agencies would, by four and one half years after enactment, be required to reserve 5 percent of their employment positions for persons entering civilian service. This provision would also have the effect of limiting the size and cost of the civilian service program. A summary follows:

1. The Selective Service System will be replaced by the Public Service System. The Director of the Public Service System will be appointed by the President. Each state will have a state director, a state headquarters, and an appeals board. Each county will have a local placement center with members serving on a voluntary basis and appointed by the President based on recommendations made by the governors of the states.
2. Every young adult will be required to register with the local placement center between his or her seventeenth and eighteenth birthdays. At the time of registration, the individual will receive information explaining the military and civilian service options available.
3. The individual will have the following options:
    a) volunteer at any time between the ages of 18 and 26 for eighteen months of active duty military service;
    b) volunteer at any time between the ages of 18 and 26 for six months of active duty military service followed by a 3 year active reserve commitment;
    c) volunteer at any time between the ages of 18 and 26 for a two year period of service in an approved civilian service position;
    d) elect any six-month period between his or her eighteenth and twenty-sixth birthdays during which to expose himself or herself to a random selection process for induction into:
        i)   the active duty armed forces for a period of eighteen months, or
        ii) the active duty armed forces for a period of six months followed by a three year period of service with the active reserve, or
        iii) the civilian branch of the Public Service System for a period of two years.
4. Individuals who do not volunteer for public service and who choose to submit to the lottery will be allowed to indicate their preference for military, military reserve, or civilian service. Each month the Director

will determine the manpower needs of the three divisions of the Public Service System and will select that number of registrants required, assigning them to the division for which they have indicated a preference and for which they are qualified. If the division that the registrant has selected has been filled for that month, he or she will be assigned to another division. Those individuals meeting the established standards for conscientious objection to military service will be assigned to the civilian division. If an individual has remained in the lottery pool for the six-month period and has not been selected for service his or her obligation will cease, except in the event of a national emergency.

5. The current system of veterans' benefits will be made available only to those volunteering or selected for military active duty for a period of eighteen months or more. Military pay rates will not be affected by this Act. Those volunteering or selected for civilian service will receive a subsistence wage during their period of service.

6. Every federal agency will be required to designate a minimum of 5 percent of its employment positions to be filled by Public Service registrants. The Congress will annually earmark certain funds in the budget for each agency for these civilian service positions. Included in the Act is a four-year phase-in period, designed to provide for gradual placement of individuals into those positions created by attrition and promotion within the agencies. The Act establishes a Civilian Placement Bureau which will process the monthly personnel requests of the federal agencies and assign those selected for civilian service to the positions for which they are best suited and for which the individual has indicated a preference.

7. Those persons who are found to be mentally or physically unfit for service will be exempt from participating under this Act, as will those individuals who meet strict standards of conscientious objection to the entire program. Those who are temporarily unfit, pregnant women and mothers caring for children, and those with family hardships will be deferred for so long as is necessary.

8. Individuals who knowingly fail to register will be liable for misdemeanor penalties not to exceed six months in jail and/or $500. Those who fail to complete service after being selected in the service lottery will be denied any future federal employment, any loan or loan guarantee, grant or scholarship for educational purposes, any federal home mortgage loan or loan guarantee, and any loan or loan guarantee under the Small Business Act.[16]

The Tsongas, Cranston, Panetta, and Schroeder Initiatives of 1979-80

Former Peace Corps Volunteer Paul E. Tsongas, Senator from Massachusetts, introduced in 1979 a bill that would have created a Presidential Commission on National Service. At least seven of the 25 members of the Commission would have been between the ages of 17 and 25. The Commission would have conducted hearings and conferences throughout the United States to stimulate discussion of national service, and would have submitted its report to the President within two years. A similar bill was introduced in the House by Representative Leon Panetta of California.

With the strong support of Senator Alan Cranston of California, hearings were held on the Tsongas bill; it was attached as a rider to a bill on domestic violence, and it passed the Senate in September 1980 by a vote of 46-41. The Panetta bill failed to reach the House floor for a vote and the Tsongas-Cranston-Panetta initiative collapsed when the Tsongas rider was dropped in a Senate-House conference.

Meanwhile, President Carter was conducting a limited study of national service under the terms of an amendment to the Defense Authorization Act of 1980. The Amendment was introduced in September 1979 by Representative Patricia Schroeder of Colorado, together with Congressmen McCloskey and Panetta. The national service part of the amendment read as follows:

> The President shall prepare . . . recommendations with respect to the desirability, in the interest of preserving discipline and morale in the Armed Forces, of establishing a national youth service program permitting volunteer work, for either public or private public service agencies, as an alternative to military service. . . .[17]

President Carter's report and recommendations were issued on February 11, 1980. The report expressed satisfaction both with the opportunities for voluntary service and for the training and employment of disadvantaged youth. The report examined various national service models and concluded that the type represented in the Cavanaugh and McCloskey bills was the most promising in the light of the legislative mandate. However, Carter's report saw no need for any form of national service at that time. The Carter report did contain an ominous warning not only to national service advocates but also to supporters of federally supported youth employment and education programs. It said:

> Any program that would compete for the same pool of qualified individuals as the military must be viewed as deleterious in its impact on the morale and discipline as well as on the force levels of the Armed Forces as currently staffed.[18]

The above statement makes one wonder how many prospective young students and employees will be compelled to be idle in the 1980s so that they, and others, might serve as a manpower pool for the convenience of the armed forces.

FOR THE 1980s: AN ANALYTICAL MODEL

Having reviewed a number of specific proposals, it is apparent that, with all the variables involved, there is almost no end to the number of national service models that could be constructed. A useful technique for dissecting the legislative models presented above is to identify the important issues and then construct a continuum for each issue. Seven such continua are presented below; they represent the following issues: voluntariness, universality, size, unit cost, employment opportunities, educational value, and relationship to the military. (We would like to emphasize that the value of service performed is also an essential element of any national service program; however, because all the proposals equally recognize its importance, value of service is not included as a dimension in this analysis.) With these seven continua identified, the legislative proposals can be systematically compared and contrasted. To illustrate this approach to analysis of national service proposals, the legislative proposals of Hatfield (1969), Bingham (1970), McCloskey (1979), and Cavanaugh (1979) are analyzed below. A summary is presented in figure 6.1.

Voluntariness

Hatfield's bill is totally voluntary. Bingham's and McCloskey's require registration of everyone but they also permit registrants to opt for civilian service. Cavanaugh's bill requires registration and, in some cases, mandatory civilian service. Placing each of these bills on the voluntariness continuum gives the picture in figure 6.1, where Hatfield's bill ranks high, Bingham's and McCloskey's bills are in the mid-range, and Cavanaugh's bill ranks low.

Universality

Universality refers to the extent to which a national service experience is open to everyone. A universal program would be equally open to young people regardless of socioeconomic status, and would not discriminate against either advantaged or disadvantaged youth. The Bingham, Hatfield, and McCloskey bills are high in universality since any young person wishing to serve would be guaranteed a position. Cavanaugh's bill limits civilian service positions to 5 percent of federal agency employment. It seems likely that this restriction would lead to competition and "creaming" of the most qualified applicants for civilian service jobs. Thus, the Cavanaugh proposal, although open to everyone officially, would likely skew the civilian service population toward the most qualified applicants. In sum, Bingham's, Hatfield's and McCloskey's proposals rank high in universality, while Cavanaugh's falls in the mid-range.

		Bingham		
Voluntariness	Hatfield	McCloskey		Cavanaugh
	High			Low
Universality	Bingham Hatfield McCloskey	Cavanaugh		
	High			Low
Size	Hatfield	McCloskey	Bingham	Cavanaugh
	Large			Small
Unit Cost			Cavanaugh Hatfield McCloskey	Bingham
	High			Low
Employment Opportunities	Hatfield McCloskey	Bingham	Cavanaugh	
	High			Low
Educational Value	Hatfield	Bingham	Cavanaugh McCloskey	
	High			Low
Relationship to the Military	Bingham Cavanaugh McCloskey			Hatfield
	High			Low

Fig. 6.1. Comparison of the National Service Proposals of Bingham, Cavanaugh, Hatfield, and McCloskey on Seven Key Dimensions.

Size

Universal opportunity does not mean that all young people would choose to serve, any more than universal suffrage means that all eligible citizens choose to vote. The ultimate size of voluntary national service is difficult to estimate because the major determinant is the array of choices open to young people, and this array cannot be confidently forecast. There will be a choice between military and civilian service, but what will be the effect of the job market and the international situation? Each of these factors could strongly influence young people to either select or reject some form of national service. Eberly has testified that, under conditions prevailing in 1979, the McCloskey bill, after a four or five year build-up, would have produced an enrollment in the Civilian Service Corps of approximately 1 million young people.[19] Although the Bingham bill has an option plan similar to McCloskey's, the Bingham requirement for sponsors to pay the prevailing wage to the National Service Agency would make sponsors more selective than those in the McCloskey bill. A steady-state enrollment of some 600,000 seems likely with the Bingham bill. Hatfield's bill, which permits part-time enrollees, might well produce a large number of participants, perhaps 1 million or more in a time of no conscription. Without any draft credit, it would be comparatively less attractive during a period when people were being drafted. A reasonable estimate for the Hatfield bill is some 1.5 million enrollment, equaling a full-time equivalent of about 500,000. Cavanaugh's proposal, restricted to 5 percent of federal agency employment, would yield a civilian service program of about 100,000.

Unit Cost (Federal Funds)

The cost per participant per year is lowest in the Bingham bill since employers who engage national service participants would pay the prevailing salary to the National Service Agency, which in turn would pay only a subsistence stipend to the participant. All four bills call for a subsistence-level stipend, which for a single person approximates 75 percent of the minimum wage. This brief analysis does not examine unit cost factors outside civilian service; if it did, the McCloskey bill's unit cost would be reduced because it calls for a substantial reduction in military pay. For comparability, the Hatfield bill is figured at unit cost per full-time equivalent. For comparisons of total program cost, one would, of course, multiply unit cost by program size.

Employment Opportunities

There are several aspects to employment opportunities including work experience, career exploration, and the prospect of future employment. The quality of work experience would depend heavily on the participant's supervisor and sponsoring agency, and to a lesser extent on the administration of the program. While each of the legislative proposals has a strong potential for a high quality of work experience, there is no basis for distinguishing among them at this time. Career exploration is primarily a function of the variety of opportunities available. Being restricted to federal agencies, Cavanaugh's bill would yield the least variety. The Hatfield and McCloskey bills would offer a broad array of opportunities, and the Bingham bill somewhat fewer opportunities because of the limiting feature of having sponsors pay the prevailing wage to the National Service Agency. Overall, the prospects for future employment would depend most heavily on the state of the economy and whether the job market was expanding or contracting.

Educational Value

The educational value of national service would be found in three areas. First would be the educational value of the service experience. All four proposals offer the potential for substantial learning experiences, but Hatfield's must be given top rank because service-learning is an organic part of the Hatfield plan. Second would be the education and training given to national service participants. None of the bills gives as much emphasis to this feature as did, for example, the Oberlin College plan of 1944 (see pg. 100). One apparent reason is the great increase of federal aid for education and training since 1944. Still, Bingham's bill calls for education and training for National Service Corps members, and training for service assignments, at the very least, would take place under the other three bills. Third would be post-service educational benefits, or a GI Bill for National Service. All four bills rank low on this feature since they do not make provision for post-service benefits for those performing civilian service. Again, the likely reason for this absence has been the generosity of federal aid to education during the 1970s. Given the austere prospect for such help in the 1980s, it is reasonable to expect new proposals for linking post-secondary educational aid to a period of military or civilian service.

Relationship to the Military

Only Hatfield's bill is devoid of any link to the armed forces. The other three contain provisions for a military draft but do not require it. Thus, they are situated slightly to the right of the highest military linkage, which would be a draft that did not permit persons to volunteer for the armed forces. (Volunteering was suspended for a time during World War II in order to prevent men in essential civilian jobs from volunteering for military service.[20])

To address a related issue, each of the bills with a military linkage (Bingham, Cavanaugh, and McCloskey) would also almost certainly increase the representativeness of the armed forces. As long as society does not require young people to serve, most of the upper socioeconomic classes give little consideration to entering the military. With some kind of option plan in effect, surveys indicate that there would be a marked increase in the number of persons volunteering for military service. Because of the GI bill incentive for volunteering under the McCloskey bill, this proposal probably would produce an armed force which most nearly reflects society. The Hatfield bill would not have much effect on the composition of the armed forces.

The seven continua above might be used in several ways. First, the reader can order the seven key issues according to his or her priorities, and then determine where each proposal falls in this individualized priority-ranking. Second, as new national service models are proposed, the reader can analyze them, place them along the continua, and then decide how they compare with the four bills considered above. Third, as national service projects are undertaken, these projects can be evaluated to determine where actual experience places them on these key dimensions. Finally, the dimensions can be used to evaluate the impact of selected national service proposals if and when they are implemented.

Now, keeping in mind these seven central issues in considering national service, what is the best model for the 1980s?

NOTES

1. National Service Secretariat, *A Plan for National Service* (New York: National Service Secretariat, 1966, mimeographed).

2. Ibid., p. 30.

3. Morris Janowitz, "American Democracy and Military Service," *TransAction* 4, no. 4 (March 1967): 59.

4. Ibid.

5. Ibid., p. 10.

6. Charles C. Moskos, Jr., and Morris Janowitz, "Volunteer National Service: A Prerequisite for Federal Employment" (1978, unpublished).

7. Edward F. Hall, "The Case for Compulsory National Service," in *National Service: A Report of a Conference*, edited by Donald J. Eberly (New York: Russell Sage Foundation, 1968), p. 470.

8. Ibid., p. 475.

9. Ibid., p. 471.

10. Ibid., p. 472.

11. Harris Wofford, "Toward a Draft Without Guns," *The Saturday Review* (October 15, 1966).

12. Ibid., p. 53.

13. Mark Hatfield, "S. 1937-Introduction of the Youth Power Act," *Congressional Record* 115, no. 64 (April 22, 1969): S3987–S3988.

14. Jonathan Bingham, "A National Service Plan to Replace the Military Draft System," *Congressional Record* 116, no. 14 (June 10, 1970).

15. Paul N. McCloskey, Jr., "National Youth Service Act," *Congressional Record* 125, no. 30 (March 13, 1979): E1070-1071.

16. John Cavanaugh, "Cavanaugh Introduces Public Service Act," news release (April 10, 1979).

17. *Presidential Recommendations for Selective Service Reform: A Report to Congress Prepared Pursuant to P.L. 96-107* (Washington: U.S. Government Printing Office, February 11, 1980), p. 5.

18. Ibid., p. 52.

19. U.S. Congress, House Committee on Armed Services, *Hearings on Military Posture and H.R. 1872*, 96th Cong., 1st sess., 1979, p. 1105.

20. George Flynn, *The Mess in Washington* (Westport, Connecticut: Greenwood Press, 1979), p. 194.

Chapter 7
A Proposal for National Service for the 1980s

Donald J. Eberly and Michael W. Sherraden

The seven dimensions described in the previous chapter can serve as a framework for building a national service plan for the 1980s. In this chapter, the authors examine each of these dimensions and state in italics where they stand on the respective dimensions. A similar procedure is followed in the chapter's conclusion, where the authors describe a series of steps for moving toward a national service program. Taken together, the italicized sentences describe the authors' national service proposal for the 1980s.

THE VOLUNTARY-COMPULSORY ISSUE

We propose a voluntary program. Civilian youth service activities should be restricted to persons entering of their own volition. This is a volatile issue, however, and one that is often misrepresented. Voluntariness is often presented as a dichotomous issue where there are only two possible kinds of national service, one 100 percent voluntary and the other 100 percent compulsory. The truth, however, lies somewhere in between, and the national service debate is enhanced by placing this question in perspective. A few historical examples may help illustrate.

After calling for "a conscription of the whole youthful population," William James went on to suggest some of the most onerous tasks in society to which "our gilded youth would be drafted off, according to their choice. . . ."[1] What was he really advocating, a compulsory program or a voluntary one? Or, as seems most likely, was he advocating a system of voluntary choice within a framework of compulsory service? Given at least some element of compulsion, how would James have enforced it? What penalty would be paid by those who refused to serve? James left these and other questions unanswered.

Without reference to William James' essay of a decade earlier, the well-known horticulturalist Liberty Hyde Bailey published his national service proposal in 1919. Bailey included women as well as men in his proposal, but he did not quite resolve the voluntary-compulsory dilemma:

> If any man is his brother's keeper he cannot delegate the responsibility. Every man and woman will give of himself and herself, or the common opinion of mankind—which at the same time is the greatest punishment and corrective—will condemn him. In the time certainly coming, if the person does not volunteer for public service he will be drafted; but the conscription, I hope, will be more universal and useful than merely the bearing of arms by males.[2]

In September 1944, the faculty of Oberlin College was concerned about national defense, national leadership, international relations, and youth development and education. They proceeded to endorse in principle a national service proposal which called for all young men and women to spend a year in training for service of national importance.[3] What is most surprising about this statement is that the endorsers—a liberal college faculty—saw no need to agonize over the voluntary-compulsory issue. "All young men and women" would participate. Why was this?

Clearly, the important thing for these early advocates, as for many national service proponents who followed them, was that there be universal opportunity for civilian service. The degree to which such service should be voluntary or compulsory was of secondary consideration, and the problem of meting out penalties to persons refusing to serve in a compulsory system was not mentioned by James, Bailey, or the Oberlin College faculty.

In recent years, some have argued that a voluntary program would inevitably "cream" the better candidates for national service, leaving very few opportunities for disadvantaged young people. We agree that a voluntary program, if conceived and managed improperly, could be discriminatory. However, it need not be discriminatory, as experience with Job Corps indicates. Job Corps participants are all disadvantaged, predominantly minority young people, and few Job Corps enrollees have completed high school. If Job Corps can reach this population, then a national service program, by establishing appropriate recruitment, support, and job placement guidelines, should be able to reach disadvantaged young people. Most likely, national service would reach even larger numbers of disadvantaged young people because it would be better publicized and because no young person willing to serve would be turned away.

On the other hand, if national service were mandatory, it is very likely that participant commitment would be lower and the quality of work would suffer. Concurrently, the educational and maturational value of the experience would be jeopardized. There is also some danger that, in a mandatory program, middle and upper class young people might disproportionately find ways to avoid service. Certainly the experience with the draft during the

Vietnam War provides reason to be skeptical of the universality of a mandatory program. Moreover, the enforcement problems of a mandatory program would be enormous, so enormous that we believe a mandatory program is, above all else, impractical. Conscription for civilian service would automatically establish a negative psychological response among many young people. There would be resistance and outright opposition. In a democracy, a mandatory program could succeed only if popular support for it were strong enough nearly to obviate the need for enforcement.

The issue of voluntariness of national service also relates to other parts of the proposal for the 1980s. If the military draft should be restored and civilian service be equated to military service, would some young people eligible for the draft feel "compelled" to enter civilian service to avoid the military? If educational entitlements were to favor those who had completed a period of national service, would those who could not otherwise afford further education feel "compelled" to join national service?

There is, finally, the constitutional issue. Would a compulsory nonmilitary service program violate the Thirteenth Amendment which prohibits involuntary servitude? Attorney Anita Martin said in 1967 that compulsory civilian service would appear to violate the Thirteenth Amendment. She noted, however, that "there are no permanent legal barriers to nonmilitary conscription since the Constitution can always be amended."[4] A different viewpoint was expressed in President Carter's 1980 report to Congress on the subjects of Selective Service and national service. According to Carter's report, the Department of Justice, in concurrence with the American Law Division of the Congressional Research Service, found that "Congress probably has no independent constitutional authority to compel participation in national service *per se* unless it is linked to the power to raise and support an army and provide and maintain a navy." The report concluded that Congress could, without initiating a constitutional amendment, implement a national youth service program having the general characteristics of either the McCloskey or the Cavanaugh bill.[5]

The voluntary-compulsory issue has many facets and there is no possible arrangement that would be equally acceptable to all interested parties. National service, under any set of choices, would not be a nirvana. Some elements of compulsion, such as registration and the threat of early discharge for those failing to live up to their service agreements, would exist even in the voluntary program we propose.

UNIVERSAL VS. LIMITED SERVICE OPPORTUNITIES

Occasionally, a proposal is put forward as national service that falls short of the promise of national service. Such proposals include a national service limited to the elite, a national service limited to the poor and unemployed, or a national service designed solely to sweeten the military draft or otherwise for the convenience of the armed forces. Each of these limited views of national service is undesirable. *We propose a universal national service in which the country tells all young people their help is needed, asks them to contribute a period of service, and makes administrative and financial arrangements such that every young person who offers to serve is able to serve.*

The one inevitable concession to a limited service program would come at the development stage in the very beginning. Not everyone who wanted to join would be able to join at the outset of the program. In order to prevent discrimination against a particular socioeconomic class, the initial program could be limited geographically. Thus, eligibility during the first year would be limited to persons in specified cities or counties or states. These first sites in particular would be carefully monitored to be sure that neither intentional nor accidental discrimination occurred in the job development and placement process. Another approach would be to limit participation to persons born on certain days of the month. For example, if eligibility were restricted to persons born on the 15th, 21st, and 25th of each month, the persons represented by the 36 birthdates would comprise 10 percent of the age cohort.

One way to assure universality of opportunity would be to award national service vouchers to all 18-year olds. This could be accomplished through such avenues as voter registration, draft registration, or motor vehicle bureaus. The voucher would entitle the holder to a full year of financial support and medical coverage in exchange for a year of civilian service. Accompanying the voucher would be a set of instructions for becoming a national service participant. The young person would be directed to a place where openings were listed in a book or, more likely, on a computer. The young person would interview for any positions of interest and, when one was found which both the young person and the organization official perceived as a good match, these two persons would describe their respective duties and agreements on a short form, sign it, and deliver it to a local national service official. This official then would countersign the agreement, in which case the young person would begin service the next day or whenever specified on the form; or the official would reject it as invalid, in which case the young person and agency official would have to rewrite the agreement. Reasons for rejection would include (1) less than full-time work, (2) inadequate explanation of responsibilities, (3) forbidden duties such as religious proselytizing or political campaigning, and (4) absence of a training program in cases where the young person is assigned to duties beyond his current level of skill.

Who would exchange vouchers for a year of service? Most likely there would be more women than men, unless there was a male-only military draft, which would increase the number of men entering civilian service. The most popular age for entering national service would be 18-20, with the proportion declining fairly rapidly after age 21 to age 25. All socioeconomic classes would be well represented, although the proportion of minority persons, unemployed persons, and poor persons would probably be slightly higher than their proportion in the population as a whole. It has been estimated that the educational backgrounds of participants would be roughly one-third high school dropouts, one-third high school graduates, and one-third persons who have attended college.[6]

The creation and use of national service vouchers to match the service needs of society with the employment, experiential, and idealistic needs of young people would bring together these two important parts of our social economy that are presently, in large measure, cut off from one another. Furthermore, national service vouchers would give young people a greater voice in determining national priorities. After making individual choices for work in the fields of conservation, or education, or health, or whatever, the sum total of these choices would, to a certain extent, represent the collective voice of young people in contributing to the nation's well being.

SIZE

1980 was the peak year for the youth population. There were some 30 million 18-24 year olds with an average of 4.3 million persons in each year cohort.[7] In 1980, the distribution of persons 18-24 in the four activities that would be most directly affected by national service was approximately as follows: 16 million were employed; 8 million were in school or college; 2 million were unemployed and seeking work; and 1 million were in active military service.

The "baby boom" population surge has already passed through the nation's schools. With an average of only 3.6 million persons in the 8-14 year cohort in 1980, it is not surprising that schools have been closed and teachers laid off. What is surprising is that the decline in population was so little anticipated; some schools built in the early 1970s were boarded up almost as soon as construction was finished. The 8-14 year olds of 1980 will become the 18-24 year olds of 1990 and, barring a major catastrophe or immigration surge, they will number some 25 million persons. This is the ceiling figure. However the pie may be sliced, in 1990 there will be 5 million fewer young people who may be recruited for employment, higher education, military service, or some form of national service than there were in 1980.

The implications of this substantial decline are nowhere near as clear as some have suggested. For example, some observers contend that youth unemployment will disappear as a problem and youth crime will be greatly reduced. This may happen, but this scenario overlooks the possibility of an economic decline of greater severity than the decline in the youth population, or labor market changes so dramatic that far fewer people are absorbed into traditional employment.

Others have forecast increased enrollments in higher education in this decade; but one of the first consequences of an economic decline could be a substantial reduction in federal aid to higher education, leading to a sharp drop in higher education enrollments. And what are the implications of the population drop on military recruitment? Will enlistments fall with the declining population? Will enlistments rise because of some external threat and increased patriotism? Will enlistments fall because of a booming economy, or rise because of a falling economy?

On the supply side of the equation, the only safe prediction is that the youth population will decline steadily during the 1980s. Whether there will be more or fewer young people with little to do will be a function of trends in youth employment, education enrollments, and military enlistments, all of which are subject to radical and unpredictable changes in size.

On the demand side of the equation, as noted in Chapter 1, the need for national service workers, all of whom would serve outside the traditional labor market, remains at the 3 to 4 million level where it has been since 1964, and shows no signs of falling in the 1980s. An analysis of a 1978 partial survey undertaken for the U.S. Department of Labor is consistent with both the qualitative and quantitative findings of earlier surveys.[8]

The need for national service participants should not be confused with the current demand. On the basis of several surveys, Eberly estimated in 1969 that, in contrast to a need for 3 to 4 million national service participants, not more than 250,000 could be absorbed in three months.[9] It takes time to translate a need into an actual position. A trainer and a supervisor must be identified. Necessary equipment and supplies must be located. Most organizations, both public and private, prepare their budgets a year or so in advance. Once adopted, budget flexibility is quite limited. As national service becomes a reality, organizations could begin to plan ahead for their participation in the program, and needs would gradually be translated into real positions. ACTION's experiences with test projects in Seattle and Syracuse are consistent with this analysis. As noted in chapter 3, the Seattle project identified 1,200 positions in three months and the Syracuse project 2,465 positions in two years. When extrapolated nationwide on the basis of population, these figures correspond to 100,000 positions in three months and 1,100,000 in two years.

It would, however, be a mistake to set targets for the size of national service or to push the growth of the program. To do so might lead to a distortion, perhaps an elimination, of one or more of the principles set forth in this chapter. Nevertheless, estimates are necessary for planning purposes. Eberly testified in 1979 that under conditions existing at that time, especially high youth unemployment and no draft, the number of national service participants could reach 100,000 by the end of the first year of operation, 300,000 by the end of the second year, and 1,000,000 by the end of the third year. At that time, the enrollment would level off, although it would fluctuate according to such factors as the economy, the draft, the size of the youth population, and the popularity of national service.[10] *We propose that the Congress authorize national service to grow at the rate suggested by Eberly for the first three years, with authorization for at least one million participants in later years. With these authorization levels, Congress would establish upper limits for the growth of national service, but would not require that the program reach these limits. Thus, national service would be allowed to develop at its own pace and would reach a size appropriate to its performance.*

THE COST OF NATIONAL SERVICE

The cost issue lends itself to a more straightforward analysis than would appear from a glance at national service literature. Advocates and opponents of national service differ markedly in their presentation of cost estimates. Advocates tend to deal primarily with unit costs, saying that one person in national service for one year would cost, say, $8,000. The reader or listener is then left with the task of multiplying the unit cost figure by the enrollment in national service. Opponents, on the other hand, tend to choose total costs, a favorite being the $24 billion estimate in 1978 by the Congressional Budget Office. As many times as we have heard that figure used by opponents of national service, we have never yet heard any of them refer to the other two CBO estimates in the same report, one of $2 billion and the other of $11 billion.[11]

The CBO made another set of cost estimates for national service in 1980, this time concentrating exclusively on the McCloskey national service bill of 1979 (chapter 6). CBO concluded that the net cost for such a program with 3 million work years over a five year period would be $13.1 billion, or $4,367 per work year. If the savings in military pay that would result from McCloskey's bill are excluded from the calculation, the work year costs would rise to $6,660.[12] While this study was an improvement over the 1978 report, a few of its assumptions were inaccurate. For example, CBO dichotomized the types of persons who would enter national service, saying they would be either economically motivated or service-motivated. This assumption was made in the face of evidence from the Program for Local Service (chapter 3) that more than 9 out of 10 PLS volunteers from across the socioeconomic spectrum were highly motivated by considerations of both service and economics.

Clearly, the major overall cost determinant is the number of persons who would be in the program. At the very least, in a residential program, each participant would be housed and fed and given a little money for personal needs. At the most, national service participants would be paid the minimum wage or perhaps even the prevailing wage. In 1980 dollars, these two extremes cost out at approximately $5,000 and $10,000, respectively. Provision also would have to be made for the costs of administration and training. Again in 1980 dollars, these estimates are in the range of $1,000 to $2,000 per work year.

Another major cost factor is not found in all national service proposals, that is, the provision of an educational fellowship for those who have served. The range for this modern-day GI Bill for national service is from zero, for those who would exclude it, to some $3,000 per service year.

When all cost factors are included, the lowest unit cost would be some $6,000 and the highest, approximately $15,000.

In 1976, noting the common cost elements in all national service proposals and exasperated with having to recalculate the costs every year from scratch, Eberly devised a formula for estimating the cost of national service in current dollars. He estimated that the unit cost of national service, without the educational fellowship, would come to 115 percent of the full-time minimum wage. By the third year, with experience and economies of scale, he estimated that the unit cost would level off at 110 percent of the full-time minimum wage. The added costs of the educational fellowship would be 30 percent of the full-time minimum wage. Eberly's reckoning was based on these assumptions: (a) one year of education or training for each year of service; (b) the year of education would cost 60 percent of the minimum wage; and (c) one half of national service participants would take advantage of the educational fellowship.[13]

Thus, in 1981 dollars, we estimate that unit costs for national service would be some $8,000 without the educational fellowship, and just over $10,000 with the educational fellowship.

This is a sensible formula for approximating national service costs. At the same time, it does not imply that national service participants would be paid the minimum wage. Such a wage scale might not be appropriate for two reasons. First, payment of the minimum wage would carry a strong connotation of an employment program. While recognizing the work experience value of national service, the classification of national service as a work experience program would be misleading and could transform it into another "jobs for needy youth" program. Second, payment of the minimum wage could lead to legal complications involving the employer-employee relationship and including such issues as the right to strike, pension benefits, and union membership. While fully respecting the employer-employee relationship, national service is primarily a manifestation of citizenship and of government's responsibility for the future well-being of the nation. As such, national service should be as free of these employment issues as have been the Peace Corps, VISTA, and the armed forces.

Although we do not necessarily advocate direct payment of the minimum wage for national service, we do clearly recognize the necessity of compensation adequate enough to attract low income young people. The provision of training and the educational fellowship are important program features in this regard. Although the minimum wage might not be paid directly, the total benefit package for national service would very likely exceed a minimum wage equivalent.

THE EMPLOYMENT DIMENSION

All young Americans should be entitled to a full-time work experience that permits them to learn about the world of work, establish a creditable work record, and earn financial support for further education and training. National service should join education, employment, and military service as a fourth cornerstone of our unwritten national youth policy. As national service is phased in over several years, the targeted "jobs for needy youth" programs should be permitted to seek their lowest level. We believe that the great majority of young people in these programs would be better served in the kind of national service program described in this chapter.

There is ample reason to support this perspective. Large numbers of young people, sincere and capable and motivated, try in vain to get jobs. In 1980, there were approximately 2 million 18 to 24 year olds unemployed and seeking work. After a while, when they have been rejected dozens of times, many of these young people become discouraged. They stop trying. Many seek admission to a government training and employment program and, if the Congressional appropriations are big enough, the paternal government permits them to enter. Such experiences are demoralizing and they are repeated millions of times each year. Although intended to be helpful, this kind of youth employment policy is very callous treatment of young people by the nation through its government.

Looking at another important employment issue, *national service positions should be designed so they do not displace regular employees, either current or potential.* At the national level, those administering the program should be as sensitive to the labor issue as President Roosevelt was when he appointed labor leader Robert Fechner to head the CCC. At the local level, labor officials and other interested parties should be invited to review the local national service openings and to challenge any that could represent a conflict.

THE EDUCATIONAL DIMENSION

All young Americans are entitled to 12 years of elementary and secondary education. In addition, *young people should be able to earn a period of education and training beyond high school. Much of the current federal aid to education programs that Charles Moskos refers to as "the GI Bill without the GI" should be shifted to support those who contribute a period of national service. As with the old GI Bill, educational benefits should be proportional to length of service.*

An intensive service-learning experience for young adults, such as may be found in national service, would, in many cases, provide an added dimension to a largely passive education. *The government should encourage the academic recognition of service experiences in a way that is educationally sound, but should neither compel nor control such linkages and recognition.*

RELATIONSHIP TO THE MILITARY

Mention of the military tends to evoke strong reactions. There are those who would avoid any consideration of the military whatsoever, wishing perhaps that it would go away. And there are those for whom the military and national defense are single-minded interests. We do not think either of these approaches is especially helpful in considering national service. Issues related to the military are complex and inevitably connected to other important issues. In this respect, the military, as a major social institution, is no different from education or employment. It is from this perspective that we consider the relationship between the military and national service.

As advocates of national service, our view is that the need for national service transcends military recruitment policies. If the military had no problem recruiting volunteers, or if there were no armed forces, there would still be a need for national service. Thus, *a civilian youth service should exist independently of the military establishment. If there is a need for the military draft, persons choosing to volunteer for civilian service should bear a relationship to the draft comparable to that of those volunteering for military service.*

Concerning military policy, this national service proposal does not take a simplistic stand for or against a military draft. So long as there is a need for an armed force, we much prefer a volunteer military. However, we do not prefer a volunteer military at the price of its becoming a mercenary armed force. A mercenary armed force could easily be more damaging than a conscript armed force. Moreover, we do not think a conscript armed force would necessarily lead to war, as some opponents of the draft have contended. On the other hand, neither do we believe the arguments of draft proponents who suggest that a very large armed force would assuredly prevent war through deterrence. In short, we find that military policy questions tend not to be as clear-cut as the more vocal discussants would have us believe.

The question of relationship between national service and the military is not simply an either-or proposition. For example, in recent years, a number of youth employment bills have been introduced in the Congress. With few exceptions, these bills have made no reference to military service. At first glance, one might conclude that they were unrelated to military service. But this is clearly not the case when one probes further and asks what happens if the bill becomes law and within a year or two virtually all young people looking for work find it? Where will the armed forces find their recruits, who come disproportionately from the ranks of unemployed young people? Since the All-Volunteer Force came into being in 1973, its recruits have been drawn heavily from the reservoir of 2 million and more unemployed young men and women. If that reservoir is depleted for whatever reason—a successful youth employment initiative, a booming economy, a declining youth population—armed forces recruitment would be adversely affected.

That would leave the armed forces with four choices. First, they could reduce the number of persons in military service, an unlikely prospect for the 1980s. Second, they could raise military pay to whatever level is required, a difficult prospect in an inflationary period and in view of the government finding that the added cost of the All-Volunteer Force was $3 billion per year from 1974 to 1978.[14] Third, they could resort to the draft. And the fourth option is some form of national service. A national service with a standby draft for military service, as outlined in the McCloskey bill (chapter 6), would be one way to assure that recruitment goals of the armed forces were met.

A voluntary national service, however, offers a more intriguing prospect. A strictly numerical analysis would suggest an effect similar to that of a large-scale youth employment program, i.e., so many young people would join voluntary national service that the armed forces would have to reduce the size of the military, raise pay, or reinstate the draft. But some students of national service, notably Harris Wofford and the Rev. Theodore M. Hesburgh, differ with this analysis. They argue that if the government expressed its trust in young people by inviting them to serve for a period in voluntary national service, before long young people would come to appreciate the government's trust by enlisting in the military in sufficient numbers to obviate the need for a draft.[15] Also, Amitai Etzioni has pointed out that "the larger the segment of the youth who are spending a year in national service (military or otherwise), the more the fear of 'losing a year' will be diminished. Thus, somewhat paradoxically, the creation of nonmilitary service may help the voluntary mobilization of recruits *for* military service."[16]

Another important issue concerning the military is representativeness of the armed force. Prior to the post-World War II era, the United States confined conscription almost exclusively to periods of war. In those days, war was conducted in a way that gave a country adequate time to shift from a volunteer military to conscription. Consequently, battlefield casualties generally weighed more heavily on the conscript force than the more narrowly recruited volunteer force. In modern warfare, however, that time lag no longer exists. Moreover, the combat arms in 1980 were nearly 45 percent black, three times the proportion of blacks in the general population. The rapid deployment of the all–volunteer combat arms into a conflict would lead to casualty rates which would cause many people to ask with John Cavanaugh, "Why should those who have benefited least from society be required to give all in defense of those who have benefited the most?"[17]

A national service program of the kind described in this chapter can be expected gradually to increase the representativeness of a volunteer armed force. Military service would be viewed as one among other possible service alternatives and, in the process, would regain some measure of the respect lost during the Vietnam era. The word "service" would take on a more positive meaning and military service would again be viewed more as a citizenship responsibility than as a last resort employment program for the disadvantaged.

EXPECTATION OF PERFORMANCE

Pursuit of the above seven dimensions along the suggested lines should yield an entity recognizable as national service. But it would not be a finished product. The right concept and the right legislation for national service are essential but not sufficient. Regardless of the administrative model (see chapter 8) adopted for national service, the program must be administered in a way that prevents it from degenerating into a make–work program or little more than an income transfer program. *The work and service performed must be genuinely needed and perceived by the public and national service participants as worthwhile.*

What is needed is a national service program with low entry standards and fairly high performance standards. Admission should be open to everyone willing to serve; continued enrollment in national service should be contingent on living up to the service agreement reached between the young person and the sponsoring agency. The participant should understand that he or she has agreed to serve someone, say, a disabled person, and that failure to show up regularly would be a severe affront to that person, and might well impair the person's health and well being. The consequence of failing to live up to one's commitment should be the same for the participant as for the sponsor.

If the integrity of the social compact is to be maintained, it must be possible to fire not only the youthful participants but the sponsoring agencies as well. This should not be done capriciously. Rather, it should come about as a natural consequence of the contract between sponsor and participant. If the sponsor fails to live up to the commitment, the sponsor should be warned; and, if the violation continues, the sponsor should be dropped from the program.

THE NEXT FIVE STEPS

No large-scale program can be planned and put into effect overnight. Preparations must be made in order to move toward national service from where we are today. The purpose should be to move deliberately and systematically toward a time when the nation and its young people recognize and fulfill their responsibilities to one another. We recommend a five-step initiative which includes study, discussion, testing, evaluation, and review.

Study

A Presidential Commission on National Service, as recommended by Senator Paul Tsongas (D-Massachusetts), Representative Leon Panetta (D-California), and others, should be created either by executive order or by legislative action. This body should be charged with studying all aspects of national service and producing a realistic proposal that could be translated into legislation. The Commission should also initiate a number of studies that would examine in more detail the likely impact of national service on citizenship, employment, education, and the other fields reviewed in Part IV of this book. This kind of presidential leadership would be almost certain to spawn national service studies at foundations, universities, and elsewhere. All of these studies would provide the basis for an active discussion of national service.

Discussion

The Presidential Commission should also spearhead the discussion of national service. The Tsongas-Panetta bill would sponsor hearings and forums around the country to stimulate discussion of national service among the public at large, and young people in particular. Here again, this initiative would lead to discussion of national service in classrooms, living rooms, and taverns; in newspapers and magazines; on radio and television.

Testing

National service should be tested on a large scale and over a long period of time.
The testing should be more extensive, for example, than ACTION's experiments in Seattle and Syracuse. If national service would ultimately enroll
approximately one million young people, then it should be tested on a comparable scale. In the typical city or county or state, this would mean one
national service participant for every 225 residents. Thus, the state of Washington, with some 4 million residents, would have roughly 18,000 national
service participants. Washington, D.C., with 635,000 residents, would enroll
some 2,800 participants. These levels would be reached after a build-up
period of three years.

   *At least a five year commitment should be made for each of the test projects
and a ten year commitment would be preferable.* This span of time would
enable evaluators to view national service as it might appear after the initial
hurdles were overcome and the glow of the Hawthorne Effect worn off. More
importantly, a long test period would yield answers to important issues that
could be obtained only over several years. Some contend, for example, that a
national service for 18 to 24 year olds is too late. The real problem, they say,
is with teenagers who are, or should be, in junior and senior high schools.
Others respond that it is uncertainty and despair over what will happen after
high school that causes many of the problems among younger teens. The
certainty of admission to national service would give these teenagers something to look forward to and prepare for. Clearly, this important issue
requires longitudinal study. Also, what will be the migration patterns of
young people between test sites and other areas? Will the existence of a
national service test site attract or repel young people and, if so, which young
people move into the test sites and which ones move out?

   The transition period offers an ideal time to test various features of national service. Units of city, county, and state government, as well as private
organizations, could be invited to bid for one of the initial national service
grants. Certain features, say, level of stipend, age range, medical coverage,
and duration of service, would be fixed. The grant applicant would be invited to introduce unique elements. One proposal might call for a strong linkage between national service participants and the statewide community college system. Another might choose to specialize in a certain area such as
energy; its national service participants might build greenhouses and retrofit
houses for energy conservation. Still another proposer might be a labor
union whose major purpose would be to demonstrate how to run a program
locally without infringing on the rights of labor.

   Existence of several test projects would also facilitate the transition to full
national service. If, after five years, there were 100,000 young people en-

rolled in the test projects in 20 sites, the shift to full-scale national service for 1 million persons could be accomplished within three years.

Evaluation

These test projects should be evaluated not only against one another and control groups but also against existing youth programs. A great oversight in the conduct of youth programs during the 1960s and 1970s was a general failure to make comparative studies. What needs to be done is to set up an evaluation system which includes significant outcomes of all youth programs. The evaluation might include each of the seven key issues reviewed in this chapter as well as the value of service performed by participants. Among the youth programs to be examined might be Job Corps, VISTA, Young Adult Conservation Corps, CETA Summer Youth Employment, College Work Study, Youth Incentive Entitlement, and National Service test projects. This approach would enable lawmakers to assess, in a comparative framework, a broad range of outcomes, both intended and accidental. The merits and limitations of individual programs could be viewed clearly when placed in the context of other alternatives. For too long, the United States has had a piecemeal and fragmented approach to youth policy.

To undertake such a broad evaluation would be much more difficult than simply evaluating a number of national service test projects. Every federal program acquires a cluster of legislators, bureaucrats, consultants, administrators, and sometimes clients who protect the program. Protectors of any specific program would argue that it is wrong to assess their program against any objectives not specified in the legislation, or to make comparisons across programs. But if the nation's youth are to be served, there must be some way around this dilemma.

Review

A National Youth Commission should be created and empowered to conduct the necessary evaluations of existing youth programs and national service tests, to review the results, and to make recommendations. The Commission itself would not conduct any programs, experimental or otherwise. Its purpose would be to take a wide-range view of the nation's youth programs, and to report findings and conclusions to the President, the Congress, and the people.

If the above five steps are undertaken, there would be, within a few years, sufficient evidence and crystallization of public opinion to embark with confidence on a full-scale national service.

NOTES

1. William James, "The Moral Equivalent of War," *International Conciliation* no. 27 (New York: Carnegie Endowment for International Peace, 1910).

2. Liberty Hyde Bailey, *Universal Service* (Ithaca, New York: The Comstock Publishing Co., 1919), p. 92.

3. Oberlin College Faculty, *A Plan of National Service* (Oberlin College, 1944), pp. 3-4.

4. Anita Martin, comments as a discussant in Donald J. Eberly, *National Service: A Report on a Conference* (New York: Russell Sage Foundation, 1968), p. 504.

5. *Presidential Recommendations for Selective Service Reform: A Report to Congress Prepared Pursuant to P.L. 96-107* (Washington: U.S. Government Printing Office, February 11, 1980), p. 46.

6. Donald J. Eberly, Testimony in U.S. Congress, House Committee on Armed Services, *Hearings on Military Posture and H.R. 1872*, 96th Cong., 1st sess., 1979, pp. 1103-1109.

7. U.S. Bureau of the Census, *U.S. Resident Population by Single Years of Age: 4/1/80* (Washington: U.S. Government Printing Office, June 18, 1981).

8. National Service Secretariat, "First Comprehensive Survey in 13 Years Finds Need for Several Million People at National Service Level," *National Service Newsletter* (January 1979), p. 2.

9. Donald J. Eberly, "National Needs and National Service," *Current History* 55, no. 324 (August 1968).

10. Donald J. Eberly, testimony in Committee on Armed Forces, pp. 1105-1106.

11. U.S. Congressional Budget Office, *National Service Programs and Their Effects on Military Manpower and Civilian Youth Problems* (Washington: U.S. Congressional Budget Office, 1978), pp. 83-85.

12. U.S. Congressional Budget Office, *Costs of the National Service Act (H.R. 2206): A Technical Analysis* (Washington: U.S. Congressional Budget Office, 1980).

13. Donald J. Eberly, "A Model for Universal Youth Service," Paper presented at the Universal Youth Service Conference, Eleanor Roosevelt Institute, Hyde Park, N.Y., 1976.

14. Comptroller General of the United States, *Additional Cost of the All-Volunteer Force* (Washington: U.S. Government Printing Office, 1978), p. ii.

15. Harris Wofford and Rev. Theodore M. Hesburgh, Testimony in U.S. Congress, Senate Committee on Labor and Human Resources, Subcommittee on Child and Human Development, *Hearings on Presidential Commission on National Service and National Commission on Volunteerism*, 96th Cong., 2nd sess., 1980, pp. 39-42 and 67-70.

16. Amitai Etzioni, *Toward Higher Education in an Active Society: Three Policy Guidelines* (New York: Center for Policy Research, 1970), p. II-27.

17. John Cavanaugh, quoted in *National Service Newsletter* no. 36 (June 1979), p. 3.

Chapter 8
Administrative Issues
Harris Wofford and Donald J. Eberly

However much young people are needed and however eager they are to serve, the process by which needs and resources are brought together would vitally affect the success of a national service effort. Administrative possibilities range from a highly centralized, tightly controlled hierarchy which might replace present federal youth programs, to a decentralized, loosely coordinated network of service opportunities.

There is an equally broad range of funding possibilities. There might be federal support for all costs associated with national service, or federal support for participants only, or federal support only for volunteers in specific positions.

Then there is the question of whether national service should be administered from a new or an existing agency. Should the job be assigned to an agency such as ACTION or the Department of Labor, or does it require a new entity such as the National Youth Service Foundation proposed in the Hatfield bill? Could a viable national service program exist entirely outside the federal bureaucracy? At the local level, should the national service participant be assigned to a job by a counselor or by a computer, or should the young man or woman arrange and negotiate his or her own assignment? In order to suggest the implications of different administrative models, Wofford weighs the merits and demerits of three models and Eberly details a single model consistent with the national service plan described in chapter 7.

THREE MODELS FOR THE ORGANIZATION OF NATIONAL SERVICE*
(HARRIS WOFFORD)

A stumbling block in considering national service is the problem of administering a program for a million or more participants. Even before the Reagan

---

* Parts of this section are taken from the Committee for the Study of National Service, *Youth and the Needs of the Nation* (Washington: The Potomac Institute, 1979). Harris Wofford served as co-chairman of the Committee.

era of budget–cutting, the prospect of a giant new government bureaucracy for national service repelled many if not most people. The 1979 Report of the Committee for the Study of National Service tried to get around this obstacle by recommending that the administrative structure "should emphasize decentralization and result in the smallest feasible government bureaucracy with the strongest possible ties to the private and voluntary sectors of American society, including business, labor, charitable and religious organizations."

If national service can be organized and administered as well or better through the private sector, with minimal government intervention, then it should be done that way. Its chance of securing widespread public acceptance would thereby be greatly increased. Indeed, this may be the only way that a majority of the people could be won over to the concept of national service. It is not only the old school and the born again conservatives who look askance at any proposed new government program. Young people of all political persuasions are an important part of the antibureaucratic tide, and they would be the main participants in national service. National service as a program of the American people, organized largely through the voluntary agencies of the people, would appeal to far more people, young and old, than any essentially government-run program.

The Buckley Model

The model proposed by William F. Buckley, Jr. suggests a total decentralization, with no government bureaucracy at all. In his book, *Four Reforms*, and in his newspaper column, Buckley has suggested that national service be instituted not by government draft or even with government financial support and inducement but by the nation's leading private colleges and universities. He envisions "a statement by the trustees of the ten top-rated private colleges and universities in which it is given as common policy that . . . no one accepted into the freshman class will be matriculated until he has passed one year in public service."[1]

Buckley's priority would be service by the young to the elderly, but he would not impose this prescription. Any form of work—through existing private, religious, or government agencies, or on one's own—that the colleges and universities recognize as public service would qualify. He assumes that most young volunteers could live at home and work in their communities, so that their living stipends could be minimal and could be paid by the agencies they served, or by their families.

As evidence that this approach might work, he points to the tradition of the Mormon Church, which calls on its youth to serve full time, at home or overseas, for one or two years in their late teens or early twenties. The Rev.

Theodore Hesburgh, president of the University of Notre Dame, similarly points to the successful experience of hundreds of that university's students who have worked as volunteers, usually through Catholic agencies, often living in the homes of people in the communities where they served, and receiving only bare living expenses from the agencies supervising their work.

Obviously, this approach would cut the costs of national service to any central agency by a vast amount. In 1979, the average cost of a VISTA Volunteer for a year of service was approximately $6,700, including training, supervision, and administrative expenses, as well as living stipends. The Buckley model would eliminate almost all of these costs.

But what about the young person requiring financial aid to attend the private colleges and universities imposing the service requirement? Buckley notes that "in the unusual case where the eighteen-year-old is helping to support his own family, the college could either suspend the requirement or concert with foundations to find ways to permit the young volunteers to eke out the year."

From the federal government, Buckley would ask no money and only minimal collaboration. He would expect the government to exempt this category of volunteers from the provisions of the minimum wage law, so that living stipends to volunteers could be well below that level. He also proposes that, since billions of federal dollars are going into higher education (which he opposes), such federal support should be conditioned on a requirement of public service by its freshman applicants. Buckley argues that there are already strings attached to federal aid: "No racial discrimination, more basketball for girls. God knows what else. Why not discriminate against those colleges that fail (except in special ones) to require a year's social work for matriculants?"

As a way to begin national service on a substantial scale, the Buckley model has considerable appeal. The hundreds of thousands of young people who might engage in a year or more of service before entering college should have a leavening effect on the whole generation of youth. There would be nothing to prevent non-college-bound students from participating. Since most private colleges and universities have taken steps to become more representative, a significant number of black and white, rich and poor, urban and rural students would be among the volunteers. Applicants to public universities or young people not presently planning to continue their formal education could be encouraged to participate, but would face no negative sanctions if they did not do so. The main initial constituency of volunteers would be among the better-educated and probably more highly motivated youth.

Such an aristocracy of service is the opposite of the approach taken by those who see national service as a euphemism for public jobs for unemployed youth. Buckley would start with the college-bound elite—and, first of all, with the elite going to the "ten top–rated private colleges and universities" (he did not list them). Since part of the problem of high school drop-outs and unemployed young people, especially inner-city youth, is lack of motivation and self-confidence, it is unlikely that many of them would respond, at least initially, to a call to national service on these terms.

This "trickle down" way of organizing national service might work, nevertheless, if it were tried with the strong sanction sought by Buckley. The multiplier effect of so many of the nation's "top-rated" young people could be powerful. If their work proved to be beneficial to the agencies and communities served, and if the effect on participants proved to be good for their own development as well as for the educational climate of the colleges and universities which they entered, the idea could become contagious. Then new ways could be found to enlist non-college-bound young people, and assure that their work, alongside the student volunteers, would also be rewarding.

There is, however, a fundamental case against such a beginning. Although it is in accord with the current antibureaucratic tide, it runs counter to the democratic spirit of the age. It is contrary to the concept of "national" service, as most of the advocates of such service from William James to the present have espoused it, since it would draw primarily from a pool that was not representative of the nation. The Committee for the Study of National Service recommended the following alternative proposition:

> In moving toward universal service, the system should aim to enlist at each stage a representative cross-section of American young people, drawing into work together men and women from all regions, races, and backgrounds. Though difficult to carry out, this functional integration of Americans should be an essential operating principle of the system.[2]

There is also a more practical argument against Buckley's characteristically provocative proposal. It is difficult to believe that the leading colleges and universities, singly or together, would have the conviction or the courage to require a year or more of public service from their applicants.

What might be expected of many colleges and universities (and probably the most that could be expected of them), if the idea of national service took hold of the public mind, is that they would give significant weight in the admission process to applicants who engaged in public service. Thus, even if Buckley does not persuade one to go completely his way, he points to a strong nongovernmental incentive to national service that could be provided by institutions of higher education. If one or more colleges or universities did go all the way and require such service of applicants, that could add momentum to any larger system of national service that might be underway.

The GI Bill as a Model

A model that from the beginning would make national service readily available to the whole generation of young people is suggested by the post-World War II GI Bill of Rights. Exservicemen were offered stipends for living expenses and educational institutions were offered tuition by the federal government. The number of months for which this support was available depended on the years each former GI had served in the armed forces. Living stipends were just barely adequate. The administrative structure was simple, with very little government intervention. Stipends went directly to the students once they were admitted to accredited educational institutions, and the tuition went directly to those institutions. Admissions decisions were made entirely by the institutions themselves, and the accrediting of the institutions was done by professional educational organizations.

Most private voluntary agencies that have considered national service have said that they could use and would welcome the service of young full-time volunteers, but that they could not afford to pay any substantial stipends for living expenses. Many agency executives have also asserted that the administrative expenses involved in training and supervising young volunteers would be beyond their budgets. Such a request for administrative support should be viewed as a bargaining position, since agencies would utilize volunteers without reimbursement for added administrative time. But the claim that most voluntary organizations would not be able to pay stipends to a large number of young volunteers is probably accurate. Throughout the country, voluntary social agencies are facing budget crises, and no solution to this is in sight. Therefore, unless the private sector can design some new method of securing funds for volunteer stipends, a national system for funding volunteer stipends would be necessary if the program is to be available to a large number of young people each year.

Adapting the idea of the GI Bill, one could construct a national service system in which the only government involvement was the provision of minimum living allowances to all young people accepted for service by accredited agencies of public service. The accrediting of those agencies could be done by one or more professional organizations. In fact, a broad list of service agencies likely to be acceptable for alternative service by conscientious objectors was developed in the 1960s.[3]

A further inducement to national service would be a postservice educational benefit, based on the months of service, also similar to the system developed under the GI Bill of Rights. Such educational assistance to young people could replace much of that now appropriated annually by Congress. Indeed, the Buckley proposal that federal aid for higher education be conditioned upon students engaging in public service would fit such a national service system.

This financial support from Congress would, of course, be substantial. Federal intervention and control would be minimal, however, if the government's role were limited to the provision of in-service living expense stipends and postservice educational benefits. If that were the extent of the federal role, then there would be a great need for leaders of the private sector to join in establishing some kind of overall national council or clearing center and probably some kind of nationwide network of local councils as sources of information.

A Public Corporation for National Service

National service may seem to be a simple concept, but its implementation would be complicated whether done through one centralized government (or nongovernment) agency or through many diverse national and local organizations in the most decentralized manner. The articulation of the idea, the development of effective ways to utilize volunteers, the dissemination of information that would persuade young people to volunteer, the appraisal of the service rendered and of the effect of the experience on the volunteers, and other aspects of carrying out national service call for strong leadership. If that leadership is not to come from government, it must come from some concerted source in the private and voluntary sector of society.

A public corporation for national service, chartered and funded by Congress but drawing its leadership from the private and voluntary sector—as proposed by the Committee for the Study of National Service—may be the most promising way to provide the concerted leadership needed. Innovative structures in both the private and public sectors should be examined, including the American Red Cross, the Legal Services Corporation, the Corporation for Public Broadcasting, the Tennessee Valley Authority, the Atomic Energy Commission, and the Peace Corps. Such a public corporation (or, it might be called, a foundation or institute) would be empowered to set overall guidelines and criteria for funding and monitoring the various programs in which young people may serve. It should also be authorized to establish a network of local service councils for information and counseling.

The Committee for the Study of National Service suggested a more maximalist model in which the Corporation for National Service would also be empowered to initiate and administer some service programs directly itself. It further proposed that the staff of the National Service corporation seek to initiate and assist a variety of in-service educational activities among volunteers. The volunteers could be encouraged to take available extension courses or attend night school; English-speaking and Spanish-speaking young people could learn to tutor each other in oral language skills; college-trained participants could tutor high school dropouts in basic skills or subjects they lack; the central literature of the American tradition could be read and discussed in volunteer seminars. Some of these activities could be particularly valuable for volunteers who were not planning to attend college and especially for high school dropouts.

Even without such additional functions, the National Service corporation would need to develop a kind of national network of information and communication. For this, the structure and experience of the voluntary local boards in the Selective Service System suggest a way to proceed. To assist young people in choosing the best form of national service, service councils could be established in each community, composed of citizens with experience in voluntary service, education, business, labor, and religious organizations. Members would be appointed nationally and serve without pay. The councils might well be located in underutilized facilities in local high schools. They would provide information and counseling on the various opportunities for service.

After age 16 but before leaving high school all young people should be urged to visit a local service council, and the councils would hold open meetings in schools. In addition to giving up-to-date information on national service opportunities, such councils would be well informed about job training and public service jobs available through other federal programs, and about opportunities in the armed forces.

In the development of National Service, by whatever route, the course should be gradual. The system should expand only to the extent that the service of young people is effectively used. Each of the programs to be included should plan and administer the work of the volunteers so as to achieve a substantially increased contribution to meeting one or more of the nation's needs. Those responsible for schools; day-care centers; tutoring programs; programs for the elderly; hospitals; community health centers; institutions for the retarded and the mentally ill; prisons and juvenile detention centers; neighborhood associations; city, county, and national agencies for conservation, renovation, and energy-saving; and efforts to deal with disasters of nature—and other service agencies—should be asked: What could you do better to meet your present goals if you had the full-time service of a substantial number of young people? What larger goals could you then set? Precisely how would you utilize the services of such young people? What training and supervision would be required?

The organization of national service is, in all respects, an invitation—and challenge—to the imagination. It calls for a new social invention. Looking at the unmet needs of the nation and the energy of young volunteers that might be put to work, we can see that the philosopher's adage was never more true: we must be more inventive if we are going to do our duty.

AN ADMINISTRATIVE MODEL: NATIONAL YOUTH SERVICE (NYS)* (DONALD EBERLY)

The intent of this model is to produce a national service program that is consistent with the promise of national service, cost-effective, and administratively efficient. Following this model, national service would be organized and administered in a way that would (1) foster decision making at the lowest levels; (2) bring in the federal government only when necessary; (3) keep politicians at arm's length; (4) provide for a transition from the present to a full-scale program; (5) provide room for growth and change; and (6) include participation by business and labor.

In order to prevent discrimination, both overt and covert, a certain level of federal control would be necessary. It is possible that such apparently innocent processes as recruitment and application could develop into highly sophisticated sorting and discriminatory procedures. The federal government must retain the right to review and rectify such activities.

The national service program presented here would include an underwriting approach in which federal funds would not replace other funds already available, but in which federal monies would be adequate to guarantee service positions to all young people who wanted them. In National Youth Service (NYS), funds would be administered by state or local levels of government, and they would be obtained from the federal government by means of the grant-making process. This national service program would have application and placement procedures taking place at the state or local level. At the same time, there would be enough common elements in all NYS projects to give NYS a clear image nationwide, and to permit certain generic recruitment activities to be undertaken on the national level. At the state and local levels where programs would be administered, there would be no new organizations but sometimes new coalitions of existing organizations. At the level of the sponsor, where the NYS participant would work, new organizations would not be ruled out but the great bulk of activity would be conducted by existing organizations.

Finally, the model would create a new entity at the national level to perform a new function; namely, a public corporation that would be accountable to the President and the Congress but somewhat removed from day-to-day political pressures. In brief, the system would be organized as follows:

---

* Parts of this section are taken from Donald J. Eberly, "A Model for Universal Youth Service," prepared for the Eleanor Roosevelt Institute (1976, unpublished).

- A Foundation for National Youth Service would be established by law. It would be a quasi-public organization, similar to the Corporation for Public Broadcasting, and receive appropriations from Congress.
- The Foundation would be operated by a 21-member Board of Trustees, with 12 of its members serving 3 year overlapping terms, appointed by the President with the advice and consent of the Senate. The following nine other persons would serve as ex-officio members: Secretaries of Agriculture, Education, Energy, Labor, Health and Human Services, Housing and Urban Development, and Interior; the Director of ACTION, and the Director of the National Youth Service Foundation.
- Also, an Advisory Council would be created to advise the Board of Trustees on broad policy matters. It would have 24 members with at least eight under 27 years of age at the time of appointment. Members of the Board would meet at least three times a year.
- Present federal programs providing opportunities for youth service would remain in effect. As of 1981, these would include the Peace Corps, VISTA, College Work Study, Young Adult Conservation Corps, Job Corps, and other youth programs funded by the Comprehensive Employment and Training Act. The summer Youth Conservation Corps would be modified to permit 15 to 17 year olds to engage in other than strictly conservation activities and to learn about national service opportunities. After three years of NYS operation, Congress would examine all of these programs to determine the appropriate degree of consolidation among them.
- The Foundation would invite units of state, regional, and local governments to submit grant applications, outlining plans for the operation of NYS within the specified guidelines. The Foundation would award grants on the basis of merit and the funds available. In considering proposals, the Foundation would give particular attention to the priorities allocated to job placement, accomplishment of needed service, education and training, and youth development. The ideal proposal would reveal a balance among these goals supported by participation of the respective agencies in program administration.
- Grantees would have exclusive jurisdictions, as defined in the grant application. Thus, several cities in a given state could be NYS grantees and the state government could be the grantee for the balance of the state.
- Grants would run for periods of up to three years. Upon receipt of the grant, the grantee would announce the program and invite participation by persons ages 18 to 24. At the same time, the grantee would invite participation by public and private nonprofit organizations interested in becoming NYS sponsors.
- In addition to encouraging participation in the existing youth service programs, NYS would offer participants two major options: Community Service and Environmental Service. Applicants for Community Service

would interview for a wide range of local service projects sponsored by public agencies or private nonprofit organizations. Those who wished to travel in search of Community Service projects would do so at their own expense and register with the local NYS agency.

• Most sponsors of the Environmental Service option would be federal, state, or local agencies. Most environmental projects would require travel costs as well as expenditures for supplies and equipment. Such costs would be the responsibility of the sponsor, not of the Foundation. If lodging and food were provided by the sponsor, these expenses would be reimbursed by the NYS grantee from whose jurisdiction the participant was recruited.

NYS at the Local Level

The process of identifying NYS sponsors and participants can best be described by imagining that we are in a city or state that has just received a NYS grant. To illustrate how the program might work, it is helpful to trace the process first for young people and then for the sponsoring agencies.

NYS from the Participant's Point of View.   Young people would learn of NYS from numerous sources, including word-of-mouth, newspapers, radio, television, schools, colleges, youth clubs, religious groups, and the local service councils suggested by Wofford. Where mailing lists were available, persons from 18 to 24 would be sent information packets on NYS. Elsewhere, intensive efforts would be made to make the packets easily available through a variety of channels. Should there be a registration requirement, all 18 year olds would receive the information packet directly.

By the second year of NYS, many 18 year olds would become acquainted with NYS through participation in the new Youth Conservation Corps. These YCC camps would be residential, eight-week summer camps with 100 to 200 persons at each site. Each camp would have these features: (1) The major part of the time would be devoted to performing needed conservation and community service; (2) some time would be devoted to giving necessary training to the young people and to reflecting with them on what they have learned from their service experience; (3) participants would be informed of their options under NYS when they reach the age of 18; and (4) each camp would have a socioeconomic mix of young people.

A simple, one-page application form would be included in the information kit. Persons interested in joining NYS would complete the form and send it to the local center for processing. By return mail, the applicant would receive an invitation to attend a one-day orientation session to be held within one month.

For applicants who had not yet decided which branch of NYS to join, further information and counseling would be available at the orientation session. Also, major pending legal and medical problems would be reviewed at this time, and a determination would be made as to whether the application could proceed or would have to await resolution of such problems. Each qualifying applicant would complete a one-page resume and receive a voucher and agreement form. The *resume* would serve as an introduction to the potential sponsors and would describe the applicant's educational background, work experience, and interests. The *voucher* would guarantee a certain level of financial support and health care by the U.S. government in return for the performance of needed services by the applicant and compliance with the regulations by both applicant and sponsor. The *agreement form* would provide space for the applicant and sponsor to spell out the duties of the applicant, the training and supervisory responsibilities of the sponsor, and other features of the job.

Next, applicants would have direct access to a computer terminal where they would compile a list of positions of interest to them, with the assistance of a computer operator as necessary. Applicants would then receive brief training in interview techniques and make appointments for one or more interviews with sponsors. Normally, officials from the Environmental Service would be available at the orientation session. Agreements might be completed and the voucher signed and certified by the end of the day. For persons seeking positions with Community Service agencies, it might take several days to complete a round of interviews leading to agreement between applicant and sponsor.

The final agreement would state the date of beginning service and provisions for training and transportation. NYS would normally provide for one day of training on administrative matters. Work-related training would be the responsibility of the sponsor and would be offered as part of the service period unless otherwise provided for in the agreement.

NYS from the Sponsor's Point of View.   Sponsors would be recruited in a fashion somewhat similar to that used for participants. Sponsorship would be universally open to public and private nonprofit agencies. Sponsors would be able to request NYS participants only for positions meeting certain general criteria; these would include: (1) no displacement of regular employees, and (2) no political nor religious activities. The latter criterion would not exclude political and religious groups from sponsorship; they could engage participants for such tasks as non-partisan voter registration or nonsectarian day care.

The sponsoring agency would certify that it is prepared to contribute 5 percent of the participant's stipend per work-year of service and to provide the necessary supervision and in-service training. Also, the sponsor would agree to participate in a one-day training session before receiving any NYS participants. The 5 percent contribution would be in cash but might come from outside organizations such as businesses and churches.

Sponsors' requests would be open to public review for a period of one week. Where challenges were made, the grantee would investigate them and make a determination. Those position descriptions which successfully pass through this process would be entered into a computer listing, where they would be immediately accessible to NYS applicants in the area. It is from this listing that applicants would arrange interviews and the agreement process would go forward. Should there be more than negligible abuse of this clearance process, it would be necessary to set up formal review committees, including union officials, to pass on each application for a NYS participant.

Decisions affecting the retention or dismissal of NYS participants would have to be made individually. Still, guidelines would be needed. The guiding principle would be the participant's willingness to serve. The written agreement would spell out the duties and responsibilities of both participant and supervisor. If a participant were repeatedly late for work or neglectful of agreed-upon duties, he or she would be giving a clear signal of an absence of a willingness to serve. Dismissal would be in order. By contrast, another participant who simply could not master an assigned job, even while making every effort to do so, would be provided in-service training or offered placement in a simpler job, accompanied by a renegotiated contract.

When sponsoring organizations failed to live up to the terms of the agreement, the participant would be assisted in securing another placement and the sponsoring organization would be removed from the computer listing. Participants dismissed for failing to comply with the terms of the agreement normally would be ineligible for reenrollment in NYS.

By relying on the best interests of the persons and organizations at the heart of the program to undertake most of the monitoring function, the need for red tape would be correspondingly reduced. For example, the use of vouchers and agreement forms would achieve placements satisfactory to both parties, would provide a basis for handling complaints, and would reduce costs and administrative oversight. If the service worker did not show up for work or failed to perform the duties agreed to in the contract, the sponsor would be motivated by its investment to report the service worker to the local administrator for discipline and possible discharge. Similarly, if the sponsor assigned duties to the service worker that were not in the agreement or otherwise violated the agreement, the service worker would be motivated by his self-interest (e.g., loss of anticipated work experience) to report the sponsor to the local administrator for discipline and possible discharge.

Use of the agreement form also would facilitate the process of incoming NYS participants building on the work of their NYS predecessors. New NYS enrollees could interview outgoing participants, read their reports, and review their statements of objectives. With this background information, incoming participants could better negotiate a set of worthwhile activities.

After Service in NYS

As indicated earlier, NYS would be a transition program. It would not be a lifetime job, nor would it guarantee employment upon completion. Still, NYS would include certain features that would facilitate future employment and further education.

First, NYS would be a source of information about jobs and education. This information would take the form of newsletters, job information sheets, opportunities for counseling, and referrals to such institutions as the State Employment Security Agencies and the Community Education-Work Councils proposed by Willard Wirtz and presently in operation in a number of communities.

Second, NYS would certify the work performed by the participant. Certification would be descriptive, not judgmental, and would enable outgoing participants to get beyond the initial hurdle to jobs for which they are qualified.

Third, NYS would award an education and training voucher to the departing national service worker. The voucher, a kind of GI Bill for National Service, would be good for one year of education and training for each year of service.

Fourth, the Women in Community Service and Joint Action for Community Service programs of the Job Corps would be adapted for utilization by NYS. These volunteer programs are currently very successful in recruiting, counseling, and placing Job Corps enrollees. Community placement services would provide post-NYS assistance to young people with special needs as they completed national service.

Flexibility in the Future

The NYS program would prepare for the future by allocating 5 percent of its budget to experimental projects. Chapter 2 describes the changes which have occurred with national service ideas in the twentieth century. First, national service was viewed as a way to unleash the energies of young men in constructive pursuits, and, later, as a way to demonstrate the U.S. commitment to peace, then as a draft alternative, then as a means of enabling students to acquire relevant education, then as a way to solve the youth unemployment problem. While it is reasonable to assume that the idea of national service will stand the test of time for decades to come, it is clear that any national service program would need to adapt to changing social, political, and economic conditions. A systematic program of experimental projects is the best way to meet unforeseeable contingencies five or ten years in the future. The Foundation could foster experimentation by supporting such initiatives as:

(1) a college incorporating a year of national service in its curriculum, (2) a labor union supervising national service work projects while giving specialized training to participants, (3) a sponsor such as the Red Cross contracting for national service participants for emergency work on an intermittent basis, (4) a sponsor such as a nursing home contracting for participants on a part time basis, and (5) national service participants taking the initiative to be their own sponsors or organizing their own national service teams.

NOTES

1. William F. Buckley, Jr., *Four Reforms* (New York: G. P. Putnam's Sons, 1974), pp. 17-18; and "Public Service by Youth: An Appealing Idea," syndicated Buckley column, *Austin American-Statesman* (March 17, 1979). All references to Buckley are from these sources.

2. The Committee for the Study of National Service, *Youth and The Needs of the Nation* (Washington: The Potomac Institute, 1979), p. 2.

3. National Interreligious Service Board for Conscientious Objectors, *Guide to Alternative Service* (Washington: National Interreligious Service Board for Conscientious Objectors, 1970).

Part IV:
Impacts of National Service

Chapter 9
The Impact of National Service on Youth Employment

Peter B. Edelman

The best way to examine the impact voluntary national service would have on youth employment is to begin by asking who the participants in national service would be.

If voluntary national service pays all participants a stipend adequate only to cover subsistence, it is fair to conclude that on the whole it would attract only those who could afford to participate as volunteers. Its ranks would be drawn primarily from middle income and wealthier families and, as such, would be disproportionately nonminority. If that is the type of voluntary national service that is enacted, the question of national service and employment would be easy to answer. The only "employment" issue, if the vast majority of the participants are people with good career prospects anyway, would be the need to avoid competition with the labor market in the types of volunteer slots that are created. The rule to be followed would be to avoid placing young people in service activities which someone would have paid someone else a full wage to do. Postvolunteer placement would generally take care of itself if the volunteers were mostly all people who could be expected to "make it" without any special attention to training, remediation, or job readiness during their service period. Such a concept of national service is not unthinkable. That is what the Peace Corps and VISTA have been.

But, if we are talking about a large-scale voluntary national service program, what is not unthinkable is nevertheless undesirable. It would be better, for a number of reasons, to draw people from all parts of the society. Most important, participants would benefit from working side by side with people from widely varying backgrounds. Stereotypes would be challenged and even shattered, sensitivities honed, and new challenges posed. Many who began with limited perspectives as to their life's possibilities would find their horizons, options, and aspirations broadened.

Moreover, a significant negative outcome would be avoided. If voluntary national service were an elitist activity, programs to combat youth unemployment, if they existed at all, would be separate and segregated economically and, to a significant extent, racially and ethnically as well. Separate life tracks would continue. Among other things, youth employment programs would not have as strong a political base as they would have if they were tied to national service.

Designing voluntary national service so that it is fully open to people of all income levels is a complex proposition, to say the least. For lower income participants, voluntary national service, adequately compensated, should be one option in an array of youth employment and development choices.

It is useful to think of voluntary national service and youth employment programs as two distinct activities which might have certain common elements: picture two circles which somewhat overlap each other. Most national service participants would be "pure" volunteers. Most youth employment program participants would be doing things other than service activities, especially, I would hope, getting subsidized work experience or quasi-apprenticeship training in the private sector, particularly in small businesses. Some youth employment program participants, those representing the area where the circles overlap, would choose community service as the work experience component of a course designed to produce employability and employment as the ultimate outcome.

Thus, the two overlapping circles might have two entry points. One would be direct enlistment in voluntary national service. This entry point would be for those who are looking only for a year during which they can make an appropriate contribution to their community or country. The second entry point would be through the youth employment system. This is the area which would present complications. For example, many young people who seek help in becoming employable need substantial education and training before they are ready for either a subsidized job or a service setting. Some of these young people have dropped out of school and many are years behind in basic skills. A fully developed system might place these young people in a year or more of intensive remediation, coupled in some instances with a heavily sheltered work situation, before even considering either community service or a quasi-apprenticeship assignment in the private sector. For these young people, national service would not be a viable option until they had completed a significant period of preparatory training.

An even larger number of young people function at an adequate or higher level of basic skills but lack job readiness. They often do not know how to handle an interview or a job application, how to dress appropriately for work, how to get to work on time every day, or how to respond appropriately to supervision. A short job readiness phase might be necessary for such young people as a prelude to a work or service assignment. Again, therefore, entry into the overlapping area between the two activities—youth employment programs and national service—would not be appropriate until an introductory phase had been completed.

Once these preludes were completed, service assignments should be one, but only one, among a number of work experience choices for youth employment program participants. This cannot be stressed too strongly. For many young people from low income families, a service activity would not be the most appropriate way to advance long-term employability. The vast majority of jobs in the United States are in the private sector. A full-scale youth employment program must, in my judgment, include the possibility of subsidized work experience in the private sector. On the other hand, service and employment need not be mutually exclusive. Indeed, lack of available jobs and/or need for further subsidized work experience might force youth employment program participants to choose a service activity and then be offered an additional placement in the private sector portion of the employment program when the service activity is completed.

Another key issue is compensation. As implied above, national service participants from low income families would need to be offered something more than a subsistence wage—probably the minimum wage—in order to be attracted in proportionate numbers to the service option. This implies either a two-tier, means-tested compensation structure for the service program, or it implies paying all participants the minimum wage or its equivalent.

To the extent possible, teams of national service volunteers should be fully integrated in terms of backgrounds and family income levels as well as race. This, too, would present problems insofar as some participants referred by the youth employment system would require a certain amount of skill development training even while they were in the national service component. Particularly in large cities, some volunteer teams might be composed solely of low income young people who receive extra remediation or training along with their service activities. Otherwise, the system would present the anomaly of some team members being assigned to additional classroom activities and others not.

Finally, if national service is to be fully open to participants from low income households, the issue of postservice placement must be faced, in terms of both a possible educational entitlement as one reward for service and of a systematic placement function.

This issue highlights, even more, the need for dovetailing of national service and youth employment programs. Even if it were possible to attract low income participants to national service by offering sufficient compensation, the national service scheme would still present postservice pitfalls for low income participants. A year of service activity could demonstrate faithful attendance, punctuality, and appropriate attitude; but, since its content probably would be seen as quite different from private sector work, private employers might not be very impressed by the "credential" of a completed year of service, especially if it were not accompanied by needed skill development and training. Keying national service into a parallel but partially overlapping youth employment system would be the best way to maximize ultimate job outcomes for service participants.

There are at least two other logical possibilities. One is that national service would "go it alone," creating its own training and placement efforts for those participants who needed such assistance, and leaving the youth employment structure to function on a totally separate basis. This, however, would result in considerable duplication of effort and would tend to be politically damaging to the separate youth employment efforts. The second possibility would be to subsume the entire youth employment effort under the rubric of national service. The problem with this is that it might be a case of the monkey swallowing the elephant. Youth employment efforts, as indicated earlier, should involve a wide variety of activities, including work experience in the private sector and intensive skill development and job readiness programs. Calling the whole thing "national service" would be a misnomer.

Nonetheless, this second possibility should not be dismissed if it is the most politically feasible approach to a fully developed system. It should be clear to the designers, however, that, even if they choose to call the whole thing national service, they are, in fact, designing a system which would look like the two overlapping circles described earlier.

The relationship between national service and youth employment or, more specifically, removing the barriers to full participation in national service by young people from low income families, is an extremely complex issue. It confronts the advocates of national service with a genuine dilemma: either run a "true" volunteer program which would be relatively simple to administer but would effectively deny thousands the opportunity to participate and simultaneously limit prospects for a genuine effort to combat youth employment, or undertake the very complicated task of "fitting" the national service agenda to the youth employment agenda in order to achieve the maximum synergistic effect.

Chapter 10

The Impact of National Service on Education

William R. Ramsay

The immediate reaction to questions of the impact of national service on institutions of higher education is to think of enrollment. Enrollment concerns are not without cause. College enrollment has always been sensitive to changes in military service requirements and variations in the job market. Now, with the pool of college age youth declining, enrollment is even more sensitive to expansion or restriction of other major options for young people. The addition of a major national service program for 18-24 year olds would affect enrollment. Enrollment impact, both temporary and longer range, needs to be examined. To limit attention of the educational impact of national service to its effects on enrollment in existing patterns of higher education, however, would be to miss the greatest potential impact on education: new patterns of service and learning which national service may inspire. Higher education need not see national service as competitive, but as an opportunity for creative variations in sequences and combinations of education, service, and employment.

IMPACT ON ENROLLMENT

The choices available to youth today are primarily education, employment, unemployment, homemaking, or military service. To call all of these categories "choices" is subject to question. Some are consequences of negative choices such as a decision to drop out of school or quit a job, and others are situations not of choice at all.

In 1980, approximately 16 million young people aged 18-24 were employed; 8 million were in school or college; 2 million were unemployed and seeking work; 2 million were homemakers, and 1 million were in active military service.[1] How would a national service program of 1 to 1.5 million affect these numbers? Would it reduce unemployment? Would fewer youth be employed? Would a smaller number be in school? The answer is probably "all of the above" but, without question, national service would have a particular impact on decisions by many youth to continue or not continue formal education upon graduation from high school. It would also increase "drop outs" among high school students and students who have begun higher education programs. It would tend to decrease traditional college age enrollment.

The total number of 18-24 year olds was approximately 30 million in 1980 and is expected to decline to a low of about 23 million by 1995. The number of 18-24 year olds enrolled in higher education institutions in 1980 was about 6.9 million or 23 percent of the total population of that age. If that percentage of enrollment remains constant, the number of this age group attending institutions of higher education will fall by 1.6 million students by 1995. If an additional million are taken out of this population pool by a national service program, one can speculate that those choosing national service would represent both those who would have gone to college and those who would not at the same rates. This would mean an additional loss of 230,000 students of this age group from higher education, exacerbating an already difficult admissions problem for traditional educational programs serving primarily this age group. Furthermore, any national service program is apt to be developed in conjunction with military service plans in a way which would assure the meeting of personnel goals in that area—goals that would likely be higher than present levels. With fewer youth having more options, it seems clear that the pattern of uninterrupted education through secondary school and college would be chosen by a smaller number and percentage of youth.

Net Increase Expected

Of course, at the other end of the pipe would emerge an increasing number of slightly older and more experienced young men and women seeking further education. In fact, it seems likely that the net effect of a major national service program would be to increase the percentage of youth eventually completing secondary school and enrolling in higher education, especially if the program includes educational benefits or incentives such as provided to veterans of military service. A good portion of the youth who drop out of high school or were not college bound would probably become reoriented educationally during a national service period, and those who were college bound would probably engage in higher educational programs after a period of service. Substantial possibilities would also arise for part-time or special educational arrangements during periods of national service.

The impact of national service on traditional enrollment in terms of numbers, therefore, would probably be a reduction for a few years. This would be a difficult period for colleges. But then, more importantly, an increase in enrollment would occur as the number of youth completing periods of service begins to equal those entering. The focus of educators should be on the youth in or completing service rather than on those entering. Remembering the experiences of the 1940s, it was the returning veterans who had the greatest impact on education—not the youth who entered military service a few years earlier.

More Adult Learners.   It seems obvious, then, that the longer-range impact of a major national service program for 18-24 year olds on college enrollment would be to swell the already major wave of older learners entering educational programs and institutions. The first significant step toward older learners was the influx of veterans in colleges and universities at the end of World War II. Encouraged by the GI Bill providing educational benefits, nearly 8 million veterans of World War II went to school between 1944 and 1954. Of these, 2.2 million were in college level programs. College and university enrollment in the fall of 1946 was 56 percent higher than in 1939. Half of the World War II veterans took advantage of the GI Bill's educational programs. These older entrants into the stream of higher education chose overwhelmingly to engage in "practical" courses such as engineering, business administration, and economics, with only 10 percent taking nonspecialized liberal arts courses.[2] According to a survey by Tyrus Hillway reported in the 1945 *Journal of Higher Education*, colleges responded to this new clientele by adjustments in academic load requirements, totally new programs, interdisciplinary options, refresher courses, admission requirement adjustments, greater emphasis in admissions on service performance rather than prior scholastic records, increased counseling services, changing housing offerings, and other modifications to traditional patterns.[3] Most of these changes have now become regular parts of most institutions and further changes have been instituted to respond to more recent needs of new adult and part-time learners. The delay of higher education which is likely to result from a period of national service would fit in well with this trend toward older and more experienced students who have more clearly defined educational, career, and personal goals.

What percentage of national service veterans would choose further education is unknown but would undoubtedly depend on (1) who is choosing national service in the first place, (2) what the postservice educational benefits are, (3) what programs are offered by educational institutions, and (4) the job market. It would seem likely that most of the veterans of national service would have needs, desires, and patterns more comparable to other adult learners than to the traditional age students.

More Part-Time Learners.   One pattern of adult learning that is apt to be sought by the graduates of national service, and perhaps by others during periods of national service, is part-time education. According to studies

reported in the *College Board Review*, adult and part-time learners accounted
for most of the increase in college attendance during the 1970s. Between 1972
and 1978, the proportion of students over 25 years of age increased 24.3
percent, while the proportion of students under 25 years of age decreased 9.4
percent. By 1979, more than one-third of all higher education students were
25 years and older. Two out of three of these adult learners were part time.
By comparison, only one out of ten 18–21 year olds was part time. By 1979,
more than 30 percent of undergraduate students were part time and 60
percent of graduate students were part time, approximately 10 percent of
first professional degree students were part time and 85 percent of those not
classified by degree status were part time.[4]

   In summary, the impact of national service on enrollment in higher education is projected to be a contributing factor to trends away from traditional
age, full-time enrollment in four-year uninterrupted programs and toward
older learners seeking more flexible educational patterns in terms of calendar, schedules, course offerings, crediting, and degree programs. In this
regard, national service would not offer any significantly new problems for
higher education but would offer some significant new opportunities.

Educational Responses

Educational institutions have already responded to the needs and desires of
older students in many ways that would serve younger persons completing a
term of national service. Community colleges have developed flexible programs and a wide array of offerings particularly responsive to older learners
with commitments and responsibilities beyond the educational setting. Continuing education and extension programs have moved other schools in the
same direction. Experiential learning developments, particularly with respect
to assessment and recognition of prior learning, offer additional points of
entry into higher education programs for persons approaching higher education from an experience base rather than directly from secondary education.
Some institutions have adopted, and others would adopt, these new learners
as their major focus while some institutions would remain primarily oriented
to the traditional student. The great variety of institutions and programs is
one of the strengths of higher education in this country, and not all schools
can or should attempt to serve every need or to offer the same program
responses.
   The youth in a major national service program would offer a particularly
attractive challenge for creative educational responses. These young people
would, to some extent, have a common identity much as the veterans of
military service have had an identity that allowed special responses. They
would represent a more or less common experience and have access to the

same benefits. The nature of a national service program would naturally have a major effect on the degree of this common identity and experience. The fact that a large number of youth would be collected together in common programs and locations would offer opportunities for education in both direct programming and recruitment. The completion of a period of service would be a natural break in patterns that would lend itself easily to entry or reentry into educational programs before taking on employment obligations, especially if education is reinforced by postservice educational benefits. Many institutions would find it productive to target special recruitment efforts, admission policy, and program opportunities to the national service veterans. Some institutions might find it desirable to recognize interruption of a college program for national service as an acceptable pattern, much as a junior year abroad, with provision for ease of continuation following a period of service. Others might choose to play more active roles in relating to national service programs directly. Some of these possibilities are discussed below after an exploration of learning dimensions within the national service program itself. Ideally, cooperative efforts between national service and higher education institutions would enhance both service and learning.

A LEARNING DIMENSION FOR NATIONAL SERVICE

The fascination in education with credentialing has become so great that we tend to classify as education only those experiences designed for some form of educational credit, typically classroom learning, but increasingly including internships and other such experiential designs. In planning a national service program, attention should be given to an educational dimension not exclusively concerned with credit. Due attention should be paid to deliberate, disciplined learning and assessment. Ideally, credit and credentials would follow as a result of—rather than be the purpose of—learning. The opportunities for educational advancement by youth in a service-learning mode which would open up with national service is a major challenge to program planners and educators.

Learning At All Levels

National service would attract young people with educational backgrounds ranging from high school dropouts to graduates of advanced degree programs. Education potential would be found at all levels. The education and training programs of military services have shown some of the potential for education from completion of high school by GED (graduate equivalent degree) to sophisticated graduate level training. In areas where patterns have been well established, such as GED, the educational programming would be relatively easy.

Educational System Dropouts.   At the more basic levels of education, needed by early dropouts of the educational system, some of the greatest contributions can be made. A large number of youth who did not or do not find school attendance acceptable would join a national service program. These young people would need basic learning skills if they are to develop to a fuller potential in a period of national service. The classroom mode of learning which they left might not be the educational approach best suited for their needs. A service–learning mode of education might help them make the connections between their need for skills and knowledge and their goals for living and serving. Motivation should be high in national service and the opportunity of combining disciplined learning with service assignments would be great. Many youth who have given up on education could be reoriented during national service to understand and appreciate learning, to develop basic learning skills, and to be prepared to continue education following a period of service.

Vocational and Technical Learning.   Vocational and technical training opportunities coupled with service assignments would also abound. National service would require skills and knowledge in many professional and technical areas. In at least some areas, it might be desirable to undertake intensive training. In other areas, the training might develop with the assignment. In either case, it would be important to identify discreet training areas related to assignments and to provide supporting educational materials, services, and instruments. It might be productive to seek relationships with educational institutions in developing the training dimensions of vocational and technical assignments. Military services have offered major opportunities for learning in vocational and technical areas which national service could emulate. The American Council on Education publishes a three volume *Guide to the Evaluation of Educational Experiences in the Armed Service*, which contains credit recommendations for more than 10,000 formal courses, 850 military occupations, and 105 subject standardized tests. According to information from the 1980 issue of the *Guide*, more than 80 percent of colleges and universities responding to a recent survey indicated that they award credit for military learning experiences.

Higher Education.   Higher education opportunities in national service are apt to be seen as the typical practicum or internship in which knowledge and skills learned in formal education are "applied" in a real situation. This perspective is important and many opportunities for such arrangements would be possible, but the application of knowledge and skill is only part of the picture. Learning is not as neat as this perspective implies. It is not nicely packaged in educational institutions just waiting to be applied. Learning goes on; it matures; it takes leaps; it backtracks; it is never complete; and it is in experience that it arises and develops. Institutional education is, in the final analysis, the distilled experience and insights of others; and since all experience is not yet complete and all insights have not yet been realized, learning must go on. Much is to be gained by deliberate efforts to see that learning from experience and observation continues in some disciplined fashion. Tools developed in experiential education programs could be used in national service to enhance the learning from experience and from the interpretation of experience during periods of national service. The development of portfolios, review by expert judges, and self-analysis systems could be structured into national service experiences for learning enrichment as well as for assessment related to crediting. Perhaps a new model of "interpretive" learning is needed falling somewhere between "prior" and "sponsored" learning. Developing techniques for conscious learning from service experiences designed for service rather than for learning would appear to have wide applicability. Preparing the participant to be "learning alert" and providing opportunity for and assistance in interpretation might, in the long run, be more valuable than either structuring an assignment or assessing it after the fact. The use of educational debriefing also would seem to have wide applicability in learning dimensions of national service.

In sum, it would seem important to deliberately foster learning dimensions of service experiences at all levels. Learning goals as well as service goals could be established for each participant, regardless of past educational achievement or lack of achievement. In doing this, patterns of life-long learning could be established that would serve both the participant and society well. Both service and learning would take on new excitement and meaning when productively linked together.

Organizing for Service-Learning

To accomplish these goals a national service program would need to emphasize learning as well as service and put adequate resources into the learning dimension. This emphasis should start with the basic legislation, which should be worded to avoid barriers to learning and to provide authority and policy direction for pursuing service-learning as one of the major purposes of national service. If "education" or "service-learning" or other such words or phrases are not included in the legislation on national service, it would be much more difficult to develop the learning dimensions. For example, the casting of the College Work Study program as financial aid has determined the direction of that program, but the inclusion of educational and experiential goals has made possible the use of this program in internships, cooperative education, Urban Corps, and other experiential education.

Educational Support.   A national service program should include educational leadership on its staff. It should provide for instructional programs directly operated or contracted, access to library and other educational resources, educational counseling and guidance, and other education-related services. National service personnel should be recruited and trained to meet educational goals as well as service goals. Supervisors in particular should be given training and recognition for their roles as educators along with their roles in effective supervision. Instruments to assist educational development and to evaluate its progress would be needed, calling for professional staff to develop and assist in this area. Provision for contracts, cooperative agreements, and other arrangements with educational institutions would be necessary.

National Service "Graduation."   Ideally, completion of a period of national service should also be graduation from an educational program with awareness and documentation that new levels of learning have been reached. At graduation, educational goals, needs, and desires should be articulated in a way which would make choices for continued education easy. Postservice educational benefits could play an important role in encouraging continuing education but would not be fully utilized unless some preparation had gone into post-"graduation" plans. Various forms of credentials and recognition would also be important both symbolically and in the arrangement of educational crediting by other institutions.

ROLES FOR EDUCATIONAL INSTITUTIONS

Educational institutions could play a great variety of roles in relation to national service. As suggested earlier, they would at least need to make adjustments to accommodate the graduates of national service who want to continue education in a school or college. They might also make calendar and curricular progress modifications to allow an "interruption" of education for a period of national service. Hopefully, many institutions would play more direct roles in national service.

Sponsors of National Service Programs

The most direct role would be to sponsor a national service project. If the national service program is decentralized, colleges, universities, and other schools, singly or in combination, might very well develop and direct national service projects. Most colleges and universities express their purposes in three dimensions: teaching, research, and service. National service projects could be operated as a service of the institution but could also become part of the educational program involving students in service-learning directly. The University Year for ACTION (UYA), initiated by the federal ACTION agency in 1971 to demonstrate the value of linking full-time community service with formal higher education, is an example of a productive linking of service and educational goals. A number of colleges who have operated UYA projects have institutionalized them beyond the limits of federal funding. One question for national service planning is whether or not existing programs such as UYA will be incorporated into a national service program. If colleges and schools are permitted to sponsor and operate national service projects, it is desirable that legislation and rules be broad and flexible enough to allow for creative variety among a whole range of institutions.

Contracts and Cooperation

Another form of participation by educational institutions would be by contractual or cooperative arrangements with national service agencies providing for direct roles in educational and training dimensions. Participation could be very limited, such as providing supporting instruction in basic skills or technical areas; or participation could be as broad as helping design and operate the whole learning component of a service–learning program. Educational institutions are strategically located throughout the country, and it is hard to imagine a geographic area where they could not provide educational resources to national service projects.

Off-Campus Service-Learning Periods

A third method of participation would be to build a period of national service into the college program much as cooperative education programs have built-in periods of practical employment, or junior-year-abroad programs have structured intercultural experiences into curricular patterns, or internships have provided for periods of practical experience. Such arrangements might include periods of preparation and educational responsibilities such as journals, reports, readings, and evaluation. The variety of potential assignments would make such arrangements possible in most areas of a college curriculum or a vocational school program. A number of these patterns are well established in many institutions and could be transferred to national service projects with little difficulty. While national service is in the developmental stage, colleges or other schools that wish to establish arrangements for their students to participate in national service would have a chance to influence the conditions and substance of assignments. This opportunity usually is not available for off-campus learning arrangements. One question, for example, would be whether or not parallel work and study arrangements which combined national service and college education would be possible. Another variation would be the development of service-learning teams involving a group of students (and perhaps faculty) in carrying out a service project with a built-in educational program.

Comprehensive Programs

An even closer tie between national service and higher education might be possible by integrating national service and college education. It is possible that a comprehensive education/national service package could be offered in which periods of national service and college attendance are sequenced, combined, and overlapped to provide for completion of two years of national service and four years of college in a total of four or five years. A student might enroll in national service and a college at the same time under a cooperative agreement. After a summer period of service, the student might complete a freshman year of college, followed by a second summer of service. A second year of college with a program related to service choices might be followed by a full year of service with educational relationships, reports, and other learning requirements. A fourth year might be spent back at the institution in rounding out courses for a major degree, followed by a half-year national service assignment at a senior level, and then completed by a final college semester pulling the program together and completing work for the degree. One can imagine that both service and learning might be enhanced by such an extended combination of action and reflection.

Education for National Service Leadership and Research

Another opportunity for educational institutions would be the development of curricula, including national service internships, which would prepare professionals for leadership in national service. This would be possible at undergraduate and graduate levels but would most likely fit into patterns for masters degree programs such as are found for business administration, public administration, social work, and other professions. Also, opportunities for research would present themselves and make possible faculty research and dissertation material for degree candidates. Some of this would happen with no prior planning or structure, but it could be expedited and enhanced by conscious attention. The devices used after World War II to encourage interaction between educational institutions and the newly developed atomic energy program would lend themselves to this purpose. Research participation periods for faculty, graduate fellowships, special seminars, conferences, and cooperative research are some of the possibilities.

SERVICE AND EDUCATION

In all of these possible relationships between educational institutions and national service, a great deal more value can be realized if special attention is given to the concept of service. If the proponents of national service are correct in their assumptions and successful in expressing them in programs, the effect of national service on the release of creative energy of youth would be tremendous. The idea of service is more than one more option, something to do, or a way to get ahead. It implies value in the participant and a need for his or her contribution. Service emphasizes that the young person is living, not just preparing for life. It suggests a commitment to one's society and fellow human beings. Service asks something of youth while affirming youth as important. Education in this context should be exciting. Service can give meaning to learning. Institutions which recognize the possibilities and find ways to take advantage of them would find increased vitality. National service leadership could do a great deal to encourage and guide the development of a service-learning ethic that would probably spread well beyond the confines of a national service program and influence the whole society.

Service-Learning Patterns

From an educational perspective, national service could enhance educational patterns for youth. A growing concern has been expressed over the past decade regarding the educational insulation of youth from active participation in the world of work or service. This concern has been summarized in a Carnegie Council report: "Young people received too heavy a dose of schooling for too long a period, unmixed with knowledge of the world of work or experience in work or community service. Work that takes the form of community service is particularly desirable, giving young people a feeling of involvement in community problems and of contributing to their solution."[5] Education is much more stimulating, meaningful, and eagerly sought when an experiential base provides perspective on the need for learning. Education contributes not only to the quality of work or services being performed, but to the quality of life itself. Willard Wirtz, former Secretary of Labor, has suggested in *The Boundless Resource* that "a considered break of one or two years in the formal educational sequence—taken between ages sixteen and twenty—be recognized and established as a standard optional phase of youth experience, and that a comprehensive program of Community Internships and Work Apprenticeships be instituted at the local level."[6] Another spokesman for higher education, Reverend Theodore Hesburgh, has suggested that the experience of service to others should be accepted as part of our whole educational system: "Service provides a dimension that cannot be had in a classroom."[7] National service can be seen as an opportunity for improvements in education and not simply as a means of providing needed services or solving social problems of youth.

Service-Learning and Liberal Education

These voices from higher education are not talking about increased apprenticeships or other means of better "tooling" of youth for the economic system. Experience, particularly that which is considered service, has much more profound value than job preparedness, important as that may be. Liberal education and work or service experience should not be strangers. Arthur W. Chickering has compared objectives of liberal education with competences and characteristics needed for effective performance in the world of work and has found "striking agreement." He concludes ". . . that the separation of liberal education and preparation for work is indeed unwise, if not impossible. The basic point is that when we talk about achieving the ends of liberal education and about effective preparation for work, we are tackling the bedrock task of human development."[8] The possible educational impacts of national service raise visions of unlocking the "boundless resource" of human potential.

FINANCIAL CONSIDERATIONS

The costs of a national service program would be substantial and a variety of projections have been made. A Congressional Budget Office (CBO) study published on December 31, 1980, based on the National Service Bill (HR 2206) introduced by Rep. Paul N. McCloskey on February 15, 1979, estimated the net cost per national service participant at $4,367 per year, a figure which includes savings from lower military pay. If these savings are not included, the CBO estimate is $6,660 per person per year. Without challenging or analyzing the CBO figure, this estimate is compared to sample costs and rough estimates of other "options" for youth. College education, military service, employment, Job Corps, and incarceration all have their costs and to varying degrees are publicly supported. In a list of rough cost estimates of various alternatives, national service falls at the bottom (see table 10.1).

Obviously, some of the options presented in table 10.1 are net costs to society, and other options involve services in return or preparation for future returns to society. National service appears to be a "best buy," especially because it combines immediate service with learning which would find expression in future service and value to society. The Carnegie Council report makes estimates of the financial benefits of reducing costs of crime, welfare, unwanted youth pregnancy, and other social ills which might be realized

Table 10.1.   Annual Cost Estimates of Some Youth Alternatives

Youth Situation	Estimated Annual Cost Per Person
Military Service	$21,000[a]
Juvenile Incarceration	$18,000[b]
Job Corps	$13,558[c]
College Education	$ 8,900[d]
Minimum Wage Employment	$ 6,968[e]
National Service	$ 6,660[f]

[a] Michael Hicks, Planning and Analysis Division, Manpower Reserve Affairs and Logistics, Department of Defense, telephone conversation with Donald Eberly, May 29, 1981.
[b] Carnegie Council on Policy Studies in Higher Education, *Giving Youth a Better Chance* (San Francisco: Jossey-Bass, 1979), p. 294.
[c] *Employment and Training Report of the President, 1980* (Washington: U.S. Government Printing Office, 1980), p. 38. This figure is the Job Corps service–year cost for fiscal year 1979.
[d] This figure represents average current fund expenditures at private undergraduate institutions. The data are from a survey conducted by Berea College for the year 1979-1980.
[e] Full-time employment at $3.35/hour.
[f] Congressional Budget Office, *Costs of the National Service Act (H.R. 2206): A Technical Analysis* (Washington: U.S. Government Printing Office, 1980).

through increasing options for youth including national service. The Carnegie Council report estimates that economic return to society would exceed program costs. More important than economic benefits, the social benefits would be beyond measure. To realize these benefits more fully in national service, the educational component would need to deal with values, knowledge, and development beyond just vocational skills and technical information. Liberal education should be part of the planning of educational programs of national service.

Educational Benefits

Educational benefits during national service and postservice benefits would also have their costs. Benefits such as time for educational pursuits, direct instruction, attendance at educational institutions, counseling, and other educational services should be built into the program budget. These ideally would not be wholly separate activities, but integrated with and of value to service assignments as well as to educational advancement. Postservice benefits might include monthly stipends based on years of service; allowance for tuition, fees, and books; and provision for dependents. An opportunity for accumulation of savings through personal investment would also be desirable whether for education or other postservice choices. A matching program of benefits may be useful in encouraging planning and saving for educational purposes.

Relation to Federal Financial Aid

A number of questions relating to educational benefits and present federal financial aid programs would need to be addressed. Could College Work Study funds be used for short periods of national service related to an educational institution's programs? Would a period of national service place young people in "independent" status in regard to Pell Grants and other federal aid programs? How would national service benefits and educational savings be treated in financial analysis formulas for federal aid?

Self-Help

The opportunity to emphasize self-help through national service in relation to federal financial aid should not pass unnoticed. It would be much healthier for society and more in keeping with the spirit of national service if aid were related to service. The "entitlement" to education implied by public aid should be coupled with opportunity and responsibility to contribute to society. At the extreme, eligibility for all federal grants might be tied to national service. This would be no different than present programs which tie service obligations to educational support, for example, the National Health Service Corps. Those who need financial aid to go to college but are not interested in service would have to rely on loans (which are deferred work) or private grants. Such a public policy coupling aid to service would be a major redirection of emphasis and would be strong incentive for national service choices. Other less extreme options are, of course, available. In any event, it would seem prudent to coordinate national service educational benefits to financial aid programs. The most beneficial use of financial resources would be when educational programs and national service programs are closely integrated.

SUMMARY OF RECOMMENDATIONS

A major national service program could have positive consequences for society and particularly for education. New patterns of service and learning could change attitudes of and about youth, could bring renewed excitement to citizenship, and could add vitality to education. In order to realize the fullest potential of educational possibilities related to national service, it is important to adopt a cooperative rather than a competitive posture. The focus should be on new program possibilities and new patterns for youth service and education. To encourage positive development of education within a national service program, several recommendations are suggested:

- Legislation should be flexible enough to allow different levels, styles, structures, and emphases for learning components.
- A decentralized national service with a variety of programs at local, state, regional, and national levels is preferable to one large bureaucratic program.
- Provision should be made for cooperative arrangements or direct operation of programs by educational institutions, consortia, or associations.
- Inclusion of existing programs should be considered.
- Educational goals and programs should allow for both career development and liberal education choices rather than being limited to or strongly biased in favor of one or the other.
- Provision is needed for staff and funds to promote and maintain positive interaction between national service and educational institutions.

In sum, national service programs can provide the stimulus and opportunity for a recognition of service as part of education and a rediscovery of education as a part of life.

NOTES

1. Carnegie Council on Policy Studies in Higher Education, *Giving Youth a Better Chance: Options for Education, Work, and Service* (San Francisco: Jossey-Bass, 1979), p. 7.

2. "The G.I. Bill: In 10 Years 8 Million," *Newsweek* 44 (October 4, 1954): 88.

3. Tyrus Hillway, "G.I. Joe and The College," *Journal of Higher Education* 16 (June 1945): 290-98.

4. Ronald H. Miller, "A Decade of Data on Adult Learners," *College Board Review* 114 (Winter 1979-80): 6-17.

5. Carnegie Council, *Giving Youth a Better Chance*, pp. 94-95.

6. Willard Wirtz and the National Manpower Institute, *The Boundless Resource: A Prospectus for an Education/Work Policy* (Washington: New Republic, 1975), p. 174.

7. Committee for the Study of National Service, *Youth and the Needs of the Nation* (Washington: Potomac Institute, 1979).

8. Arthur W. Chickering, "Integrating Liberal Education, Work and Human Development," *American Association of Higher Education Bulletin* 33, no. 7 (March 1981).

Chapter 11

National Service and the All-Volunteer Force*

Charles C. Moskos

By the early 1980s, there was a growing realization that the problems of the All–Volunteer Force (AVF) would not be resolved by incremental changes in current manpower policies. This gave new impetus to those who saw little prospect of a viable defense force short of returning to a form of compulsory military service. The problems of the AVF, however, also present us with an opportunity to place military service within the framework of voluntary national service for youth. The presentation of such a national service program and its impact on the AVF is the purpose of this chapter. To bring the concept of national service into the forefront of the military manpower debate is also to depart from the prevailing econometric paradigm of the architects of the present AVF.

Let us first turn briefly to the facts of the AVF experience. All four services have been hard pressed to meet recruitment goals since the end of the draft in 1973. Indeed, the most important effect of the shift to the AVF has been the sharp decline in active–duty force levels, from over 2.6 million in the peacetime years before the war in Vietnam to slightly over 2 million in 1981. To maintain an active–duty force even at this reduced level, the military must recruit between 350,000 and 400,000 annually. In 1980, approximately 310,000 males entered the military as new recruits as did about 50,000 females; around 30,000 of these had prior military service backgrounds.

During the 1980s, the number of males turning 18 each year will decline from about 2.2 million to about 1.8 million (as will, of course, a similar number of females). Of these, an estimated two-thirds will meet the physical and mental requirements for military service. Or, in other words, about one in four eligible males must join the services to maintain an active-duty force at present levels (and—at current female entrance rates—about one in 25 eligible women). As severe as recruitment problems are for the active force, there is also a need for large numbers of entrants into reserve components.

---

* A version of this chapter is published in *Foreign Affairs*, 1981, and in *Military Service in the United States* edited by Brent Scowcroft, Prentice Hall, 1982.

Army Reserve and National Guard units in the early 1980s were some 125,000 members short of the goals set by Congress. The Individual Ready Reserve—soldiers with prior military training who are to be available in the event of mobilization—was more than 300,000 below stated requirements.

Predictions that an all-volunteer military would have less personnel turnover than one based on draftees and draft-motivated volunteers have not come to pass. Despite the fact that AVF recruits are signing on for longer enlistments than was the case in the early 1960s, personnel turnover is greater now than in the peacetime-draft era. One in three entering service members do not complete their initial enlistments for reasons of job inaptitude, indiscipline, personality disorders, and the like. In the combat arms attrition is over 40 percent. On top of this attrition, desertion rates are double those of pre–Vietnam levels. The evidence is quite clear, moreover, that in the aggregate, high school graduates significantly out-perform high school dropouts, whether looking at combat performance, work productivity, disciplinary actions, or desertion rates. One of the most striking findings during the all-volunteer era is that high school graduates are twice as likely than high school dropouts to complete their enlistments.

The drop in educational levels of recruits since the advent of the AVF is thus disturbing for mission effectiveness as well as representational concerns. This is most evident in the Army, the largest of the services and the one that most directly relied on the draft. As given in table 11.1, an average of over 40 percent of male recruits have not had a high school diploma. This contrasts with 20 percent nongraduates among 19-20 year-old males in the general

Table 11.1. Educational Levels of Army Male Entrants (non-prior-service) and Overall Male Population

	Percent Non-High School Graduates	Percent High School Graduates	Percent Some College	Total Percent	Total Number
1964 Draftees	28.7	54.1	17.2	100.0	151,194
1964 Enlistees	39.9	46.2	13.9	100.0	108,303
1975	45.7	48.6	5.7	100.0	165,610
1976	44.4	51.5	4.1	100.0	164,291
1977	43.8	51.1	5.1	100.0	153,434
1978	30.0	65.5	4.5	100.0	106,512
1979	41.4	55.5	3.1	100.0	112,008
1980	51.1	45.5	3.4	100.0	135,964
19-20-year-old U.S. males, 1978	20.0	39.9	40.1	100.0	

Source: Accession data from Department of Army Statistics. Civilian data from U.S. Census Bureau, *Current Population Reports*, P-20, no. 335.

population, and 28.7 percent of draftees and 39.9 percent of volunteers in 1964, the last peacetime year before the war in Vietnam. The contrast between the educational levels of the all-volunteer Army and the peacetime-draft Army is even greater when considered in light of the proportional increase in male high school graduates from 66 percent of males aged 18 to 24 years in 1965 to 79 percent in 1979. The data in table 11.1 also reveal an even sharper decline in the proportion of Army entrants with some college from the pre– to the post-Vietnam periods.

It must be stressed, however, that the increasing minority participation in the AVF—blacks comprised about 30 percent of the Army's enlisted ranks in 1980—is *not* correlated with the declining educational levels of recruits. Since the end of the draft, the proportion of high school graduates among entering blacks has been 65 percent compared with 51 percent for whites.[1]

When all is said and done, the inescapable conclusion is that the middle class is virtually absent from the ranks of the all-volunteer Army. This is the reality that underlies the quantitative and qualitative problems of AVF recruitment. It is a social fact that the armed forces, and the combat arms especially, will never draw proportionately from middle and upper-middle class youth. But to foster and rationalize policies that accentuate the tracking of lower-class youth into the enlisted ranks is perverse. This is not to argue that the makeup of the enlisted ranks be perfectly calibrated to the social composition of the larger society, but it is to ask what kind of society excuses its privileged from serving in its military.

There can be no question, despite official reports to the contrary, that the AVF is much less representative of America's male youth than was the military of the draft era. There can also be no question that monetary inducements, notably high recruit pay and combat arms enlistment bonuses, have failed to attract a cross section of youth to serve in the AVF. The real question is whether a voluntary national service program can accomplish what marketplace mechanisms have not.

A NATIONAL SERVICE APPROACH TO THE AVF

The national service concept has its roots in "the interdependence and hence reciprocal responsibilities of a society and the individuals who comprise it."[2] Because our nation's philosophy stresses liberty of the individual, the most desirable national service program, excepting war time conscription, is one designed to permit and encourage voluntary service. Various ideas of national service have been proposed over the years, some of which have dealt directly with implications for military service.[3] The plan advanced herein is one that will foster youth service in a broad array of activities; but will, at the same time, best serve the goals of the AVF.

I take as a given that any voluntary national service program that rewards equally civilian and military pursuits undermines military manpower requirements. The onerousness and ultimate liabilities of military service require that it be put in a more privileged category than nonmilitary service. The best available survey data show that, among youth who display an interest in voluntary national service, twice as many would choose a nonmilitary option over military service.[4] Among youth who come from families in the top half of the income distribution, a staggering ten to one would select the nonmilitary option, other things being equal.

Whatever the degree of voluntarism among American youth and whatever the relative appeals of military versus nonmilitary service, two developments over the recent past have undermined the concept of national service in general, and the national service features of the military in particular. One has been the redefinition of military service in terms of the economic marketplace, a redefining process given powerful expression by the 1970 President's Commission ("Gates Commission") on an All-Volunteer Force.[5] Rather than the standard that military service ought to be a widely shared citizen experience, the AVF has operated on the principle of recruiting at the margin through the cashwork nexus. The other development has been the tremendous expansion of federal aid to college students without requiring any national service obligation on the part of the youths who benefit. The growth of federal grants and loans to college students occurred along with the elimination of the GI Bill in 1976. We have created a system of educational benefits which offers more to those who do not serve their country than to those who do.

The central issue remains: Is there a national service way to meet military manpower needs without direct compulsion or excessive reliance on cash inducements for recruits? I believe there is. First, link federal aid for higher education to a program of voluntary national service. Second, introduce a GI Bill for the AVF. Third, construct a two-track personnel and compensation system which differentiates between a short-term volunteer and one who makes a long-term commitment to the military. The interactive effects of these proposals will be to replace the present marketplace premise of the AVF with a national service ethic. These proposals will also have positive effects on the "three R's" of military manpower: recruitment, retention, and the reserves.

Educational Benefits in Conflict with the AVF

Under the Veterans Educational Assistance Program (VEAP), which replaced the GI Bill, the government matches, within prescribed limits, voluntary contributions made by service members. It is estimated that governmental expenditures for VEAP will be under $90 million annually. But, for 1980 alone, federal aid to college students in the form of grants and loan subsidies exceeded $5.2 billion. Legislation passed in 1978 removed or loosened need requirements for the bulk of federal aid to college students. Even if budget cuts to reduce student aid are implemented, we will still confront an immense sum in competition with the educational benefits offered to military members. In effect, we have created a GI Bill without the GI.

It is surprising that no public figure thought to tie such student aid to any service obligation. A program of voluntary national service should be introduced in which participation becomes a prerequisite for federal post secondary school assistance. Indeed, the educational establishment should take the lead in proposing such a linkage in order to legitimize current student aid programs.

The preferred conditions of such national service should be broad but light, rather than narrow but heavy. The aim is for inclusiveness in youth participation, but with maximum decentralization and minimum costs. The following is set forth as one way to meet these standards.

To be eligible for federal post secondary educational aid, and perhaps even job–training aid, a youth would be required to serve a short period—say, three to six months—in an unpaid capacity. Most likely, recruitment would be handled by voluntary associations, welfare agencies, nonprofit institutions, schools, recreational facilities, and the like. The range of such tasks could include grooming care for the aged in nursing homes, escort services for the aged, serving as teachers' aides, monitoring on public transit systems, and even museum cataloguing. National service could also entail self-selected tasks, for example, driving the aged to medical or shopping facilities. Military reservists would be preeminent examples of those meeting the national service requirement for federal student aid. Much attention must be given not to displace the gainfully employed. Tasks should be in pursuits for which there is a demonstrable need, but otherwise are not being performed.

Decisions as to whether or not a specific task would meet service criteria would be the responsibility of local national service boards, whose members themselves are volunteers (albeit not youth). Evaluations could also be done in conjunction with the voluntary associations and nonprofit organizations in which the youth are serving. Salaries would be received only by clerical help at regional board levels and staffers at a headquarters office. The decentralized system of the old selective service boards is the obvious parallel. On the basis of cost estimates of revamped selective service boards, total outlays for national service boards would probably be under $70 million a year. If selective service boards were transformed into more inclusive national service boards, costs would be much less, of course, than for an independent system of national service boards.

From the viewpoint of the national server, the educational benefits would be substantial. Let us assume an annual outlay of $5 billion (approximately the 1980 federal expenditures for student aid) and 1 million national servers (a figure most likely way too high). This would mean $5,000 in potential educational benefits to each recipient. (In 1980, some 2.2 million college students received federal aid for an average of about $2,500 each.)

To go a step further, one can envision a state of affairs whereby national service, an earned attribute, would replace ascribed characteristics, such as race or sex, as the basis for affirmative action. At the very least, persons who complete national service ought to have priority in public employment. In time, national service ought to become a prerequisite of federal employment. It may be that we can come to a realization that many of the things we need as a nation we can never afford to buy. If we are to have them, we must give them to ourselves.

Provisions of a GI Bill for the AVF

Along with linking federal educational assistance beyond high school to voluntary national service, we should introduce postservice educational benefits for members of the AVF along the lines of the GI Bill following World War II. A person who enlists in the armed forces and completes his or her two-year obligatory period of active duty would be entitled to educational assistance as follows: (1) the costs of tuition up to $3,000 per academic year up to a maximum of three years, (2) a monthly stipend of $300 up to a maximum of 27 months, (3) eligibility to be limited to those who receive honorable discharges or separations, and (4) such entitlement being dependent upon an appropriate reserve obligation. In this way, maximum federal educational benefits would be allotted to those who serve in the active-duty military.

The maximum direct costs of such an AVF GI Bill would probably be under $1.25 billion a year.[6] There would be, however, substantial countervailing reductions in net costs. Estimated countervailing reductions in the annual costs of an AVF GI Bill total $900 million, as shown in table 11.2.

Cutting the attrition rate in half would result in manpower savings in excess of $600 million annually. Substantial savings would occur in lowering the recruitment outlays required to enlist high school graduates. Cost reductions would also result from less lost time for unauthorized absences and desertions, the elimination of combat arms enlistment bonuses, the end of present postservice educational benefits (VEAP) and, most likely, fewer lower-ranking service members with families. With these savings, the net costs of a GI Bill would probably be well under $400 million annually—a sum much smaller than proposed increases in recruit pay and enlistment bonuses.

Moreover, because members would not be eligible for GI Bill benefits until completion of at least two years of active duty, there would be no

Table 11.2.   Estimated Countervailing Reductions in the Annual Costs
of an All-Volunteer Force GI Bill

Attrition Savings:	$600 million
(50,000 fewer attritees at savings of $12,000 each)	
Recruitment Savings:	$100 million
(50,000 category IIIA, HSG enlistees at savings of $2,000 each)	
Termination of VEAP and Enlistment Bonuses	$150 million
Other Savings:	$ 50 million
(lower reserve recruitment outlays, less lost time for AWOL and deser-	
tions, fewer soldiers with dependents)	
Total Estimated Cost Reductions	$900 million

outlays in the first phase of an AVF GI Bill. In point of fact, the initial two
years of a GI Bill program would result in considerable savings in the national defense budget.

Citizen Soldier and Career Soldier: Complementary Roles

The definition of military service in the all-volunteer context needs overhaul-
ing as much as does the machinery of military recruitment. The armed
services can set up a two-tier personnel and compensation system recognizing a distinction between a "career soldier" and a "citizen soldier."[7] (Soldier
as used here refers, of course, also to sailors, airmen, and marines).

The career soldier would initially enlist for a minimum of four years. He
or she would receive entitlements and compensation in the manner of the
prevailing system, but there would be significant pay increases at the time of
the first reenlistment and throughout the senior NCO grades. Many career
persons would be trained in technical skills, though others would make up
the future cadre in a variety of military specialties. Along with improvements
in the quality of service life, steps such as these would go a long way toward
retaining the experienced personnel needed for a complex and technical
military force.

The citizen soldier would enlist for two years of active duty (the term of
the old draftee) and be assigned to the combat arms, low-skill shipboard
duty, aircraft security guards, routine maintenance, low-level clerical work,
and other labor-intensive positions. Because there would be no presumption
of acquiring civilian skills in the military, the terms of such service would be
honest and unambiguous. Active-duty pay for the citizen soldier would be
lower—say, by one-third—than that received by the career soldier of the
same rank. Other than a generous GI Bill, the citizen soldier would receive
no entitlements such as off-base housing or food allowances. A college or
graduate education, or vocational training, in exchange for two years of

active duty would be the means to attract highly qualified soldiers who can learn quickly, serve effectively for a full tour, and then be replaced by similarly qualified recruits.

The central point is that the citizen soldier concept would reintroduce the national service ethic into the format of military manpower.

IMPACT OF NATIONAL SERVICE ON THE AVF

The crux of the issue is what will be the effects of the voluntary national service program outlined above on the AVF. Assessing the impact of any proposed program is risky, especially so when we consider how wide of the mark previous military manpower projections have been. Nevertheless, reasonably likely effects on the AVF can be anticipated on the basis of a grounded and holistic understanding of the military manpower system. It is to be underscored that the voluntary national service program advanced here was constructed to enhance the viability of the AVF.

Recruitment

The basic recruitment difficulty in the all-volunteer era has been the failure to attract anything approaching a cross section of youth into the enlisted ranks of the military, especially in the Army. Large raises in recruit pay and enlistment bonuses have proven not to be an attraction for upwardly-mobile or middle-class youth. It is important to note, moreover, that surveys of high school youth and college undergraduates consistently show that GI Bill-type incentives hold greater appeal than do straight monetary incentives for those youth presently not inclined to join the service. Table 11.3 provides some data on the relative attractiveness of various incentive alternatives. The table

Table 11.3. Propensity to Enlist by Various Incentives and by Quality Index of High School Students

	Quality Index of High School Student*		
The higher the score, the greater the indicated propensity to enlist.			
Incentive Alternatives	High	Medium	Low
Current Pay	1.25	1.49	1.56
$200 Monthly Pay Raise	1.64	2.11	2.01
$5,000 Enlistment Bonus	2.05	2.15	2.12
Current VEAP	1.80	1.97	1.91
Noncontributory VEAP	1.94	2.03	1.96
One Year Tuition for One Year Service**	2.09	2.21	2.09

* Based on composite index of high school grades and math/science courses taken.
** Survey conducted Fall 1978; this question item was not included in Spring 1980 survey.
Source: Adapted from *Youth Attitude Tracking Study, Spring 1980* (Washington: Market Facts, 1980). The table is based on a survey sample of 5,217 16 to 21 year old males.

shows that in a survey of high school students, one year college tuition for one year of service is a strong enlistment incentive, ranking as high as a $5,000 enlistment bonus; and this high rating occurs across "quality" of potential enlistees (as defined by grades and math/science courses taken).

Surveys of undergraduates at Northwestern University (private and predominantly white) and Morgan State University (public and predominantly black) in 1980 found that a four-year GI Bill in exchange for two years of military service had greater enlistment appeal than $2,500 monthly recruit pay. The relative value of postservice educational benefits and high recruit pay is also discussed by Jerald G. Bachman, John D. Blair, and David R. Segal in *The All-Volunteer Force*.[8]

The citizen soldier concept is to create the analogue, both sociologically and philosophically, of the peacetime draftee in the all-volunteer context. The biggest recruitment barrier for middle-class youth who might join the AVF is that none of their peers are doing so. Common sense as well as experience during the peacetime draft era leads us to expect that a national service approach would produce a positive recruitment synergy. As more middle-class youth choose a short term in the military for a GI Bill, still more can be expected to do likewise.

To have a genuinely attractive GI Bill in the AVF-era, however, means present federal college aid programs would have to be drastically cut back or linked to a national service obligation. The latter is to be preferred for the national good as well as the students involved. Linking national service to college student aid would also serve to place military service back into a broader national service framework, thereby reversing the present trend to define the armed forces as simply another segment of the labor market.

In terms of numbers, the armed services must recruit some 50,000 high quality recruits that they are presently not attracting to resolve the recruitment problems of the AVF. Recruiting such a number seems feasible with the implementation of a GI Bill for the AVF and a light national service obligation on the part of college students who receive federal educational assistance.

Attrition

The severest problem among first-term enlistees in the AVF is the high attrition rate and its deleterious consequences on unit cohesion. The clearcut evidence that higher educated soldiers are the most likely to complete their enlistments has already been mentioned. Any recruitment policy that attracts more high school graduates or those seeking a break in the college routine cannot but help markedly reduce the attrition rate. Limiting GI Bill eligibility to service members who successfully complete their enlistments would be another factor in the lowering of attrition.

There is one source of enlisted discontent in the AVF that had no real counterpart in the peacetime-draft era. This is postentry disillusionment resulting from unrealistic expectations as to what the military would offer. In all-volunteer recruitment, a consistent theme has been what the service can do for the recruit in the way of training in skills transferable to civilian employment. The irreconcilable dilemma is that many assignments—by no means exclusively in the combat arms—do not have transferability to civilian jobs. These are the kinds of military tasks that fit most closely into the national service framework. The two-year citizen soldier option would draw from those who, like the draftee of old, would expect no advanced training. These are the kind of service members who would be assigned to those military specialties—mainly manual and labor intensive—where recruitment shortfalls, attrition, and desertion are currently most likely to occur.

Reserves

The blunt fact is that the major impetus for reserve recruitment in the draft-era military was to avoid active-duty service. With an AVF, this motivation no longer operates. Special inducements are needed to maintain an adequate reserve force. Linkage of educational benefits with national service is one such inducement. Reserve duty clearly meets the national service standard for college aid eligibility. A "little GI Bill" for reserve duty might also be considered.

Requiring a reserve obligation following two years of active duty—as in the citizen soldier track—ought to be a condition for maximum benefits under an AVF GI Bill. For without much greater reliance on prior-service personnel, there seems no way to salvage Army reserve components in an all-volunteer context.

Retention

A major outcome of the AVF has been a dramatic compression of pay scales within the enlisted force. Raises in military pay have been concentrated at entry levels in order to aid AVF recruitment. In the 1960s, the basic pay of a sergeant major with 26 years of service was better than seven times that of an entering recruit. Since the end of the draft, that same sergeant major makes only three and one half times the pay of the recruit. The paradox is that this "front-loading" of compensation toward the junior ranks cannot be appreciated by those newly entering the service. Instead, junior enlisted members see little monetary or status improvement over the course of a military career, thereby reducing the likelihood of their choosing to remain in the service.

Over the past fifteen years, the career retention rate—usually measured after eight years of service—has declined from about 90 to 70 percent. Retention problems are especially severe in the technical specialties. Once upon a time, sergeants measured their incomes and prerequisites against those of the soldiers they led, and felt rewarded; now they see a relative decline of status within the service and compare their earnings against civilians, and feel deprived.

A national service approach to the AVF might have conflicting effects on military retention. A GI Bill could cause members, who otherwise would have stayed in, to leave the service to take advantage of postservice educational benefits. Yet, it must be noted that retention losses in technical specialties have become more pronounced since the end of the Vietnam-era GI Bill in 1976. Retention would be helped by a personnel system in which members entering a career track would receive greater compensation from the start. Without question, future pay raises should be aimed at the NCO grades rather than applied across the board.

There is historical evidence that some number of those who would not otherwise join the service except for a GI Bill will find themselves eventually entering the career force. A GI Bill could also create an entirely new source of prior-service entrants at the NCO or officer levels, individuals choosing to return to active duty after college or technical training. One might also expect, as the lower enlisted force again comes to reflect more of a cross section of youth, that military life itself would become intrinsically more attractive to career NCOs.

On balance, a national service approach would probably have many more positive than negative consequences on military retention. It may help clarify matters to think of an AVF GI Bill as the functional equivalent of conscription. For, even with a draft, retention problems would persist and have to be dealt with on their own terms; namely, by well constructed career compensation and entitlement packages along with a public recognition of the service ethic in the armed forces.

THE MILITARY IN SOCIETY

The military has always recruited large numbers of youth who had no real alternative job prospects. It will always continue to do so. But present trends toward labeling the AVF as a recourse for America's underclasses are self-defeating for the youth involved, precisely because they directly counter the premise that military participation ought to be one of broadly based national service. Whatever successes the military had as a remedial organization for deprived youth were largely due to the armed forces being legitimated on other than overt welfare grounds, such as national defense, citizenship obligation, patriotism, even manly honor. In other words, those very conditions peculiar to the armed forces which serve to resocialize poverty youth away from dead-end existences depend directly upon the military not being defined as a welfare agency or an employer of last resort. It will be increasingly difficult for the AVF to avoid such characterization, even if unfair, unless enlisted membership reflects more of a cross section of American youth. To avoid such an undesirable outcome, the choice comes down to a return to the draft or a comprehensive program of voluntary national service.

The national service framework advanced here departs from the prevailing systems analysis and econometric approaches to the AVF. The starting point is not how are empty spaces to be filled but, rather, how can a substantial number and cross section of American youth serve their country. To stretch a little and to borrow from the fashionable economic terms of the day, I am suggesting a supply-side rather than a demand-side model of military manpower. Or, to put it yet another way, how can we introduce a large dose of genuine volunteerism into the all-volunteer military. The AVF, if it is to survive, must attract those middle-class and upwardly-mobile American youth who would find a temporary diversion from the world of school or work tolerable, and perhaps even welcome.

We do not want to be so bedeviled with rival sets of numbers, so overwhelmed with data, that the key policy choices are hardly understood, much less addressed. It appears that as the technical competence of the Defense Department to deal with personnel data expands, its actual ability to deal with manpower issues declines. The grand design is to make governmental subsidies of higher education consistent, not contradictory as presently, with the ideal that citizen obligation should become part of growing up in America. Such a realization would also clarify the military's role by emphasizing the larger calling of national service.

NOTES

1. Corroboration of the finding that minority youth entering the AVF come from higher socioeconomic backgrounds than white entrants is found in an extensive survey of youth participation in the labor market. See Choongsoo Kim, Gilbert Nestel, Robert L. Phillips, and Michael E. Borns, *The All-Volunteer Force: An Analysis of Youth Participation, Attrition, and Reenlistment* (Columbus: Ohio State University, Center for Human Resource Research, 1980, mimeographed).

2. Donald J. Eberly, "Guidelines for National Service," in *The Draft: A Handbook of Facts and Alternatives*, edited by Sol Tax (Chicago: University of Chicago Press, 1967), pp. 110-13.

3. An excellent introduction to national service proposals and their relation to the military is William R. King, *Achieving America's Goals: National Service or the All-Volunteer Force?* Report prepared for Committee on Armed Services, U.S. Senate, 95th Congress, 1st session (Washington: U.S. Government Printing Office, 1977). Essential for a conceptual understanding of the issue is Morris Janowitz, "The Citizen Soldier and National Service," *Air University Review* 31,

no. 1 (Nov.-Dec. 1979): 2-16. Less enlightening is Congressional Budget Office, *National Service Programs and Their Effects on Military Manpower and Civilian Youth Problems* (Washington: U.S. Government Printing Office, 1978).

4. "National Service Programs," *The Gallup Opinion Index*. Report No. 169, (August 1979).

5. *The Report of the President's Commission on the All-Volunteer Force* (Washington: U.S. Government Printing Office, 1970).

6. The sum of $1.25 billion for total annual costs of the proposed AVF GI Bill is based on the following calculations: The sum to be received by each veteran who uses the GI Bill is estimated at an average of $10,000. This was the estimate given by the Veterans Administration for S. 2020, a GI Bill introduced in the 96th Congress which contained more generous entitlements than the one I have proposed. See *Hearings Before the Committee on Veterans Affairs*, U.S. Senate, 96th Congress, 2nd session (June 19, 1980), p. 25.

Comparative costs of the World War II GI Bill are informative. The GI Bill of that era paid up to $500 per academic year for tuition, fees, and books plus a $75 monthly stipend for a single veteran. The costs of the World War II GI Bill came to about $2,500 per veteran (2,232,000 participants in higher education at a total cost of $5.5 billion). See Keith W. Olson, *The GI Bill, the Veterans, and the Colleges* (Lexington: University Press of Kentucky, 1974), p. 59. Multiply this sum by four to take inflation into account, and we also come up with a figure close to $10,000.

In steady-state recruitment for a 2 million active-duty force, about 375,000 enlistees are required annually (less if attrition were lowered). About 60 percent of first termers—or 255,000 persons—will leave active duty as regular separations. Assume half of these—or 112,500 persons—will matriculate in college (a proportion higher than the national average). $10,000 times 112,500 approximates $1.25 billion.

7. For a more extended discussion of the two-track military personnel system proposed here, see Charles C. Moskos, "Saving the All-Volunteer Force," *Public Interest* No. 61 (Fall 1980), pp. 74-89. Note that in a lower-paid "citizen-soldier" track for 100,000 entering service members each year, cost savings would be several hundred million dollars annually.

8. Jerald G. Bachman, John D. Blair, and David R. Segal, *The All-Volunteer Force* (Ann Arbor: The University of Michigan Press, 1977), pp. 145-48.

Chapter 12

The Economic Value
of Service Projects

Michael W. Sherraden and Donald J. Eberly

Today's youth have been drastically underestimated.[1]

One of the most compelling reasons for initiating a national service program, as suggested in our proposal in chapter 7, is the economic value of the projects that would be performed. The energy and enthusiasm of young people is a valuable resource, much of which is currently wasted, while there are a great many jobs that need to be done. In simple economic terms, it is short-sighted to allow so much energy to dissipate, sometimes destructively, when it could be focused on constructive service projects with long–term positive returns.

The purpose of this chapter is to examine evidence concerning the potential of national service to provide returns to society. After assessing the worth of several federal youth programs, the conclusion is reached that the value of the service can, over the long run, more than compensate for the initial costs of the program. In other words, we do not view national service as a way to "keep youngsters busy" or "keep them out of trouble." Rather, our view is that national service is a way of accomplishing work and providing service, and doing so on an economically efficient basis. Thus, a major rationale for national service is that it is a step toward a more productive and prosperous society.

To a certain extent, this is a radical perspective. In recent years, the nation has grown to expect very little from either young people or government programs. It is almost assumed when a job is created by government that someone is on the dole, that inefficiency prevails, that little useful work is accomplished. For example, this perspective has burdened the CETA Summer Youth Employment Program (SYEP), known in previous years as the Summer Neighborhood Youth Corps and the Summer Program for Economically Disadvantaged Youth. SYEP was ostensibly designed to promote employment opportunities for disadvantaged young people. In reality, however, SYEP has been administered more like an income transfer program. Income support has replaced useful and productive employment as the primary program emphasis. For example, SYEP may retain a young person in the program even though he or she may regularly fail to show up for work or arrive late. Such practices are a disservice to the young people as well as to society, which is paying the bill for a very unsound learning experience. To put it simply, SYEP has not expected enough. The shift toward income support rather than useful work is in large part responsible for the inefficiency and massive criticism of SYEP and many other CETA efforts. Emphasizing support for the disadvantaged rather than emphasizing opportunities for productive work is a prescription for public criticism and program failure. As Chrystal Nix observes in the quotation at the beginning of this chapter, it is also a drastic underestimation of what young people have to offer.

David Lilienthal, former chairman of the Tennessee Valley Authority, often said, "The real energy problem in the United States is a waste of the basic energy, human energy."[2] We have complacently ignored a vast potential of human energy, both youth and adult, which is, in many respects, the most flexible and certainly the most creative source of energy on the planet. Lilienthal observed that human energy—drive, brainpower, creativity, imagination—puts other energy to work. Utilize this energy, he said, and you can solve the problems of homes and factories and develop a rich culture and a sound government.

As evidence that this potential human energy can, in fact, be transformed into productive work and service in a national service program, it is helpful to examine the achievements of some past and current programs in the United States.

FRANKLIN ROOSEVELT'S CIVILIAN CONSERVATION CORPS

The Civilian Conservation Corps (CCC), described in chapter 3, was probably the most popular and successful program of the New Deal. A major reason for this popularity was that the CCC was productive. "What started as a 'make-work' project rapidly developed into the most comprehensive program for the management and conservation of natural resources that any nation had ever undertaken."[3] A lot of work was accomplished in the CCC and the public could see that the program was worthwhile.

The CCC undertook a wide variety of conservation-oriented projects, of which many continue to yield benefits today. Among the CCC's accomplishments were planting over 2 billion trees covering 21 million acres; building 46,000 vehicle bridges and 126,000 miles of minor roads; constructing 62,000 buildings other than CCC camp buildings; restoring 4,000 historic structures; and putting in almost a million miles of fence, 89,000 miles of telephone line, and 69,000 miles of fire breaks. The CCC developed 800 new state parks and logged more than 12 million man-days preventing and fighting forest fires. Forty million acres of farmland benefited from erosion control.[4]

"Of all the forest planting . . . in the history of the nation, more than half was done by the CCC."[5] The 21 million acres of trees planted by the CCC was, at the time, the greatest undertaking in tree planting in the history of the world. Another major contribution was the development of state and national parks and recreational facilities, as noted by one observer in 1942:

> The Corps has built roads, picnic grounds and campgrounds, overnight cabins, horse and foot trails and bridges, swimming, hiking and camping facilities, safe water and sanitation systems, telephone lines, parking areas, dams to impound water for swimming and boating, and fences and guard rails. Some camps have been assigned to restore historic sites such as Gettysburg battlefield and colonial areas of Virginia. There is no doubt that the program has given great impetus to the state park movement throughout the country, and that it has been largely responsible for the increase in state park acreage by almost one hundred percent since 1933.[6]

Most of the major development work in the National Park system was also done by the CCC and there has been relatively little since.[7]

"Establishment of the Corps made available for the first time to Federal, State, and local governments an adequate supply of labor and funds with which to meet many conservation problems."[8] At the end of the first two years, the Secretary of Agriculture testified that the CCC "pushed forward conservation progress from ten to twenty years." The Secretary of the Interior made the same estimate in comparison with what could have been done "under the old order that prevailed prior to the initiation of the Civilian Conservation Corps."[9] Almost everyone agreed that the CCC was "the greatest boon ever to come to conservation in this country."[10]

Regarding value of the work projects completed, the CCC *Final Report* states:

> It has been variously estimated that the actual dollar value of the work performed by the CCC enrollees would be from 82 to 90 percent of the cost of doing it under the best of competitive conditions—and this labor was performed with men who had never had previous work experience and who, in too many cases, were "down and out" prior to enrolling in the Corps. . . . It is also often overlooked that between 25 and 30 percent of the entire cost of the program was

never received directly by the enrollees but was sent to their dependent relatives.[11]

Thus, if payments to relatives are subtracted from CCC program costs, the
value of CCC work projects was well over 100 percent of expenditures.
Moreover, many CCC work projects have appreciated in value over time,
often far outpacing the overall rate of inflation. Note, for example, the tree
planting that was done in the Capital Forest area near Olympia, Washington:

> During the early 1920s and into the 1930s the Capital Forest area . . . was
> completely devastated by intensive private logging operations. The land was
> abandoned as being of no further value to its owners and was taken over by the
> state. During 1934-1939, 90,000 acres of this land was reforested by the CCC at
> an approximate cost of $270,000. In 1960 commercial thinning began and the
> first returns on this investment began to be realized. Today [1981] the acreage is
> being harvested with the timber value placed conservatively at $7,000 per acre
> or $630,000,000 total.[12]

In the above example, two points stand out. First, private logging operations
raped the land and left it abandoned. The timber companies did not have the
foresight to replant the area. Second, the CCC did replant the area and the
return on a $270,000 investment was valued at $630 million in 1981. This
represents a 2,333-fold increase in value. It is abundantly clear from this
example that the tree planting of the CCC was worthwhile. Similarly, the
country continues to reap benefits from CCC work in improved croplands,
grazing lands, and recreational facilities.

The thoughtful reader, at this point, may be wondering if all of these CCC
"accomplishments" are not a bit overstated. After all, CCC spokespersons
would naturally wish to put the best light on Corps' activities; perhaps tallies
of CCC productivity are stretched here and there. Is it possible that some
"accomplishments" have been recorded which are nonexistent? During more
than two years studying CCC records in the U.S. National Archives and
elsewhere, Sherraden found no evidence of tampering with the productivity
figures. There were apparently no objections or serious questions raised by
Congresspersons, the press, or others regarding productivity data. Almost
nothing in the historical record would indicate that CCC enrollees "leaned
on their shovels" for nine years. The productivity data seem to reflect the
reality of the CCC's achievements.[13]

Two important points help account for the rather remarkable work record
of the CCC. First, the Civilian Conservation Corps was large. Program size
averaged 300,000 enrollees. Altogether, more than 3 million young men were
in the CCC. By comparison, the Job Corps averaged about 20,000 enrollees

during the 1970s. The CCC was at least ten times as large as similar year-around programs which exist today. Of all the men in the age range eligibile for the CCC, approximately one in eight enrolled in the CCC at one time or another.[14] A program of this magnitude certainly has the potential to accomplish a lot of useful work.

The second point to bear in mind when thinking about the CCC's productivity is that program administrators, from the Director in Washington to work project leaders in the camps, were serious about doing conservation work. Productivity was a major goal of the CCC. It is clear from Advisory Council Minutes, Camp Inspection Reports, and other CCC data sources that productivity was always considered extremely important.[15] In sharp contrast to a program such as the CETA Summer Youth Employment Program, the CCC was geared to do work. The principle of a 40 hour work week was firmly upheld in the CCC and work projects were specifically defined. Time spent in emergency work, new camp construction, camp maintenance, and other nonconservation efforts was, for example, considered "lost time." It is indicative of the genuineness of the CCC's work efforts that a large percentage of letters from communities to the Director's office mentioned the importance of a work project that was being done or could be done by a nearby CCC camp. Table 12.1 tabulates these letters from communities to the CCC Director's Office. In a random sample of 202 letters, 85 percent are favorable toward the CCC, usually requesting to keep or acquire a camp nearby, and often mentioning the value of the work projects. In contrast,

Table 12.1. Interests of Communities Near CCC Camps as Indicated by Correspondence to the CCC Director's Office

	Number	Percent
Request for camp	84	41.6
Request to keep existing camp	45	22.3
Request for specific work project to be carried out by existing camp	15	12.4
General praise, need for jobs or business, or other remarks indicating positive impact of CCC camp	18	8.9
Total positive letters	172	85.1
Total negative letters (Complaints, Concerns, etc.)	27	13.4
Total letters on neutral subjects	3	1.5
Overall total	202	100.0

Source: U.S. National Archives, General Records, Correspondence of the Director, Series 300, Community Correspondence. These data represent a 10 percent random sample of all letters in this file. The term "correspondence" has a special meaning in these data, sometimes indicating a petition or multiple letters on the same subject at the same approximate time from the same community. Table originally appeared in Michael W. Sherraden, "The Civilian Conservation Corps: Effectiveness of the Camps," Ph.D. dissertation (The University of Michigan, 1979), p. 218.

again, due to a very poor performance record in many communities, the CETA Summer Youth Employment Program often has difficulty finding agencies that will accept the enrollees as workers, even though the labor comes free to the agency.

What factors contributed to the CCC's productivity? Sherraden has examined a number of possible variables and has reached two conclusions. First, the organization of the work project, including use of appropriate clothing and equipment and transportation to the work project site, was the most prominent group of variables associated with productivity. In other words, doing work requires paying attention to how the work will get done. This would appear to be almost a truism, yet it is a lesson which has sometimes escaped modern youth employment efforts. To take the unfortunate example of the Summer Youth Employment Program once again, it is often true that SYEP enrollees cannot, for "safety" reasons, use power equipment, even a lawn mower, while CCC participants were known to drive bulldozers and other heavy equipment. It is little wonder that productivity differences result from these two very different approaches. SYEP simply has not been designed to get work done. It has been designed to keep young people occupied and out of trouble, but for very little else.

A second important conclusion it that characteristics of CCC enrollees did not greatly affect productivity. CCC camps were productive with urban as well as rural enrollees. Neither did enrollee age or race make much of a difference in productivity.[16]

For those who try to account for the CCC's remarkable record of productivity by saying that CCC enrolless were skilled, experienced, and competent workers, we can say assuredly that this was not the case. It is a misconception that CCC enrollees were healthy, hard-working young men thrown temporarily out of work by the Depression. Most CCC enrollees were poor and hungry young men of below average intelligence who had never had a regular job before and who had few or no work skills.[17] One CCC official in 1936 put it this way: "In some instances their morale has been broken by the depression. Many are undernourished, poorly clad, and disillusioned. All have been unemployed, many have never had a job and some of them have been slowly drifting toward delinquency."[18]

The Depression, after all, was not a fleeting event. Even when the CCC was first established in 1933, the economy had already been depressed for over three years. On the average, CCC enrollees had experienced nine years of the Depression by the time they entered the program. Most were not even old enough to have worked in pre–Depression years. They did not bring employment experience to the job. Very few CCC enrollees knew what it was like to work a forty hour week, follow orders, and collect regular pay. They were not skilled and able workers. CCC enrollees were poor, unskilled, and inexperienced; they were as scruffy and as disadvantaged a group of young people as any which exist today—and still the CCC was productive.

PRODUCTIVITY IN THE YOUTH CONSERVATION CORPS AND YOUNG ADULT CONSERVATION CORPS

Parts of the foregoing sections have been critical of the CETA Summer Youth Employment Program because it has operated more as an income support program than a work program. We would like to note, however, that all modern youth employment efforts have not fallen into this pattern. One example is the Youth Conservation Corps (YCC), a summer program which has focused on conservation work and environmental education. Initiated in 1970, YCC has been targeted toward a broad range of youth and the program emphasizes productivity. YCC productivity appears to have been substantial. Annual Reports indicate that the appraised value of works projects has been reasonably close to the overall costs of the program. For example, during the summer of 1974, the appraised value of YCC work projects was 76 percent of total dollars spent; for 1975, the appraised value of YCC projects was 108 percent of total costs of the program; and for 1976, the value of the projects was 84 percent of program costs.[19] In looking at these figures, it is also important to bear in mind that YCC has had educational goals as well. One full day per week has been devoted to environmental education rather than work projects. Thus, the very respectable YCC productivity figures have been achieved within the constraints of a four day work week.

YCC also has been successful in terms of satisfaction among participants. However, the program has been criticized for not enrolling a fair proportion of urban, black, and economically disadvantaged young people.[20] This criticism is partially justified. As we have pointed out, however, there is a danger in expecting a youth employment program to have only social welfare goals. Because YCC is a universal program, i.e., open to anyone regardless of economic status, and because YCC is serious about doing useful work, this program does not suffer from a "welfare" image. Instead, it is popular among participants and the public.

The Young Adult Conservation Corps (YACC), created as part of the Youth Employment and Demonstrations Projects Act of 1977, has been the closest modern attempt at replication of the goals of the old CCC. Young people ages 16 through 23 have been employed in conservation work and other projects with the U.S. Forest Service, the National Park Service, and State Park Departments. Productivity, i.e., emphasis on getting the work done, has been a prominent YACC objective.

Evidence indicates that YACC has been productive. Total allocations in fiscal year 1979 were $227.5 million and the total appraised value of work accomplished was $226.4 million. Altogether, YACC is returning to the nation a dollar earned for a dollar spent. YACC accomplishments include thousands of acres of trees planted, thousands of acres of timberland improved, millions of miles of roads and trails built and maintained, thousands of acres of range and cropland protected by erosion control, development and maintenance of hundreds of recreational facilities, and so on.[21] Below is a statement made in a Senate Committee Hearing by John L. Fulbright, Jr., Director, Office of Youth Programs, Department of the Interior, which evaluates YACC accomplishments in the Department of the Interior:

> In fiscal years 1978 and 1979, enrollees in Interior programs performed work valued by the Department at $51 and $83 million respectively. This represented returns of $1 and $1.10 for program operating dollars expended. While these measures of cost-effectiveness are important, they are not indicative of the importance of work performed by the young men and women in YACC. At numerous sites around the country, enrollees have helped with solar energy modifications to agency buildings. In San Francisco, Mr. Chairman, enrollees dismantled old barracks at Fort Mason and salvaged valuable redwood timber for use on other projects. This year, proclaimed the "Year of the Coast," enrollees in the State grant program in Rhode Island are working on a variety of marine projects including stocking programs, shellfish transplanting, and fishery reproduction activities to mention just a few.
>
> Services that participants have provided go beyond regular Federal and State agency missions. They have worked to clear roads after blizzards, clean up after floods and hurricanes, and have dealt with other emergency situations in numerous communities across the Nation. Some community enrollees have helped restore valuable historic sites and buildings.
>
> Mr. Chairman, these are but a few examples of the excellent work and service of YACC participants throughout this country in urban, rural, and remote areas.
>
> I would also like to mention that these work programs frequently bring training to these young people, even though YACC is not mandated as a training program per se. Moreover it frequently is training which will be recognized in the world of work at large. . . . In Providence where enrollees are growing trees and plants for city parks, several have received State certification as arborists. Beyond those on-the-job related activities, camp level staff in numerous locations have made arrangements with local educational institutions so that participants could complete a high school education or its equivalent. Marin County, Calif., is one of such efforts to enhance enrollees' preparation for work after they leave the program.[22]

These results occurred with a substantially disadvantaged population—out of school and unemployed young people. Looking at YACC's record, one can only conclude that real productivity is quite possible, even normal. The first step is simply to be serious about getting the work done. As Fulbright has noted, much of the job training takes care of itself.

A LESSON FROM JOB CORPS

Job Corps, created as part of the Economic Opportunity Act of 1964, is primarily a job training program for economically disadvantaged young people between the ages of 16 and 21. The focus is on vocational training rather than work and service. Nevertheless, Job Corps has an important lesson to teach us which applies to this discussion of useful work and the potential of young people to contribute to society.

In the early years of Job Corps, the program was controversial. Program goals were unclear; dropout rates were high; and Job Corps withstood a barrage of negative publicity.[23] Partly as a result of this inauspicious early performance, Job Corps was pared down in the late 1960s to about one-fifth of its originally projected size. The program learned to live with austerity. In this climate, the urgent need for remedial education, specific job training, and connections to jobs became more clearly defined and operationalized. "Training and education were narrowed to specific job requirements. The key seemed to be the ability to gain access to jobs rather than efforts to alter attitudes and values of enrollees."[24]

As Job Corps began to focus on specific job opportunities and seriously began placing enrollees in jobs, the program began to succeed. By 1975, a major review of the program said it was "a social experiment that worked."[25] According to government statistics, the Job Corps placement rate for fiscal years 1977, 1978, and 1979 averaged 93 percent, i.e., 93 out of every 100 enrollees available for placement were placed in employment, military service, school, or further job training.[26] It is all the more remarkable that this placement rate has been achieved with a disadvantaged population, 85 percent of whom had not completed high school, and 50 percent of whom were reading at below seventh grade level when they entered the program. Following Congressional recognition of Job Corps' effectiveness, appropriations were approved in 1978 to double the size of the program.[27]

The lesson which Job Corps offers is that any youth program should be very clear about what it is trying to do. In the early years, Job Corps tried to reform enrollees as well as to give them job training. Enrollees did not respond well to the reform efforts and it is likely that this adversely affected the job training component. In later years, however, when enrollees could see that Job Corps training would lead to a better future, dropout rates began to diminish and enrollees responded very impressively.

And what are the economic returns? Even though Job Corps concentrates on job training rather than service projects, it is still possible to calculate economic impacts. Fortunately, Job Corps is a rare exception in that reliable data are available to assess overall economic impacts. Job Corps is the target of one of the most comprehensive research efforts ever focused on a single social program. This research effort, which incorporates a longitudinal design following a sample of enrollees and a comparison group, has confirmed that former Job Corps enrollees make more money, are less likely to be unemployed, are less dependent on welfare assistance and other public transfers, are less often arrested on criminal charges, are more likely to receive a high school diploma, and are more likely to attend college than a comparable group of youngsters who have not enrolled in Job Corps. These positive impacts, translated into economic terms, represent an excess of program benefits over costs:

> The findings from a comprehensive evaluation of the social benefits and costs of Job Corps suggest that public investment in Job Corps is economically efficient. Our benchmark estimate is that the value of benefits in fiscal year 1977 exceeded costs by almost $2,300 per corps member, or by approximately 45 percent of costs. Furthermore, the program is found to be economically efficient under a wide range of alternative assumptions and estimates. Because over 40,000 youths enrolled in Job Corps during fiscal year 1977, our benchmark estimate of the net social benefit for the entire program is approximately $90 million for that year.[28]

Thus, Job Corps more than pays for itself by reducing a variety of social costs. Economic benefits go far beyond the simple value of work projects.

In many ways, Job Corps enrollees of today are similar to CCC enrollees of the 1930s—they come from impoverished backgrounds, they do not have work experience, and they had limited success in school. The CCC and Job Corps demonstrate that economically disadvantaged young people, like everyone else, do well when the program is clear about what it has to offer and what it expects from enrollees. There is a vast and simmering potential locked up in our youth population, white and nonwhite, urban and rural, rich and poor. Job Corps, like the old CCC, had demonstrated that this potential can be realized to effectively meet the needs of both young people and society. It is not at all necessary to continue to write off thousands of young people as social and economic burdens. The task before us is to provide more opportunities for young people to contribute.

THE OPPOSING VIEWPOINT

Not everyone agrees that a national service program can, or would, yield positive results. Some have pictured a national service program as a make-work boondoggle. One of the more articulate statements expressing this viewpoint is by Lewis Crampton, Former Commissioner, Massachusetts Department of Community Affairs, Newton, Massachusetts, testifying before a Senate committee:

> I think a large, comprehensive national service program will inevitably give rise to the creation of millions of meaningless make-work jobs. This clearly is an issue that you know about, and I know this is something you wouldn't want to have happen. But I think that the likelihood of such occurrences is pretty good, given our recent experiences with the CETA program in and around the cities. Furthermore there are real possibilities for abuses. Look what happened to CETA in our own State, Senator. We had a State legislator transporting people—CETA program people—from his town to another town to work on a political campaign for a friend of his.
>
> With the kind of loosely supervised, volunteer organization bureaucracy that is likely to be set up to administer this program, the potential for the same kinds of abuses occurring elsewhere certainly exists.
>
> Another major objection to a large-scale program is that the task of matching available jobs with available people under a comprehensive national service program is simply beyond the capability of any existing bureaucracy. In some cases, we will have lots of people looking for jobs and no jobs available, while some communities will have no people and a surplus of available jobs. Who is going to transport these people to a job site? Will it be necessary for some people to live away from home in order to participate in this program? Who is going to pay for that?
>
> Indeed, even the military service has its own problems of matching jobs with people within its own self-contained environment. I doubt that national service, in whatever form emerges except as a small program, is likely to have much success either.[29]

Crampton's concerns must be considered; and as we examine his misgivings, we are best guided by past and current experience. Regarding the possible "creation of millions of meaningless make-work jobs," certainly the CCC of the 1930s and the YCC and YACC of the 1970s cannot be accused of this fault. Crampton cites "the CETA program in and around the cities." While this vague reference is hard to pin down, he is probably referring to the Summer Youth Employment Program. It is unfortunate that the abuses of some misguided and mismanaged CETA programs have received so much attention, while the more successful programs such as YCC and YACC, the California Conservation Corps, and the Program for Local Service in Seattle, to name some of the major ones, have received comparatively little coverage. Most Americans are not even aware of these programs. The nation has developed a certain inability to recognize success, especially in a government program. Perhaps it is the times. Perhaps America has been so down on itself that positive results go unnoticed. Whatever the explanation, it is high time that we begin to focus on programs which work rather than programs which do not work. It is time to orient ourselves toward solutions and successes rather than problems and failures.

Regarding the issue of matching people and jobs, the Program for Local Service (see chapter 3) may serve as an example. Below is a statement from Pascal J. DeBlasio, former director:

> Could they be matched together? The answer to that was also "Yes." We found that individuals could be matched with an absence of bureaucratic paperwork and time. They were matched using the voucher system in which the individual participant selected a placement from a pool of opportunities in the community.
>
> We found that young people involved in the Program for Local Service probably knew more about the needs of their own communities than did staff— or any outsider. They could figure out many innovative ways to serve community needs.
>
> The program worked very simply. We recruited a large pool of potential volunteers. We went to potential sponsoring organizations to create a pool of opportunities which were compiled in a catalog. The potential volunteers then chose placements from the catalog. Applicants filled out a voucher— memorandum of agreement—created a match, and as soon as that voucher was signed, payment of a living allowance was started.[30]

Apparently PLS in Seattle did not experience job matching problems. Similar matching procedures can work in other communities. One of the chief advantages of a decentralized service program which addresses local needs is that it avoids large bureaucratic organization.

Overall, was PLS economically worthwhile? An early evaluation found that it was: "The evaluation found the worth of service performed by the average participant to be $7,000, almost double the unit cost to ACTION of funding the program. It also found the unemployment rate to have fallen from 70 percent at entry to 18 percent six months after completion of service."[31] Because of the dramatic change in pre-PLS and post-PLS unemployment rates, the program clearly provided economic returns beyond the actual value of work performed. Skeptics of national service, who engage so often in vague criticism, would do better to look at concrete experience and economic realities of programs such as PLS.

CONCLUSIONS

We have attempted to show, not by assertion but by evidence, that the economic value of service projects can be substantial. Indeed, there is reason to believe that a national service program would pay for itself in the value of its work and service projects alone, and more than pay for itself if additional economic benefits are considered, such as increased employability of participants, decreased crime, decreased reliance on income transfer programs, and so forth. Related to this general conclusion, we have several additional observations.

First, we would like to emphasize a distinction between inexperience and incompetence. Many young people may lack experience, but they are not incompetent. In the postindustrial United States, we have developed a labor market which has left many young people uninvolved. Opportunities for constructive contribution have been too few. But this does not mean that those who are uninvolved are also unable. On the contrary, many young people have responded enthusiastically and with competence when provided a chance to assume a responsible role in society.

Second, of the programs sponsored by the federal government which address youth unemployment problems and/or provide work and service, the programs which have stressed development of competence and productivity—for example, YCC, YACC, and Job Corps in later years—have been successful. On the other hand, youth programs that have been characterized more by income support and social control than by performance—most notably, the Summer Youth Employment Program—have been visible failures. Based on these experiences, we are opposed to dressing up income support programs and pretending that they are employment and service programs. There is nothing to be gained from this masquerade and there is much to be lost. The negative evaluations of the CETA Summer Youth Employment Program and its predecessors will take a long time to overcome.

Third, as we note elsewhere, there is no shortage of genuine work to be done. It doesn't make a great deal of sense to engage in make-work or busy-work. Although this may appear to be a fairly obvious conclusion, it is not a line of thinking that has always penetrated youth employment programs in the past.

Fourth, there is in the United States a preoccupation with productivity of the average working person, while too little attention is paid to levels of unemployment and underemployment and their impact on overall production. Indeed, the common definition of "productivity" is based on output per working person (either within an industry, an economic sector, or the overall economy). The nation has developed a kind of tunnel vision in believing that it is better off when the average working person produces more, thus increasing "productivity." But this perspective tends to ignore a larger and more salient reality, which is that, in the long run, overall production is what matters most. It is not difficult to see that the nation is worse off when productivity of the average worker increases by 2 percent while, at the same time, an additional 3 percent of the labor force becomes unemployed. Who supports the additional unemployed workers?

Overall production is the key variable because, one way or another, everyone is supported—if not by legitimate employment income, then by income from government programs, private pensions, crime, "subterranean" employment, or some other source. And all of these sources of support are derived, directly or indirectly, from overall production.

What does this concern with overall production have to do with national service? Young people, like everyone else, are supported one way or another, whether they are in school, employed, hanging out on the street, in the army, robbing liquor stores, or in jail. From a macroeconomic perspective, there is a burden on the economy of food, clothing, shelter, and so forth for every person. Economically, the question is, what do young people provide in return? It is reasonable to expect that many more teenagers and young adults can make a productive contribution? We think it is.

As a final observation, the traditional cost-benefit framework for looking at national service is inadequate, and the bulk of the error is in nonquantifiable long-term benefits. In other words, technical evaluation methods are likely to understate the real value of national service. Bernard Anderson, while Chairman of the National Council on Employment Policy and as a member of the Committee for the Study of National Service, stated it this way:

> While many of the benefits of the program, such as the value of service to society produced by youth, can be measured, many more benefits to individual participants and to society at large cannot be measured with tools currently available. How can one place a quantitative value on the enrichment of the spirit, the strengthening of the fiber of personal commitment, or growth in a sense of community? Such benefits of National Service are unlikely to enter into the calculus of economic returns, and for that reason, conventional cost-and-benefit analysis applied to the program will be seriously flawed.
>
> In approaching the economic justification for National Service, one must place the question within a broad framework of analysis that emphasizes the potential enrichment of the nation's strength and vitality that might emerge from a comprehensive service program involving thousands of youth. That framework of analysis will enable one to view National Service in the larger context of investment in human development. Costs incurred today can then be discounted against benefits that will accrue only partially in the short run. Continued, and perhaps increased returns, can be expected over the lifetime of program participants and will be revealed in many forms difficult to contemplate at the time initial costs are incurred.
>
> What is clear is that investment in National Service can only be perceived as a short-term commitment directed toward long-term benefits. The investment will contribute to the nation's good; to its sense of human values; to its sense of community through which one person cares about the well-being of his neighbor; and to the reduction in anti-social behavior born of cynicism, selfishness, and the lack of purpose in life. If the spirit of service and a sense of national

goals are restored in the professions, unions, businesses, and other institutions, the nation's well-being will be served. It is difficult to imagine that the attainment of that goal would not have significant effects on the nation's productivity, and in turn, its economic vitality. For those to whom the economic calculus looms large in the consideration of National Service, this should be economic justification subject to little debate.[32]

Ultimately, evaluation of national service must rest on the long-term perspective which Anderson has described. The United States has not always been good at taking the long-term view. Short-term arithmetic tends to dominate decision-making processes, and this is unfortunately true for private business and consumers as well as government. As the nation attempts to deal with its economic difficulties, however, the general public, the business community, and major social institutions are beginning to realize that short-term economic thinking is inadequate. With this realization, the nation would do well to consider national service as a sound long-term investment.

NOTES

1. Chrystal Nix, "An Alternative Proposal to the Draft," reprinted in U.S. Congress, Senate, *Hearings: Presidential Commission on National Service and National Commission on Volunteerism*, March 13, 1980 (Washington: U.S. Government Printing Office, 1980), p. 62.

2. David Lilienthal, quoted in "To Lilienthal, Human Energy was Nation's Greatest Asset," *St. Louis Post-Dispatch*, January 18, 1981, pp. 1 and 4.

3. Hubert H. Humphrey, "Plan to Save Trees, Land, and Boys," *Harper's Magazine* 218 (January 1959): 53-57.

4. U.S. Civilian Conservation Corps, *Final Report of the Director of the Civilian Conservation Corps, April 1933 through June 30, 1942* (Washington: U.S. Civilian Conservation Corps, 1942).

5. William E. Leuchtenberg, *Franklin Roosevelt and the New Deal, 1932-1940* (New York: Harper and Row, 1963), p. 174.

6. H. L. Caravati, "Civilian Conservation Corps in Education–Recreation Field," *Recreation* 34 (February 1942): 650-51.

7. Peter Mowitt, U.S. National Park Service, Personal Interview with Michael Sherraden, Washington, D.C., February 8, 1978.

8. Howard S. Carpenter, *The Civilian Conservation Corps, 1933-1942: A Review* (Washington: U.S. Department of Labor, 1961, mimeographed).

9. Kenneth Holland and Frank Hill, *Youth in the CCC* (Washington: American Council on Education, 1942), citing Congressional Hearings.

10. J. D. Guthrie, "CCC and American Conservation," *Scientific Monthly* 57 (November 1943): 401-12.

11. U.S. Civilian Conservation Corps, *Final Report.*

12. Human Environment Center, "Background Information on YACC Activities in Washington and Oregon" (Washington: Human Environment Center, 1981, mimeographed).

13. Michael Sherraden, "The Civilian Conservation Corps: Effectiveness of the Camps," Ph.D. Dissertation (University of Michigan, 1979).

14. U.S. Department of Labor, *Annual Report of the Secretary of Labor, Fiscal Year Ended June 30, 1938* (Washington: U.S. Government Printing Office, 1938).

15. Sherraden,"The Civilian Conservation Corps," pp. 179-212.

16. Ibid.

17. Holland and Hill, *Youth in the CCC*.

18. Howard Oxley, *Education in Civilian Conservation Corps Camps* (Washington: U.S. Civilian Conservation Corps, 1936), p. 5.

19. U.S. Department of the Interior and U.S. Department of Agriculture, *Youth Conservation Corps, Annual Reports* (Washington: U.S. Government Printing Office).

20. Garth Mangum and John Walsh, *Employment and Training Programs for Youth: What Works Best for Whom?* (Washington: U.S. Government Printing Office, 1978), p. 60.

21. U.S. Department of Labor, *Joint Annual Report to the President and Congress, Young Adult Conservation Corps* (Washington: U.S. Department of Labor, 1979, mimeographed).

22. U.S. Congress, Senate Committee on Labor and Human Resources, *Hearings: Presidential Commission on National Service and National Commission on Volunteerism*, 96th Cong., 2nd sess., 1980, p. 141.

23. Christopher Weeks, *Job Corps: Dollars and Dropouts* (Boston: Little, Brown, 1967).

24. Mangum and Walsh, *Employment and Training Programs for Youth*, p. 84.

25. Sar Levitan and Benjamin Johnston, *The Job Corps: A Social Experiment that Works* (Baltimore: The Johns Hopkins University Press, 1975).

26. U.S. Department of Labor, *Job Corps in Brief* (Washington: U.S. Department of Labor, annual reports).

27. As of this writing, in the spring of 1981, the continued expansion of Job Corps is questionable. The Reagan administration has proposed a 15 percent reduction in the program, which, in light of Job Corps' record of achievement, is one of the more short-sighted proposals of the new administration.

28. Mathematica Policy Research, Inc., *Evaluation of the Economic Impact of the Job Corps Program: Second Follow-Up Report* (Princeton, New Jersey: Mathematica, 1980), pp. vi-vii.

29. U.S. Congress, Senate, *Hearings: Presidential Commission on National Service*, p. 162.

30. Ibid., p. 271.

31. Donald Eberly, "A Call for National Service," *Voluntary Action Leadership* (Summer 1979), pp. 27-30, citing Kappa Systems, Inc., *The Impact of Participation in the Program for Local Service on the Participant* (Arlington, Virginia: Kappa Systems, Inc., 1975).

32. Bernard Anderson, "Is National Youth Service Economically Justifiable?" in *National Youth Service: What's at Stake?* (Washington: The Potomac Institute, 1980), pp. 26-27 and 29.

Chapter 13

The Impact of National Service on Participants

Michael W. Sherraden and Donald J. Eberly

In the preceding several chapters, some impacts of national service on employment, education, the military, and the economy are examined. At this point, to round out the picture, it is useful to look at the immediate impact of national service on the young men and women who would serve. How might national service affect participants? Addressing this question requires a bit of conjecture since we cannot be absolutely sure how young people would respond or exactly what they would gain from a national service experience in the 1980s and beyond. There are, however, two approaches to this question which go a long way toward an informed assessment.

One approach is simply to ask young people what they think about national service. Diane Hedin takes this approach in Chapter 14. Hedin, in a very illuminating manner, reviews the results of surveys and other research, including her own research in Minnesota, designed to "read the pulse" of America's young people on the issue of national service.

Another valuable approach is to turn to previous experience with national service–like programs in the United States. How have young people responded to these programs in the past? Have there been benefits to participants? In this chapter, the authors select three programs—the Civilian Conservation Corps, the Job Corps, and the Program for Local Service—and present data related to the programs' impacts on the young people who signed up. (General descriptions of these national service-like programs are presented in chapter 3.)

THE CIVILIAN CONSERVATION CORPS

As the first and among the largest federally-sponsored civilian youth service programs in the United States, the CCC of the 1930s was a valuable experience for many young men. The positive impact on individuals was tremendous. As one gauge of the CCC's popularity, it is noteworthy that most enrollees signed up for a second term. Although the standard enrollment period was six months, the average period of service was ten months, and black CCCers stayed an average of fifteen months.[1] These enrollment statistics indicate that the CCC had widespread appeal and acceptance.

The reasons for the CCC's popularity among participants were many. Economic support for the family back home (most of the $30 monthly pay was automatically sent home) and "three squares a day" were undoubtedly the most important attractions,[2] but the CCC offered enrollees other benefits as well. These included health, education, reduction of criminal activity, preparation for employment, and personal satisfaction.

Health

The young men who signed up for the CCC were not always in the best of health. Many were not accustomed to eating regular meals, much less did they have access to professional medical care. In the CCC, by contrast, nutritious meals were provided and a doctor was assigned to each camp on at least a part-time basis. It is not surprising, therefore, that statistics related to health improvements among CCC enrollees are impressive. The CCC did have physical examinations for screening out unhealthy applicants at entry, but the standards were minimal:

> The main purpose of these physical examinations was to weed out men with contagious diseases which would make them a menace to others and to exclude boys whose physical disabilities were so severe as to prevent them from doing hard work without injuring themselves or others. As compared with the Army, the Navy, or most insurance companies, the CCC standards for physical acceptance were very low. Even the relatively low physical standards for acceptance were often "overlooked" by wise physicians in the cases of thousands of men whose superficial defects . . . were largely traceable to malnutrition and poor living in general. These were defects which could be and were quickly remedied in the CCC.[3]

Thus, CCC enrollees were not always completely "fit" at the outset; but, due to a balanced diet, inoculations against major diseases, and a policy of immediate and thorough treatment of even minor sickness or illness, health improvements were significant.

> In most cases the impact of CCC life on enrollees was profound. These effects are most clearly and easily noted with regard to the physical changes in enrollees. Repeated tests of hundreds of thousands of men showed that a very few months of service in the CCC increased the average weight per man between 11 and 15 pounds. . . . In all instances the average gains recorded were vastly

greater than could have been expected under normal conditions during a similar period of time.[4]

CCC youths, on the average, showed greater increases in height and weight than did college students or soldiers in the regular Army in the same age group.[5] Increases in overall physical condition and development were among the more significant accomplishments of the CCC.

The CCC also had lower accident, venereal disease, and illness rates than the Army had at the same time. "An ever-increasing campaign against accidents proved effective. The Corps-wide accident rate per 1,000 enrollees dropped from 16.81 in 1934 to 4.80 in 1940 and the rate of accidents per million man-hours of work fell to just over one third what it had been."[6] CCC enrollees contracted venereal disease at the rate of 18 per thousand. This compared favorably with the Army rate of 87 per thousand of World War I, and 140 per thousand in the Spanish-American War.[7]

Lower accident and illness rates soon led to lower annual death rates. Between 1933 and 1935, the annual death rate per thousand CCCers was 2.7, "or about one-third of that among unselected men of a similar age group according to the American Experience Table of Mortality."[8] At the end of the CCC's nine year history, "there were between 3,500 and 4,000 men alive and healthy who would have been dead under usual expected mortality."[9] Certainly, these statistics are strong endorsement of the CCC's health benefits to enrollees.

Education

The educational program was not a high priority. President Roosevelt and CCC Director Robert Fechner did not want education to interfere with the primary goal of conservation work. Nonetheless, the CCC did have an educational program and an educational adviser in each camp. In September 1935, for example, 31,012 courses were being taught: 5,399 elementary; 7,840 high school; 2,324 college; 11,430 vocational; and 4,019 "general."[10] Although not officially required, at least half of all CCC enrollees were taking classes at any given time. Probably the greatest educational contribution of the CCC was in combating illiteracy among enrollees. In 1936 Howard Oxley, the CCC Director of Education, estimated that "out of 350,000 men enrolled in the Corps, over 10,000 cannot read a newspaper or write a simple letter." Oxley went on to say that "since the CCC started, at least 35,000 men have been taught to read and write."[11]

Crime Reduction

The CCC has also been credited with reducing juvenile crime: "Reports submitted by the men and women who selected young men for the Corps and kept in touch with former CCC enrollees offer convincing proof of the value of the CCC as a means of reducing juvenile delinquency. . . . Data reaching the Office of the Director from Department of Justice officers and heads of prisons and reformatories showed that the Corps has been a factor in reducing juvenile crime."[12]

Law enforcement authorities supported these conclusions: "Judge M. Broude of Chicago estimated that the CCC was largely responsible for the 50 percent reduction in crime in that city, because it took the boys off the streets and inculcated in them a sense of values. The New York Commissioner of Correction attributed a similar decrease in juvenile crime to the beneficial effect of the Corps."[13]

Testimony before the House Committee on Labor in 1937 indicated that the CCC was not only reducing juvenile crime, but was also responsible for a decrease in the number of juveniles institutionalized for criminal activity.[14]

Preparation for Employment

Although the CCC had no formal program of vocational training, enrollees nevertheless were prepared for the world of work. Far more than "make work," CCC projects were productive efforts in which participants learned skills, work habits, work safety, cooperation, and pride in a job well done. In 1941, one observer noted that "certain large employers give preference, wherever possible, to CCC enrollees not only because of their work experience, but because of their dependability and their training in safety regulations. In the Sixth Corps Area . . . the automotive industry openly expresses such a preference."[15]

Personal Satisfaction and Self-Esteem

In large measure due to the genuineness of the CCC's work efforts, many enrollees left the Corps with a sense of personal satisfaction and increased self-esteem. One study found that work projects were by far the most appealing aspect of camp life in a sample of 2,500 CCCers in Missouri.[16] Another study of former CCCers in Cleveland reported similar results:

At least three-quarters of the boys found a reasonable degree of satisfaction in their work and seemed to feel that it was work which had value from the standpoint of the community and the general public. . . . One group of boys said they gained their real understanding when they saw the finished product. . . . Pride in accomplishment and in participation was expressed in various ways. Several expressed it in terms of helping to preserve a portion of the nation's resources. "I feel almost as if I owned that land. Someday, when those trees I planted grow large, I want to go back and look at them," said one. Another said, "that there work we did will really do some good some day."[17]

Also contributing to self-fulfillment among CCCers was the knowledge that they were providing much needed economic support for their families. In many cases, income from a son's CCC work was the major source of support. Although the amount was not large, it was enough to keep many families afloat and hold them together during very difficult times.

JOB CORPS

Job Corps, which began in 1965, is a job training program for disadvantaged young people; it is not a work and service program. However, Job Corps has had significant impacts on the lives of participants in ways which might also be expected from a national service program. It is reported in chapter 12 that former Job Corps enrollees are less likely to be unemployed, make more money, are less frequently arrested, are more likely to receive a high school diploma, and are more likely to attend college than a comparable group of youngsters who have not enrolled in Job Corps. It is also noted that these positive impacts, translated into economic terms, represent a substantial excess of program benefits over costs.[18]

There are, however, additional positive impacts of Job Corps on the lives of the enrollees. A study entitled *The Noneconomic Impacts of the Job Corps* was conducted over three years by the Department of Labor and Abt Associates.[19] A battery of tests were given to a sample of 489 young men and women in two Job Corps groups ("persisters" and "dropouts") and a comparison group who signed up for Job Corps but never attended ("no shows"). The persister group, i.e., Job Corps enrollees who stayed in the program at least three months, improved in more areas than the other two groups.

The most striking improvements were among a group of five measures for "social–attitudinal impacts." Job Corps persisters improved significantly on all five of these measures. These included attitude toward authority, self-esteem, criminal justice system involvement, family relations, and use of leisure time. Table 13.1 summarizes the results for the social-attitudinal measures.

These results indicate convincingly that the Job Corps program has a positive influence in how enrollees feel about themselves and how they get along with others—friends, family, and authority figures. No cost-benefit analysis will ever capture the value of such impacts, but they are nonetheless very important in the lives of the young people who are affected.

Table 13.1. Summary of Results of the Job Corps Noneconomic Impacts Study, Social-Attitudinal Measures

Area of Study	Three Months or More in Job Corps (Persisters)	Less Than Three Months in Job Corps (Dropouts)	Did Not Attend Job Corps (No Shows)
Attitude Toward Authority	Improved	No Change	No Change
Self-Esteem	Improved	No Change	No Change
Criminal Justice System Involvement	Improved	Improved	Improved
Family Relations	Improved	No Change	No Change
Use of Leisure Time	Improved	Mixed	No Change

Source: U.S. Department of Labor, Employment and Training Administration, *The Noneconomic Impacts of the Job Corps Program* (Washington: U.S. Government Printing Office, 1978), p. 19.

THE PROGRAM FOR LOCAL SERVICE

ACTION's Program for Local Service was located in Seattle during 1973-1974. This small national service experiment was carefully evaluated by an outside contractor to assess the effect of the PLS experience on the following attributes: (1) career exploration; (2) plans for future education; (3) academic credit; (4) value of experience for future employment; (5) understanding of the complexity and function of organizational structures; (6) self-confidence and self-worth; (7) civic pride; (8) decision-making ability; (9) understanding between ages, races, and social strata; (10) ability to work with people; (11) fulfillment of service responsibility; (12) awareness of human needs; and (13) motivation.[20]

The contractor administered a number of tests and questionnaires to PLS participants at the time of entry, again at eight months into the service period, and finally eight months later, or four months after the end of the one year PLS service. For some of the measures, interviews were held with participants' supervisors.

Career and Education

There were several indicators of a positive impact of the PLS experience on the career and educational plans of participants. In the eight–month survey, two out of three persons responded positively to the question, "Has your experience in PLS influenced or changed your career plans or educational plans?" At the same time, one in four participants reported that they already had, or possibly would, receive academic credit related to their service in PLS. This was a surprisingly high number since, unlike some other ACTION programs, PLS did not actively promote academic recognition for learning acquired during service. These results indicate that the PLS participants made their own arrangements for course credit. Participants also gave a high rating to the value of the experience for future employment, as shown in table 13.2.

In addition, there was an increased interest in understanding the complexity and function of organizational structures. When asked whether participants had grown in this respect, supervisors replied that 71 percent had shown observable increases. Among the participants themselves, the proportion which replied that this component of PLS was very important to them increased from 43 percent at entry to 50 percent after eight months of service.

In a self-anchoring career-progress scale, PLS participants estimated that they were significantly better off than if they had not joined PLS, and their long-range career expectations were also significantly higher than participants believed they would have been without PLS.

Finally, participants were asked about their future plans and were surveyed four months after leaving service to determine what they were doing at that time. The results are summarized in table 13.3. The increased interest in getting a job is remarkable since only 15 percent of all participants had a job just before entering PLS, while 70 percent were unemployed and looking for work. Four months after leaving PLS, the proportion of those who were unemployed and looking for work had dropped to 17 percent.

Personality Attributes and Attitudes

The line of inquiry addressing personality attributes and attitudes produced several "possible benefits," but only one "definite benefit," as shown in table 13.4. The increased awareness of human needs was found in all areas on which participants were questioned. The areas covered were hunger, crime, unemployment, drug abuse, substandard housing, racial discrimination, old

Table 13.2. Participant Ratings on Value of the Program for Local Service (PLS) Experience for Future Employment

Question: How would you rate the value of your PLS experience for future employment?

Very valuable	62%
Somewhat valuable	30
Only slightly valuable	7
Not at all valuable	1
Total	100%

Source: Kappa Systems, Inc., *The Impact of Participation in the Program for Local Service Upon the Participant* (Arlington, Virginia: Kappa Systems, Inc., 1975).

Table 13.3. Planned and Actual Postservice Activities of Participants in the Program for Local Services (PLS)

	Future Plans At Entry	Future Plans Eight Months Later	Status Four Months After End of PLS Service (Sixteen Months After Entry)	
Get a job	40%	47%	Employment	55%
Get H.S. Diploma	2%	3%	Unemployed and seeking work	17%
Enroll in a job training program	4%	4%		
Attend college	31%	34%		
Enroll in grad school	7%	8%	Student	25%
Enlist in armed forces	2%	1%	Armed forces	1%
Other/Don't know	33%	6%	Other	17%
	(Percentages do not total to 100 due to multiple answers)			

Source: Kappa Systems, Inc., *The Impact of Participation in the Program for Local Service Upon the Participant* (Arlington, Virginia: Kappa Systems, Inc., 1975).

age problems, health care problems, and lack of educational opportunities. Almost daily exposure to one or more of these problems evidently left its mark on those who served in PLS.

Table 13.4. Impact of the Program for Local Service on Personality Attributes and Attitude Measures

Self-confidence and self-worth	Possible benefit
Civic pride	Inconclusive
Decision-making ability	Possible benefit
Understanding between races, ages, and social strata	Possible benefit
Ability to work with people	Inconclusive
Fulfillment of service responsibility	Improbable benefit
Awareness of human needs	Definite benefit
Motivation	Inconclusive

Source: Kappa Systems, Inc. *The Impact of Participation in the Program for Local Service Upon the Participant* (Arlington, Virginia: Kappa Systems, Inc., 1975).

CONCLUSION

The Civilian Conservation Corps, the Job Corps, and the Program for Local Service have had impacts on the lives of participants in a variety of ways. Specific results vary from program to program, but the general picture is that participants have gained self-confidence, social maturity, employability, and avoidance of criminal behavior. In the Civilian Conservation Corps, there were very significant gains in health as well. It is also noteworthy that positive impacts have resulted from these three very different programs, a fact which indicates that national service might take a variety of forms and still lead to positive outcomes for those who choose to participate.

NOTES

1. John Salmond, *The Civilian Conservation Corps, 1933-1942: A New Deal Case Study* (Durham, North Carolina: Duke University Press, 1967), p. 101.

2. Michael Sherraden, "The Civilian Conservation Corps: Effectiveness of the Camps," Ph.D. dissertation (University of Michigan, 1979), pp. 117-78.

3. U.S. Civilian Conservation Corps, *Final Report of the Director of the Civilian Conservation Corps*, April 1933 through June 30, 1942 (Washington: U.S. Civilian Conservation Corps, 1942), p. 54.

4. Ibid., p. 55.

5. U.S. Civilian Conservation Corps, *Annual Report of the Director of the Civilian Conservation Corps, April 1933 through June 30, 1942* (Washington: U.S. Civilian Conservation Corps, 1941), p. 19.

6. Kenneth Baldridge, "Nine Years of Achievement: The Civilian Conservation Corps in Utah," Ph.D. dissertation (Brigham Young University, 1971), p. 246; citing CCC *Annual Reports*.

7. Salmond, *The Civilian Conservation Corps*, p. 144; citing *Time* 33 (February 6, 1939): 11.

8. "Two Years of CCC Work," *Monthly Labor Review* 41 (July 1935): 53-56.

9. U.S. Civilian Conservation Corps, *Final Report*, p. 58.

10. Lyle K. Henry, "The Civilian Conservation Corps as an Educational Institution," *School and Society* 43 (January 11, 1936): 62-66.

11. Howard Oxley, *Education in Civilian Conservation Corps Camps* (Washington: U.S. Civilian Conservation Corps, 1936), p. 5.

12. U.S. Civilian Conservation Corps, *Final Report*, p. 77.

13. Salmond, *The Civilian Conservation Corps*, p. 112; citing *The New York Times* (October 2, 1936 and January 17, 1937).

14. U.S. Congress, House Committee on Labor, *Hearings on H.R. 6180, A Bill to Make the Civilian Conservation Corps a Permanent Agency*, 75th Cong., 1st sess., 1937, p. 5.

15. Henry C. Lanpher, "The Civilian Conservation Corps—Its Program and Recorded Accomplishments," Ph.D. dissertation (University of Chicago, 1941), p. 135.

16. Clarence Aydelott, "Facts Concerning Enrollees, Advisors, and Educational Program in CCC Camps in Missouri," Ph.D. dissertation (University of Missouri, 1936), p. 86.

17. Helen M. Walker, *The CCC through the Eyes of 272 Boys: A Summary of a Group Study of the Reactions of 272 Cleveland Boys to their Experience in the Civilian Conservation Corps* (Cleveland: Western Reserve University Press, 1938), pp. 32–33.

18. Mathematica Policy Research, Inc., *Evaluation of the Economic Impact of the Job Corps Program: Second Follow-Up Report* (Princeton: Mathematica, 1980).

19. U.S. Department of Labor, Employment and Training Administration, *The Noneconomic Impacts of the Job Corps Program* (Washington: U.S. Government Printing Office, 1978).

20. Kappa Systems, Inc., *The Impact of Participation in the Program for Local Service Upon the Participant* (Arlington, Virginia: Kappa Systems, Inc., 1975); prepared under contract to ACTION. All of the data presented on PLS are from this report.

Chapter 14
The Views of Adolescents and Young Adults on Civic Obligations and National Service

Diane Hedin

It would give the young a chance to learn about other cultures, others' problems, while helping out the world. It would force us to accept more responsibility.

I have higher goals than to go into the service. It's OK for a dummy, but not for me.

We have all around good feelings about national service. It's a good way to get people involved in our community and our country and to help others. Besides, money isn't everything.

I'd pick civilian service over the military. Mosquito bites don't hurt as much as bullets.

The statements above give a flavor of the divergent opinions young people hold about national service. No short chapter can fully capture the complexity and ambivalence with which adolescents and young adults think about their obligations to their country. Clearly an accurate understanding of young people's willingness to participate in a program of voluntary national service would be most helpful to the ongoing debate. Young people's support and enthusiasm are the keys to successfully carrying out such a program. While there have been a series of surveys and polls about youth's views on national service, the findings are by no means conclusive. Some indicate that a majority of teenagers are interested in volunteering for such a program; other surveys show less than 15 percent would be willing to serve. Some surveys indicate that an equal number would opt for military as for civilian service; others show that more than 90 percent would choose civilian service. Some polls indicate that most young people have a strong opinion

on national service; other studies indicate that young people are very confused even about the meaning of national service.

Since the "hard" data on youth's views on a program of national service
are somewhat contradictory, it is useful first to look broadly at their ideas
about service to society and their sense of social responsibility. Having a
picture of the gestalt in which young people perceive their civic obligations
will perhaps make their specific opinions about national service more under-
standable. This chapter looks first at the general perceptions young people
have about social justice, community service, and civic obligations. Next,
opinions about the concept of national service are explored. Finally, potential national service volunteers are discussed along with the conditions under
which they might serve.

YOUTH PERCEPTIONS OF CIVIC
AND SOCIAL RESPONSIBILITIES

Decreasing Connection to Community and Society

As a way to channel youths' altruism and idealism, national service may be
an idea whose time has come and *gone*. The more politically and socially
active young people of the late 1960s and early 1970s seemed readier to offer
their time and energy toward solving community problems. Adolescents and
young adults of the 1980s—more career-oriented, more cynical, more
detached—seem to care less about social inequities. A 1981 study by the
National Center for Education Statistics indicated a sharp decline in the
percentage of high school seniors concerned about "working to correct social and economic inequalities." In 1972, 27 percent of students surveyed
thought it was important or very important; by 1980, that percentage had
declined to 13 percent.[1]

This trend away from a concern about social issues and responsibilities is
also evident in a series of studies of college students reviewed by Edward
Wynne.[2] While none of these studies specifically asked about the young
person's commitment to doing something about social problems, they did
ask about some of the underlying attitudes that impinge on this commitment. What these studies reveal is that the trend toward self-interest has been
slowly increasing for more than 25 years and is not just a recent phenomenon.
Between 1948 and 1968, freshman classes at Haverford College in Philadelphia took the Minnesota Multiphasic Inventory (MMPI). The longitudinal
data revealed that successive classes of students became less sympathetic to
cooperative and group activities. More and more, they expressed attitudes
reflecting withdrawal from contact or cooperation with others.[3]

Attitude tests measuring similar issues were administered to students at Dartmouth College in 1952 and 1968 and at the University of Michigan in 1952 and 1969. One of the statements to which students responded was "human nature is fundamentally cooperative." Agreement declined from 66 to 51 percent at Dartmouth and from 70 to 55 percent at Michigan. Students were also asked to identify the private and public institutions, e.g., school, church, family, to which they felt related. The number and intensity of these identifications declined 9 percent at Dartmouth and 20 percent at Michigan over the 16-year period. Apparently, students felt less related to and part of basic social institutions over this period of time and have become increasingly alienated.[4]

Finally, Yankelovich's surveys of college students in 1969 and 1973 showed similar trends toward increasing self-concern and away from concern with others. For example, the importance of "privacy" increased from 61 percent in 1969 to 71 percent in 1973. On the other hand, a value that stresses the individual's obligation to the society, "patriotism," declined from 35 percent in 1969 to 19 percent in 1973.[5] From this series of studies, Wynne concludes that young people have become increasingly individualistic, withdrawn, and alienated; and that they expect more and more from society but are simultaneously less and less willing to participate.

A 1979 study of high school students in Minnesota provides some support for these older data which show a decline in social obligation and responsibility.[6] In response to the following question, "What do teenagers believe they owe their community and country," the majority (53 percent) said "nothing." While most did not elaborate, beyond saying they owed their country "not much," or "not a damn thing," others offered explanations. Some argued that, since they had not received many services nor been allowed to be involved in decision making, they were justified in offering little in return:

What has this country ever done for us? They take our money and just use it for stupid things.

I don't owe anything to the country when it's so bad. I think I owe something to my mom and dad, but that's all. We pay enough taxes and think the country owes us.

The government does not listen to us and they do as they please.

Some argued that, because they were still young, they should be exempt from any form of civic responsibility:

Teens don't think they owe anyone anything. At this point in our lives, we care about what is for *us*. Maybe later, the outlook may change and as adults we may feel that we should give support so that the community can remain strong.

We don't owe this country anything. If anything, they owe us! They're screwing up the world for us, who will have to live in it.

We believe we don't really owe our country much; we're more on our own.

This rejection of civic and social obligations was not the only response, however. Three other themes emerged. The next most frequent response (28 percent) was that young people should have a certain set of attitudes about their country, i.e., a good citizen was characterized as being loyal, patriotic, respectful, faithful, supportive, involved, and concerned. A relatively small number of students (9 percent) said that youths should actively help create a better society, with the emphasis on tangible contribution in contrast to merely having the proper beliefs and attitudes. For example, one group of high school students made comments such as these:

Teenagers should help the community in times of hardship such as sandbagging during a flood.

Teens could contribute new ideas and opinions which help shape the country.

It is the responsibility of teenagers to keep improving the community—taking care of the environment, lending a hand to community services, get involved in parks, vote, get to meetings like the city council, church groups should get together and pick up garbage.

Finally, about 10 percent of the respondents used this general question on civic responsibilities to voice their opinions about whether young people should fight or die for their country. Those who talked about these issues were generally opposed to a peacetime draft and were not willing to die for their country. Some typical responses include:

I know I owe it something, but not my life.

Some of us feel we owe our country something, but not serving in the army.

Things have changed. A long time ago, guys thought they had to go into the army. I don't think they care so much any more about their country.

Making a Difference

While the studies cited above reveal a decreasing sense of connection to social institutions and a movement toward self-concern, at the same time there is another trend toward young people viewing themselves as competent and capable of making a difference. The Haverford studies found that, between 1948 and 1969, the proportion of students who "thought they could work great benefit to the world if given a chance" rose from 40 to 66 percent while the proportion of entering freshmen who thought they knew more than experts rose from 20 to 38 percent.[7] More recent data suggest that this trend has continued. In a study of teachers' views on changes in children and adolescents over the past two decades, teachers reported that the young were more assertive and outspoken. Teachers described children and youth as more expressive, more sure of themselves, more willing to challenge authority, more likely to openly express dislike of school, more at ease with adults, and less fearful of adult authorities.[8] This belief in themselves is reflected in the Minnesota Youth Poll on National Service and the Draft, in which respondents were asked what they could do for their community and country. They were able to generate long lists of problems on which they could work, ranging from solving world hunger to reducing school vandalism. Some of the respondents expansively asserted that young people could solve any problem:

> Basically, teenagers can do a lot about quite a few things—really, we could do something about almost any problem.

> If there's a problem, we'll solve it. We are restricted as teenagers, but we are also lazy.

The most common target of this youthful energy was problems and concerns of their peers and younger children, e.g., drugs and alcohol abuse, delinquency, learning disabilities, etc. The theme of self-interest is revealed again in the kinds of community problems identified. Some argued that the problems of teenagers came first:

> I don't want to sound mean and cruel, but I think we should take care of our own [teenagers'] problems first.

> First teens must be able to take care of themselves, *then* others.

Others argued that they would have more knowledge about and influence with people their own age and, therefore, they would be more successful working with age mates:

> We could bridge the gap between adults and young kids. When adults talk, sometimes it seems like preaching, where older kids like us are looked up to.

It is not surprising that young people prefer to work on the problems of adolescents and children. It is a function of their stage of development;

learning to relate to and be accepted by peers is a hallmark of adolescence. However, this is not the only reason. The very nature of the social structure makes it difficult for teenagers to have interest in anything outside themselves and their peer groups. In many respects, teenagers are isolated from the rest of society; they are expected to stay out of the way of adults; they are forced to observe but not participate in adult life. National service is one mechanism for reducing this isolation. As such, it is a program that envisions adolescence neither as a time zone in which the person acquires immunity from social responsibility, nor as a time when one is exempt from helping others or contributing to the general welfare. Rather, adolescence is viewed as a time when a person is rightfully expected to contribute to the betterment of the society. To what extent do adolescents and young adults agree with this perspective? The following section reviews available data on youthful views about the value and appropriateness of national service.

SUPPORT FOR THE CONCEPT OF NATIONAL SERVICE

At the level of general approval or disapproval of the concept, a substantial majority of young people approve of a voluntary national service program. The Gallup Poll in 1979 asked teenagers (13-18 years old) and young adults (18-24 years old) if they "would favor or oppose a system of voluntary national service in which young people (both men and women) after high school or college would be given opportunities to serve for one year, either in the military forces or in nonmilitary work here or abroad, such as VISTA or the Peace Corps?" Gallup found that 71 percent of teenagers and 77 percent of young adults supported a program of voluntary national service.[9]

High school students in Minnesota, through the Minnesota Youth Poll, were also asked in 1979 their opinions of national service. They were given the following description:

> The government is considering starting a national youth service. It would involve 1 or 2 years of service or community work. You would be paid just enough to live on. The kind of work might be working in hospitals and schools, cleaning up slums, building nature trails, working with the poor and the elderly, helping in disasters like tornadoes and floods, helping other nations like the Peace Corps. What do you think of this program?[10]

This description differed from the Gallup Poll question in several ways. It asked youths' views on nonmilitary service only and it did not state whether it was a mandatory or voluntary program. The initial reaction to this question was frequently positive. Many said it sounded "neat" or "great," but these positive reactions were often followed by qualifiers. Often, it was thought to be a good program if conditions such as the following were met:

a) if it were voluntary; b) if it were for a shorter period of time; c) if it paid more; or d) if recruits for the service were drawn primarily from special populations such as the poor, the delinquent, and the unemployed. The low pay and the fear of the program being mandatory were of strongest concern:

> If it didn't pay more, there wouldn't be enough teenagers willing to go in it.

> If it were mandatory, it would be too much like communism or socialism. It should be up to each person to decide to join.

While the majority of Youth Poll respondents expressed qualified approval of a program of national service, there were some who totally rejected the concept. Opposition was expressed in objections such as the following:

> It's a step into socialism—having government-funded work.

> No one likes it. Teenagers believe that they could make their lives more worthwhile if they worked themselves.

> Just enough to live on—forget it. We don't want just bare subsistence.

In another study conducted in North Carolina, approximately 400 young people, ages 14 to 19, representing a cross section of young people in the state, were asked their views on national service. However, the general question implied a mandatory program. Specifically they were asked: "Should everyone before age 25 give some kind of national service to their country, either nonmilitary like the Peace Corps or VISTA, or in the military?" Only 28 percent supported this idea, while 45 percent disapproved and 25 percent were not sure.[11]

Voluntary vs. Mandatory Service

From these data, it appears that the acceptability of national service to young people depends to a large extent on its being a voluntary program. Two of the studies cited above had specific questions on whether national service should be voluntary or mandatory. The North Carolina study found an overwhelming majority supported a voluntary program: 91 percent of females and 81 percent of males wanted a voluntary program. Slightly more black males favored compulsory service, but the overwhelming majority supported voluntary service.[12] The Minnesota Youth Poll found similar results with 90 percent favoring voluntary national service. Objections to a mandatory program can be placed into four major categories: it is inconsistent with a democratic society; reluctant volunteers sullenly giving "service" would negate the positive aspects of the program; young people have different abilities and needs and such a program would be inappropriate for some; and adolescents are particularly resistant to compulsory duties.[13] The following are illustrative comments:

> I don't think a democracy like the U.S. should force people into things like that.

> People won't do a good job if they are forced to do this.

> It shouldn't be compulsory because people have different goals set for themselves and they shouldn't be made to participate in an organization that might not benefit them for what they want to be.

> People at that age don't want to be told what to do. They want choices.

Gallup polls have also found less support for mandatory programs. However, young adults (18-24 years old) have been more favorable to required service than were the teenagers surveyed in North Carolina or Minnesota. In 1979, Gallup found 42 percent of young adults in favor of compulsory service for men, and 29 in favor of compulsory service for women.[14] In contrast, only about 10 percent of the teenagers surveyed in Minnesota and North Carolina favored mandatory service.

Moreover, because Gallup has asked questions about national service periodically over the past decade, it is possible to look at changes in support for national service over time. In 1971, 61 percent of 18-20 year olds favored mandatory service for young men. Since 1973, the year the draft ended, there has been a decline in support for a mandatory service. In 1973, 51 percent of 18-24 year olds favored mandatory service but by 1979, only 42 percent were in favor. On the other hand, support for *voluntary* service has increased among the same samples of young adults.[15]

WHO WOULD JOIN NATIONAL SERVICE?

A voluntary national service is the model that young people overwhelmingly support. Supposing that the program would be voluntary, how many young people and which ones would be likely to sign up?

Gallup surveyed both teenagers and young adults, asking them, "Do you think you, yourself, would be interested in volunteering for national service or not?" Overall, 22 percent of 13-18 year olds said they would definitely be interested; 30 percent said they might be interested; 41 percent said they would not be interested; and 7 percent were unsure (see table 14.1). Among teenagers, males definitely were more interested than females (24 percent vs. 19 percent). Nonwhites were almost twice as likely to be definitely interested than were whites (37 percent vs. 19 percent). Young people with blue-collar

Table 14.1. Gallup Poll of 13-18 Year Olds on Support for National Service and Interests in Volunteering

Support for Concept of Voluntary National Service Program

	% Favor	% Oppose	% No Opinion
National	71	20	9
Boys	74	18	8
Girls	69	22	9
Whites	72	19	9
Nonwhites	65	25	10
White-collar household	73	19	8
Blue-collar household	72	20	8
East	76	14	10
Midwest	72	22	6
South	69	21	10
West	67	28	10

Interested in Volunteering?

	% Yes, Definitely	% Yes, Might Be	% No	% Not Sure
National	22	30	41	7
Boys	24	32	37	7
Girls	19	29	46	6
Whites	19	31	42	8
Nonwhites	37	25	36	2
White-collar household	19	30	45	6
Blue-collar household	25	30	39	6
East	23	32	40	5
Midwest	21	30	42	7
South	23	33	38	6
West	17	24	50	9

Source: George Gallup, "Who's for National Service?" in *National Youth Service: What's at Stake?* Report of a Conference sponsored by the Committee for the Study of National Service (Washington: The Potomac Institute, 1980), pp. 15-22.

occupational backgrounds were more interested than were those whose parents had white-collar occupations. Finally, teenagers living in the East, Midwest, and South were slightly more likely to join than were those in the West (about 23 percent vs. 17 percent).

Young adults (18-24 year olds) were substantially less interested in joining national service than were teenagers. Overall, 15 percent reported that they definitely were interested; 20 percent said they might be interested; 57 percent were not interested; and 8 percent had no opinion (see table 14.2). Young men expressed more definite interest than young women (20 percent vs. 12 percent).

Table 14.2.   Gallup Poll of 18-24 Year Olds on Support for National Service and Interest in Volunteering

Support for Concept of Voluntary National Service Program

	% Favor	% Oppose	% No Opinion
National	77	14	9
Men	80	16	6
Women	74	13	13

Interested in Volunteering?

	% Yes, Definitely	% Yes, Might Be	% No	% No Opinion
National	15	20	57	8
Men	20	26	47	7
Women	12	15	64	9

Source: George Gallup, "Who's for National Service?" in *National Youth Service: What's at Stake?* Report of a Conference sponsored by the Committee for the Study of National Service (Washington: The Potomac Institute, 1980), pp. 15-22.

Gallup found far more enthusiasm for joining national service among adolescents than did the study of Minnesota students.[16] The data from the Minnesota Youth Poll were analyzed by region, and it was found that approximately 20 percent of rural young people would consider joining, 15 percent of those from the suburbs, 12 percent of urban respondents, and 5 percent of inner city young people.[17]

Two major reasons were offered by the Minnesota high school students who wished to join national service. By far the most frequent was to gain personal benefits, followed by more altruistic motives such as a wish to help others and improve their community. Young people saw the benefit for themselves primarily in terms of social and psychological development, including taking on new responsibilities, developing career and job skills, and seeing a wider slice of life. Some of the comments included:

It would be good because teenagers can get the experience early they need later in life.

It would give the young a chance to learn about other cultures, others' problems while helping out the world. Force you to accept more responsibility.

It would give kids their first job experience.

Representative comments from those who saw national service as a way to act on their altruistic impulses included:

Because if it would help this messed-up world, for sure we would.

We believe in helping others. It could help make America pretty.

The most typical reasons young people cited for deciding not to join were
that they could secure a better-paying job and that national service would be
a detour from their future plans. Suburban students were particularly concerned about interrupting their post high school educational plans. An image emerged of young people viewing life's possibilities as a race track, and
joining the national service would be an annoying detour from the race:

It is only a temporary job but it is a detour from doing what you really want to
do.

Who wants to waste two years? It's not in my plans for the future.

There is some evidence, though it is very limited, that national service would
have more appeal to the "best and the brightest." Seventy-five student leaders from the Midwest were asked the same questions used in the Minnesota
Youth Poll.[18] These students, selected by their school principals and teachers,
had evidenced outstanding leadership skills in their schools and communities. Two students per school were selected from Omaha, St. Louis, Kansas
City, and Indianapolis. They were invited to attend an intensive summer
workshop. The majority (54 percent) said they would volunteer for national
service; 42 percent said they would not; and 4 percent were unsure. As with
the Minnesota young people, the major reasons for joining were to improve
their community and country and to gain experience and knowledge for their
personal development. The reasons for not joining were similar to those of
suburban young people in the Minnesota study. Many of those who would
not volunteer seemed already to have formed clear educational and career
plans. They were concerned that these would be interrupted and disrupted
by a year or two of service:

I have a certain thing to do and there is no point in wasting a whole year of
school.

A related objection was that national service was more appropriate for other
youth, with less potential than the respondents:

I have higher goals than that.

It's OK for a dummy, but not for me.

Similarly, in a 1980 survey of 70 youth leaders from Minnesota, the overwhelming majority stated that they would participate; 76 percent said they

would choose civilian service; 14 percent would select military service; and only 10 percent would opt not to serve at all.[19] This survey, however, was taken at the end of eight hours of speeches and discussion about national service. Two factors are probably responsible for the extremely positive reaction. First, youth leaders feel a heightened obligation to serve their country. Second, when young people have an opportunity thoroughly to explore this topic, a fuller understanding leads them to greater support for national service.

The Civilian vs. Military Option

In several of the studies of national service, young people were asked about their preference for civilian vs. military service. Gallup found that of all those in 1979 who were interested in volunteering (the categories of definitely interested and might be interested were combined), an equal proportion of 13 to 18 year olds would choose military as would choose civilian service. However, when the data were broken down by sex, race, and area of residence, large differences were revealed. Males were twice as likely to choose military service. Teenagers from blue-collar families and nonwhite teenagers were far more likely to choose military service over nonmilitary service.

Among 18 to 24 year olds, of those who were interested in joining national service in 1979, young adults were twice as likely to opt for nonmilitary over military service. Young men were only slightly more likely to choose military service than were young women. In contrast to the teenagers in the Gallup Poll, who were equally as likely to choose military as nonmilitary service, the young adults—both men and women—consistently chose civilian service by a two to one margin.[20]

The North Carolina and Minnesota studies indicated that teenagers favored civilian over military service by an even greater margin than did the Gallup Poll. The North Carolina study (see table 14.3) indicated that females overwhelmingly chose nonmilitary service over military (46 percent vs. 2

Table 14.3. Service Options Chosen by North Carolina Teens

	Nothing	Military	Non-Military Overseas	Non-Military in State	Not Sure
Question: If national service for those under 25 was not compulsory, but opportunities existed for service, which would you do?					
Males	14	20	7	18	26
Females	11	2	19	27	20

Source: Hope Williams and John Lawrence, "North Carolina" in *National Youth Service: What's at Stake?* Report of a Conference sponsored by the Committee for the Study of National Service (Washington: The Potomac Institute, 1980), pp. 66-69.

percent). Males were slightly more likely to choose nonmilitary service, 25 percent to 20 percent for the military. It is worthwhile to note, however, that nearly one-fourth of all respondents were "unsure" of which to choose. These results suggest that national service is a confusing and ambiguous idea for many teenagers.[21]

The Minnesota Youth Poll found that high school students favored nonmilitary service over military service by a seven to one margin.[22] Sometimes the choice was viewed as the lesser of two evils, with civilian service chosen:

We'd still be alive. Mosquito bites don't hurt as much as bullets.

Because you wouldn't lose your life. And if you did, you'd know what it was for. In wars, you never really know why.

More often, the national youth service program was seen as a positive alternative with respondents strongly preferring the opportunity to help others, rather than fight them:

Instead of killing people, you're helping people.

I'm more interested in that kind of work, one-to-one, feel as if you're doing a lot more, working for peace still.

A number of youth based their choice of national service on pacifist beliefs:

People can solve problems without physical and mental harm to others. Don't believe countries should fight each other. Don't believe people should kill other people.

We are firmly against war and all related aspects—would refuse to join military.

Of the small percentage of respondents who would choose military service over national service, the reasons given were "better benefits" and "to defend the country."

Gallup has asked questions about preferences for civilian and military service over the past decade; these data are available for young adults but not for teenagers. The proportion of young men preferring civilian over military service was the same in 1972 as 1979, as shown in table 14.4. There was a substantial increase in 1976 for military service, but this increase disappeared by 1979. The proportion of young women preferring nonmilitary service over military service remained the same from 1976 to 1979, as shown in table 14.5.

Table 14.4 Young Men's Preferences for Military and Nonmilitary Service in 1972, 1976 and 1979

	Military	Nonmilitary	No Opinion
1972	32	64	4
1976	41	50	9
1979	31	60	9

Source: George Gallup, *The Gallup Poll: Public Opinion 1972-77* (Wilmington, Delaware: Scholarly Resources, Inc., 1978); and George Gallup, *The Gallup Poll: Public Opinion 1979* (Wilmington, Delaware: Scholarly Resources, Inc., 1979).

National Service as an Alternative to the Senior Year

The data indicate that most young people prefer civilian service, and that avoiding the military might serve as an incentive for them to enter national service. We wondered if there were other incentives that could also encourage youth to participate. One option that was explored in the Minnesota Youth Poll was whether teenagers would see joining national service as a viable alternative to the senior year of high school. The following question was posed:

> Some people have suggested that joining a national youth service program could be an alternative to the senior year of high school. You would receive your credits and diploma by enrolling in a national youth service program. Under these circumstances, would you join this program?[23]

Looking at the responses by area of residence, students in the inner city would be the most likely to join if it were an alternative to the senior year, urban were next, followed by rural, with suburban students being the least likely to join.

Table 14.5 Young Women's Preferences for Military and Nonmilitary Service in 1976 and 1979

	Military	Nonmilitary	No Opinion
1976	18	72	10
1979	19	73	8

Source: George Gallup, *The Gallup Poll: Public Opinion 1972-77* (Wilmington, Delaware: Scholarly Resources, Inc., 1978); and George Gallup, *The Gallup Poll: Public Opinion 1979* (Wilmington, Delaware: Scholarly Resources, Inc., 1979).

While some students seemed a little suspicious of the plan ("it sounds too good to be true" or "it seems like a bribe"), they did see some clear benefits. Joining the national service, first and foremost, would allow them to get away from school. Moreover, some thought they would learn more practical and useful information and skills, and would be paid for going to school—a very attractive offer:

We've been in school for 13 years and we could use a break. The average high school student would do anything to get out of a year of school.

You can find out what the world is really like and not looking through a closed window. You'd learn a lot more about life, not just classroom stuff you wouldn't use again. It would be a great education.

You'd get credits and money at the same time. Work outdoors and enjoy yourself more than being kept to a schedule.

The main objections to giving up the senior year of high school were: (1) they would be deprived of valuable academic learning; and (2) they would miss the "fun"—friends, activities, and sports—of high school life:

You wouldn't be able to take courses you need for a job or college.

The senior year is too much fun. It's the best of all. I don't want to end up in the boonies. We'd miss all the parties.

One group summed up the relative benefits of the senior year of high school vs. the national service by arguing that school provides a particular kind of academic information while the national service would contribute to social and psychological maturity:

You wouldn't learn as much in the national service program as you would in school, but you might grow up faster mentally.

INCENTIVES FOR PARTICIPATION

The Minnesota Youth Poll results indicated that students thought the benefits from participating in national service should be similar to those for serving in the armed forces. These benefits included educational incentives such as lower tuition and scholarships for post high school education, job preference and placement, retirement benefits, medical and health care, and a cash bonus upon completion of service. Another theme, though much less frequently expressed, was that there should be no material benefits at all—

the intrinsic reward of helping people was sufficient. Others suggested that another form of nonmaterial benefits such as certificates of service, references, and "commendations from the President" would be desirable.[24]

SERVICE PREFERENCES

The National Service Secretariat in 1971 declared that the *"raison d'etre* of a national volunteer service is the need society has for the service of youth. Main areas are energy conservation, tutoring, health and mental health, and various kinds of community and family service. By serving in these fields, young people can serve society and at the same time gain work experience and connections to future jobs."[25] Several studies have asked young people to which community problems they prefer to devote their energy.

Gallup, in 1979, asked young adults who had already said they would volunteer for nonmilitary work in the United States what areas they would find most interesting. The rank order is shown in table 14.6. It is interesting to note that in several areas, males prefer "men's work," i.e., outdoor and construction work, while females prefer "women's work," i.e., working with children in day care centers, and other nurturing roles in hospitals and with the elderly.

In the 1980 conference of Minnesota student leaders, conservation, energy, and the environment sparked the greatest interest.[26] The students suggested

Table 14.6. Preferences for Nonmilitary Service Jobs Among Young Adults (18-24 Years of Age)

	% National	% Men	% Women
Conservation work in national forests and parks	9	16	3
Tutoring of low achieving students in school	7	9	6
Day care for young children	3	0	3
Assistance for the elderly	2	2	3
Hospital work	2	1	3
Help in floods and national disasters	2	2	1
Repairing and painting run-down house	2	2	0
	27*		

* This percentage represents the total proportion of young adults who said they would be interested in nonmilitary service.
Source: George Gallup, *The Gallup Poll: Public Opinion 1979* (Wilmington, Delaware: Scholarly Resources, Inc., 1979), p. 156.

that, if they became involved in the energy issue during their stint in national service, their major focus should be on public education about energy conservation and "living with less." They argued that, while specific programs such as weatherization and insulation of houses are important, they are merely stop-gap efforts without more basic changes in people's attitudes about conservation.

Education of children and adolescents was the area of second highest interest. Conference participants thought that their major contribution would be to increase individualized attention for the academic and personal needs of children and teenagers. They said they could provide a model for younger children to reinforce the notion that the purpose of school is learning, and they could strengthen children's self-concept by identifying individual talents and providing some ways for them to demonstrate competence.

Working with elderly persons was another strong interest area. The student leaders suggested that the primary emphasis of this work would be to become personally involved with and develop caring, empathetic relationships with older persons. The students also thought that their approach ought to be working *with* the elderly, not providing services *for* them. Specifically, they said they could take on the following activities—driving, escorting, friendly visiting, doing home maintenance chores, staffing recreational programs, and preparing directories of services for the elderly. These suggestions from high school students about what they could actually do in their communities indicate that there is a reservoir of talent and ideas among the young.

CONCLUSION

Young people's views of their civic and social obligations emerge as multifaceted and multidimensional. Simple characterizations of this age group as "idealistic" or "cynical" or "apathetic" or "altruistic" must be abandoned altogether or recombined into a more complex perspective. Below are some tentative generalizations and conclusions about youths' perspectives on social responsibility.

First, many youths believe that they are capable of *doing* something about community and national problems. They are idealistic in the sense that they strongly believe that the young have some special talents and competences to ameliorate social problems. At the same time, some appear to be almost immobilized and unable to participate in public affairs because of feelings of powerlessness or their own self-interest.

The theme of self-interest looms large. For example, young people tend to see the value and purpose of service to their country primarily in personal terms—tangible material benefits such as wages, skills gained, job placement and preference, travel, and the like. The social value of community service in terms of improvement of the quality of life or the solution of pressing human problems is mentioned far less often. This, however, may be a function of young people's stage of development; self-interest, egocentrism, and the quest for a personal identity are hallmarks of adolescence. Moreover, teenagers may be simply following their adult models, who in the 1970s appear to have been more self-absorbed and narcissistic.

Another characteristic of adolescence, the wish to be independent and in control of one's life, looms large in these discussions. The vehement opposition to any form of mandatory service—military or nonmilitary—is a profoundly important theme. Both the strength of the antidraft sentiment and the resistance to being controlled and regimented by the government should be noted by policymakers.

While a program of voluntary community service should help to reduce the barriers between young people and the larger society and allow young people to become genuine contributors, the participation of large numbers of youth in such a program would be hampered by several factors. First, it may be too late by the end of high school for young people to catch the "spirit of service." By then, many are too cynical, too discouraged, and too anxious to get on with their lives to give a year or two of service to their country. Making national service an alternative to the senior year of high school as well as encouraging youth participation through schools and youth groups during childhood and early adolescence may be necessary to ensure that substantial numbers of young people are "ready" for national service.

Second, the whole issue of national service is clouded and confused by the possible revival of the draft. It is very difficult for young people to consider the possibility of voluntary community service apart from military service. This confusion is obvious in several of the studies described above. Some students, even after a full hour of discussion, never understand the difference between military and nonmilitary service. Moreover, strong antidraft and antiwar feelings seem to promote cynicism and suspicion about the government's motives in promoting national service. For example, it is seen by some as the "back door" to reinstating conscription.

Given these findings—the confusion about what national service is, the strong desire by youths to have control over their lives, the wish to participate and "make a difference" in their communities, the suspicions about the government's motives—my major conclusion and recommendation is that young people around the country be encouraged to discuss and debate these issues. Young people should be given all available information about the options and proposals currently under discussion. Only through such a process of public debate by young people, both among themselves and with adults, can a just and democratic decision be reached about service to the country.

NOTES

1. U.S. Department of Education, *The High School and Beyond*, Preliminary Report, cited in *The New York Times* (March 29, 1981).

2. Edward Wynne, "Facts About the Character of Young Americans," *Character* 1, no. 1 (1979): 1-7.

3. Douglas Heath, *Growing Up in College* (San Francisco: Jossey-Bass, 1968), p. 63.

4. Dean R. Hogue, "College Student Values," *Sociology of Education* 44 (1970): 170–79.

5. Daniel Yankelovich, *The New Morality: A Profile of American Youth in the 70s* (New York: McGraw-Hill, 1974), pp. 14-15.

6. Diane Hedin, Janis Arneson, Michael Resnick, and Howard Wolfe, *Minnesota Youth Poll: Youth's View on National Service and the Military Draft*, Misc. Report no. 158 (St. Paul: Agricultural Experiment Station, University of Minnesota, 1980), pp. 6-7.

7. Cited by Heath, *Growing Up in College*, p. 63.

8. Diane Hedin and Dan Conrad, "Changes in Children and Youth Over Two Decades: The Perception of Teachers," *Phi Delta Kappan* 61, no. 10 (1980): 702-03.

9. George Gallup, *The Gallup Poll: Public Opinion 1979* (Wilmington, Delaware: Scholarly Resources, Inc. 1979), pp. 153-57; and George Gallup, "Who's for National Service?" in *National Youth Service: What's at Stake?* Report of a conference sponsored by the Committee for the Study of National Service (Washington: Potomac Institute, 1980), pp. 15-22.

10. Hedin et al., *Minnesota Youth Poll*, pp. 9-11.

11. Hope Williams and John Lawrence, "North Carolina," in *National Youth Service: What's at Stake?*, pp. 66-69.

12. Ibid., p. 67.

13. Hedin et al., *Minnesota Youth Poll*, p. 13.

14. Gallup, *The Gallup Poll: Public Opinion 1979*, p. 154.

15. Gallup, *The Gallup Poll: Public Opinion 1972-77* (Wilmington, Delaware: Scholarly Resources, Inc., 1978).

16. The reasons for the differences between Gallup and the Minnesota Youth Poll data probably lie in the methods used to gather information. The Gallup Poll is a telephone survey, in which individuals are interviewed by professional interviewers. The Minnesota Youth Poll uses a group discussion method, in which teenagers sit in small, self-selected groups of four to seven individuals, without an adult present, and talk about an issue in depth. One member of the group acts as both a discussion leader and recorder. There is the possibility of bias in both methods. In survey research, such as in the Gallup Poll, the respondent is confronted with a question to which he is expected to have an opinion. It may be that he has never thought about the issue before, but still feels obliged to offer an opinion. A sense of pressure to respond may account for the very small proportion of youth having no opinion on whether to volunteer—a far smaller proportion, for example, than found in the paper and pencil survey done in North Carolina. There is also the possibility, particularly with adolescents, that they offer an answer which best fits the interviewer's notion of what is the right answer.

In the group discussion format, young people are influenced by one another. Responses might be influenced by what is considered to be socially acceptable to peers. However, these "public" as opposed to "private" ideas of teenagers have theoretical and practical value. Public statements probably furnish a realistic presentation of the adolescent's everyday world since the conditions under which young people's opinions are formulated, expressed, and acted upon often are in the peer group, not under conditions of anonymity and isolation. Hence, opinions expressed in the group discussion format may be a more accurate reflection of future behavior regarding national service than opinions given to an interviewer unknown to the young person.

17. Hedin et al., *Minnesota Youth Poll*, p. 10.

18. Diane Hedin, "Opinions on National Service by Youth Leaders," unpublished manuscript (University of Minnesota, 1980).

19. Diane Hedin and Joyce Walker, *Minnesota Youth Conference on National Service, Proceedings* (Center for Youth Development and Research, University of Minnesota, 1980).

20. Gallup, *The Gallup Poll: Public Opinion 1979*, p. 154.

21. Williams and Lawrence, "North Carolina," p. 66.

22. Hedin et al., *Minnesota Youth Poll*, pp. 14-15.

23. Ibid., pp. 11-12.

24. Ibid., p. 13.

25. National Service Secretariat, "Ten Point Statement on Voluntary National Service" (Washington: National Service Secretariat, originally issued in 1971, mimeographed).

26. Hedin and Walker, *Minnesota Youth Conference on National Service, Proceedings.*

Part V:
Conclusions

Chapter 15

National Service at Launch Point

Donald J. Eberly and Michael W. Sherraden

Our assumption in this final chapter is that we have progressed to some point in the future and National Service is about to get under way. We are imagining that, for whatever combination of reasons, the people of the United States have reached a consensus to proceed with a program called National Service. We say "consensus" because we do not believe National Service is a program that can be introduced against the will of young people, or the military establishment, or higher education, or business, or labor, or John Q. Citizen. Perhaps National Service was introduced following the report of the Tsongas-Panetta Presidential Commission on National Service and an extensive nationwide debate on the subject. Perhaps National Service was introduced at the same time the country decided it had to bring back the draft. Perhaps National Service came about more indirectly, with businesses, governments, and universities saying that they would give preference in employment or admission to persons who had completed at least one year in some form of civilian or military service. Whatever the reasons for its adoption, it is useful now to forecast the future course and impacts of National Service on the basis of the evidence presented in previous chapters of this book.

Even with a consensus favoring National Service, there are some skeptics and dissenters. They are attacking National Service from many directions. Some contend it will further erode the U.S. military posture, while others perceive National Service as a step toward the eventual militarization of America. Some ask whether there is enough real work to be done and whether those completing their year in National Service will not simply return to the ranks of the unemployed. There are concerns in some quarters that National Service will have a problematic effect on the labor market—a large pool of relatively cheap labor might erode the present wage structure. Some suggest that National Service will eventually collapse from the weight and complexity of its bureaucracy. Others say that National Service will cost too much, and still others ask, "Who will join, anyway?"

Our answers to these and other questions are presented in two parts. First is the development stage of National Service, a period of three to five years during which National Service grows from zero to several hundred thousand, perhaps even a million young people. Second is the mature program period, an indefinite period when the design of National Service is well established and program size no longer changes markedly over the long term.

THE DEVELOPMENT STAGE

The rate of growth of National Service will be controlled by several factors. Congress will almost certainly impose a budgetary ceiling on National Service expenditures year by year. For example, Mark Hatfield, in his 1969 legislation, proposed ceilings of $150 million, $500 million, and $900 million during the first, second, and third years of the National Youth Service Foundation. Congress can give its strongest support to National Service not by giving it unlimited funds, but by funding National Service at its optimal rate of growth. We have suggested (chapter 7) that the highest feasible growth rate would be about 100,000 participants at the end of the first year, 300,000 at the end of the second year, and upwards of 1 million at the end of the third year.

Young people themselves will probably restrain the growth of National Service. Diane Hedin (chapter 14) remarks on the skepticism expressed by some teenagers toward the national service idea. As exciting as the Peace Corps was in its early days, less than one person in a thousand eligible for the Peace Corps actually applied to join it from 1961 to 1964. We expect there will be enough venturesome young people from all walks of life to launch National Service at the level of 100,000 enrollees, but we do not expect a stampede of applicants unless some kind of crisis erupts.

As National Service gets underway, the number of service positions will probably constitute the greatest constraint on its rate of growth. Eager National Service officials may be tempted to view the congressionally set limits as quotas and attempt to fill them to capacity. If they do so with make-work positions, it will be a great mistake and may destroy the program. It will be better to enroll only 20,000 participants in the first year, with each of them performing a needed service, than to enroll 100,000 with some of them doing useless tasks or, as has occurred in past youth programs, doing nothing and still collecting their pay.

As we noted in chapter 1, it will take time to translate community and national needs into actual positions. It will take time to recruit supervisors and to get work descriptions approved. It will take time to prepare prospective fellow workers to accept even one National Service participant. If the incoming director of National Service decides to adopt Eberly's administrative model (chapter 8), it will take time for nonprofit organizations and local governments to appropriate the money that will be required to obtain National Service enrollees. It will be time well spent. It will give National Service a solid foundation from which to grow and prosper.

We foresee a high rate of growth in the third year of National Service for three reasons. First, the first-year enrollees will be passing judgment on their National Service experience to their friends, relatives, classmates, and co-workers during the second year. This first-person word-of-mouth evidence is the best recruitment tool for just about every kind of endeavor. What works for employment and education will also work for National Service.

Second, Hedin tells us that "when young people have an opportunity to explore [national service], their fuller understanding leads them to greater support for it" (chapter 14). Even young people who do not encounter former National Service participants will be exposed to media reports on National Service. What once may have been dismissed as just another wild idea will become a reality, and many young people will find themselves giving National Service serious consideration during the second year, and then enrolling during the next year.

The third reason for the high rate of growth in the third year is that the full budget cycle for public and private organizations will be completed by the third year. During the first year of National Service, personnel in many organizations will submit budget requests for supervisory personnel and matching funds to their governing bodies. There will be discussions and hearings and delays; after a year or two, some requests will be granted; and what was a budget request in the first year of National Service will become a firm commitment by the third year.

A sharp definition of National Service activities will take place during the transition period. We expect the Board of the National Service Foundation to offer enrollment to all eligible members of any federal programs which qualify. As of 1981, these would include the Peace Corps, VISTA, and the Young Adult Conservation Corps. The Job Corps could qualify by incorporating a service component together with its training component and extending the length of enrollment to at least one year.

As new projects are submitted at the local and state levels, it will be obvious in most cases to local administrators whether to approve them for National Service. There will be some borderline cases, and these will make their way to the board for decision.

There will be problems. A local grantee may fail to consult with local labor unions and become the target of union wrath. Another, thinking that National Service is a jobs program like CETA, may try to control the assignments of National Service participants and wonder why so few applicants are entering the program.

In order to cope with the problems that arise, the administrators of National Service will require a lot of flexibility in the early years. Bureaucrats have a reputation, somewhat deserved, of trying to solve a single problem by writing several pages of regulations. This syndrome can be avoided by an alert administration and adequate flexibility for local responses to local needs and conditions.

THE MATURE PROGRAM

After National Service has reached its full size, it will enter what we might call the mature program stage. During this period, National Service will continue to develop programmatically but the number of participants will remain fairly steady. Successful approaches will be identified, supported, and disseminated. National Service will have begun to settle into the fabric of society. In the sociological sense, National Service will have become a social institution. At this stage, we envision the following program features.

Voluntariness

National Service will remain a voluntary program. Circumstances under which American young people would consent to be drafted for civilian service would be so compelling that most young people would volunteer for service anyway. This does not rule out certain mandatory features that may be associated with entry into National Service. Registration may be mandatory. The military draft may be reinstituted. But entry into civilian service will be voluntary.

Universality

Any young person who is willing to serve may join National Service. The socioeconomic profile of National Service participants will approximate that of the total youth population. A major function of the National Service headquarters staff will be to monitor local programs and investigate those whose enrollment profile appears to be distorted. They may find an innocent reason for it; if they find discrimination, however, corrective action will be necessary.

Size

The Gallup Poll data presented in table 14.1 indicate that 15 percent of 18 to 24 year olds would definitely be interested in joining a voluntary national service program, and another 20 percent might be interested. If all of the "Yeses" and half of the "Maybes" decide to join, that will be 25 percent, or about 1 million persons per year. This is in accord with our earlier estimates and appears to be the most reasonable figure for conditions prevailing in the period 1975 to 1980, which was a time of peace, high youth unemployment, and high rates of federal aid to higher education. A major change in any of these conditions could significantly increase or decrease enrollment in National Service.

Economic Impact

Of the various scenarios by which the nation might have arrived at National Service, the most likely one relates to the failure of the All-Volunteer Force (AVF). The AVF might have been seen as too incompetent for maintaining a strong military posture. The public might have changed its mind about the draft, and decided that U.S. military adventurism would be better deterred by an equitable draft than by a volunteer, almost mercenary, armed force. Certainly, there have been complaints about the cost of maintaining the AVF. In 1980, former Defense Secretary Melvin Laird estimated that several billion dollars a year will be needed to maintain an AVF, over and above the $3 billion a year incremental cost of the AVF from 1973 to 1977.[1] Perhaps the nation has now decided that the cost of the AVF is too high and has replaced the AVF with a relatively low-cost national service system patterned after McCloskey's bill (chapter 6), designed in part to save tax dollars.

In whatever form, there is also a possibility that National Service will be slightly inflationary in the short run. In the long run, however, National Service benefits will equal or exceed program costs (chapter 12) and thus exert no long-term inflationary pressure. The reason for the short-term inflationary pressure will be that expenditures for service projects will not always provide immediate returns. That is, the National Service impact on overall productivity will be, in part, delayed. Examples of delayed returns in productivity might include reforestation projects, which will pay off in 30 to 40 years; home insulation projects, which will pay off in three to five years; and rehabilitation work with disabled people, which will pay off over a lifetime of increased independence from government support and increased productivity. National Service cannot be adequately viewed as a short-term investment.

National Service will be strongly countercyclical. When the economy improves and jobs become plentiful and attractive, National Service enrollment will fall. When jobs become scarce, more young people will choose National Service.

Certainly, National Service will cause the youth unemployment rate to fall sharply, and the overall unemployment rate will also fall somewhat. A more serious question is what happens to participants after the year in National Service. Does the participant get a job, go on to further training or education, of fall into the ranks of the unemployed? We agree with Peter Edelman (chapter 9) that there is no simple answer to this question; it is an issue that must be closely monitored and carefully studied. We are confident, however, that a year in National Service will leave the great majority of participants significantly better off than if they had not entered. We suggest as a hypothesis that persons in National Service will be, on the average, significantly more advanced in terms of educational and employment opportunities than persons of corresponding backgrounds who did not enter National Service.

Service Rendered

The totality of service performed by National Service participants in any year will represent the common ground between what local and state and national groups say they want done, and what young people choose to do. We expect at any time that there will be about three times as many positions to fill as there will be young people seeking to fill them. As a result, young people will be able to exercise discretion in their choice of service, and the sum total of their individual decisions will define the profile of work accomplished. We predict that about 25 percent of the participants will choose conservation work; another 25 percent will work in the field of education; about 20 percent will provide personal and social services to the very young, the very old, and the handicapped; and the remainder will choose to work in such areas as health, housing, transportation, libraries, and recreation.

As noted above, we are confident that the value of services rendered by those in National Service will equal or exceed the cost to government of supporting them. It will be somewhere between the 1:1 return for the Young Adult Conservation Corps, with its relatively high expenditures for supplies and equipment, and the nearly 2:1 return of the Program for Local Service experiment in Seattle (chapter 12).

Education

William Ramsay (chapter 10) describes a severe educational problem posed by the introduction of National Service. National Service is coming into existence (assume sometime in the 1980s) at a time when college and university enrollments are already falling due to a decreasing youth population and less federal aid to higher education. The more rapid the introduction of National Service, the sharper will be the enrollment decline in institutions of higher education.

To address this problem, Ramsay, Hedin (chapter 14), and Moskos (chapter 11) suggest answers worthy of further study and testing. Ramsay recommends active participation by educational institutions, including the operation of National Service projects. Faculty and staff members who would otherwise be engaged in a teaching role would be challenged to examine community needs and to manage local National Service operations. In the process, these educators, some of whom will resist the idea, will discover that it is a learning experience for them as well as the young people.

Hedin alerts us to the possibility that 18 to 24 may be too late for many young people to enter National Service. She suggests serious consideration of National Service as an alternative to the senior year of high school. At a time when the idea of compulsory education is under attack and one student in four never graduates from high school, Hedin's suggestion is well worth testing. We encourage the administrator of National Service to use some of the 5 percent experimental fund to test this idea at several cooperating high schools.

Moskos, Ramsay, and others support some form of GI Bill for National Service. So do we. Not only is it logically sound as a proper reward to those who have contributed a period of service, it is also politically opportune because it comes at a time when federal aid to higher education is being curtailed.

Alleviation of Social Problems

National Service will have an impact on social problems in two ways. First, the entry of young people into National Service will greatly reduce social problems in which they might otherwise have become entangled. Much of the temptation to commit crimes will disappear as young people have steady work, an assured income, and a sense of being useful and productive. It is likely that both homicides and suicides among young people will decline. Also, youth unemployment will fall as unemployed young people enter National Service.

Second, National Service participants will affect those social problems which they choose to tackle. For example, some will fight illiteracy; some will engage in outreach programs to improve personal and public health conditions; some will work to alleviate drug and alcohol abuse.

The Issue of Social Planning

To those opposed to any form of social planning, we acknowledge that the National Service program will be a form of social planning or, as some might call it, social engineering. However, it will be social engineering by design, not by default. While the terms social planning and social engineering often carry negative connotations, a planned social program may be attractive when compared with the alternative. For example, who decided to create the twilight zone of uncertain status that Clark Kerr and his colleagues have called "compulsory youth"? What session of Congress passed the "compulsory youth unemployment program" under which at least 2 million young people were forced to be unemployed and looking for work during the

1970s? We do not believe that market mechanisms have a monopoly on wisdom, and we have no hesitancy in recommending a planned alternative to major social dysfunctions.

As National Service administrators ponder the question of social planning, we suggest they take as their guide Adlai Stevenson's view of Woodrow Wilson: "He taught us to distinguish between governmental action that takes over functions formerly discharged by individuals and governmental action that restores opportunity for individual action."[2] The appropriate role of National Service is the restoration of opportunity for individual action.

The Military Impact

Apart from making the armed forces more representative of the American people, and, as Charles Moskos argues (chapter 11), possibly making a return to the draft unnecessary, we see National Service as having a limited effect on the size and cost of the military. Since 1940, military requirements have been the first concern of the President and the Congress, and these requirements have been generously supplied. There will be little competition for tax dollars. When National Service reaches its plateau enrollment of 1 million persons, its budget will not exceed 5 percent of the Pentagon budget.

We expect National Service to increase the representativeness of the armed forces regardless of whether or not there is a formal linkage between the two. If there is a linkage, we are sure that Pentagon supporters will structure National Service in a way that encourages middle class and college-bound young people to spend some time in the military. If there is no linkage between the two, there is reason to believe that National Service, after a few years, will elevate the regard young people have for their country, and military enlistments by all socioeconomic classes will become more commonplace. As 16-year old Jennifer Boyd said in 1979, "How can we love a country we have not served in some way?"[3]

It is conceivable that National Service will obviate the need for an increase in the size of the armed forces, although this can never be determined by a controlled experiment. In the early years of the Depression, there was widespread unrest and talk of revolt. It is reasonable to wonder what turmoil might have ensued, and what additions to the armed forces would have been required, had not the nation enlisted 8 million young people in the CCC and the NYA. Clearly, these young people and the nation were better served by their productive civilian activities than they would have been with some of the 8 million drafted into the military to quell the revolt of the remainder of the 8 million. Just possibly, National Service will be the right thing for the nation and its young people in more ways than can be easily measured.

While it is not very likely that National Service will greatly affect the size and cost of the military, the military may, on the other hand, have a significant impact on National Service. For example, when Eberly first put his ideas about National Service on paper, he suggested that young men be given their choice of military or nonmilitary service only after they had been drafted. While that approach would have meant some testing of National Service since it was made at a time (1958) when the draft was in effect, it would have meant the collapse of National Service in 1973 when the draft ended. Also, it would have restricted civilian service to those young men who had been called for the draft. There would have been no universal opportunity to serve.

If the draft is restored without a National Service linkage, there would still be some impact on National Service through the operation of the alternative service program for conscientious objectors. Roger Landrum (chapter 5) has shown how differently programs for conscientious objectors may operate in two neighboring countries, France and West Germany. In the United States, the alternative service policy seems to shift with each war. In World War II, most conscientious objectors served in Civilian Public Service Camps operated by the Mennonites and other historic peace churches. In the Korean War and its aftermath, most conscientious objectors had to find their own jobs with public service agencies. In the Vietnam War, California Governor Ronald Reagan broke new ground by creating a state-funded, state-operated program specifically for conscientious objectors. It was called the California Ecology Corps and, with the assistance of an active placement bureau for conscientious objectors, over half of all persons performing alternative service either lived in California, went to California on their own, or were sent there by their draft boards. In 1981, the Selective Service System shifted gears again by promulgating its intent to seek federal funds to pay persons in alternative service.

While having great respect for the idea of conscientious objection, we believe that the alternative service requirement for objectors is a public policy position inferior to that of National Service. Alternative service is a compulsory program, not a voluntary one. The order assigning men to alternative service parallels the order assigning draftees to military service.

Also, the statutory method for becoming a conscientious objector imposes an extremely complex choice at an age when a young person's conscience is still very tender. The young person considering the CO claim must make a choice between taking a stand in opposition to war and the realization that, if his claim is successful, someone else will go into the armed forces in his place. It is a tough decision to make. The question posed by National Service is more straightforward, namely, "How do you think you can best serve your country?"

Finally, alternative service is dependent upon a program of military conscription. A high official of the West German alternative service program said in 1980 that it was providing such important services on such a large scale, especially to the elderly, that if West Germany were to drop conscription there would be a very strong demand for continuation of alternative service in some form. If the work done is that important, civilian service deserves a legal authority independent of conscription authority.

Administration and Funding

National Service has been designed in such a way that it will collapse if it fails to approach its promise. By requiring sponsors to put up cash and to provide in-service training and supervision, Eberly (chapter 8) expects sponsors to drop out if they do not get a satisfactory return on their investment. By limiting participation to those young people who volunteer for National Service, we can expect that young people will stop volunteering if the program doesn't work for them.

In some cases, federal funds will support National Service indirectly. This will happen when a school or library or other sponsor utilizes some kind of federal aid for its support of one or more National Service participants. If the block grants recommended by President Reagan become commonplace, they could become a source of support for National Service at the state and local levels. Block grants have a degree of flexibility not found in many categorical programs. The demise of the Program for Local Service (PLS) in Seattle, Washington offers a pertinent case study: ACTION Director Joseph Blatchford was removed from his position as a too liberal Republican soon after Nixon's 1972 reelection. His successor, Michael Balzano, was not sympathetic to the National Service idea and set in motion plans for the reduction in size and phasing out of Seattle's PLS. Meanwhile, the state of Washington became more and more enamored of PLS and both houses of the state legislature unanimously passed a youth service corps bill, modeled on PLS, in June 1977. The legislature directed the state to spend up to $3,500,000 of state-controlled CETA-funds on the youth service corps.[4] Alas, the funds were not ultimately controlled by the state. The U.S. Department of Labor overruled on the grounds that PLS was not targeted toward unemployed young people.

We are also concerned with the ways in which National Service money flows. If all National Service expenditures come from a single source, the program will become isolated from the society it is supposed to serve. However, if a significant share of the money flows through agencies committed to the services to be performed, National Service will be subject to a high degree of accountability. Whether participants do their conservation work with the Sierra Club or the National Park Service, when those organizations provide the supervision, training, supplies, and equipment, they will be satisfied with the work done by the young people or they will cease to be National Service sponsors.

THE DISTANT FUTURE

We have attempted to describe the likely appearance and impact of National Service during its first two stages, the development stage and the mature program stage. We recognize, however, that even a "mature" program does not continue unchanged forever. Change is constant. What then, will be the third stage, the distant future, for National Service? We perceive at least six distinct possibilities:

1. National Service may come to a sudden end, as a result of U.S. participation in war, as did the fostering of national service by Franklin D. Roosevelt in 1941 and by Lyndon B. Johnson in 1966.
2. National Service may die a rapid death as a result of bad management, corruption, or some other unpredictable cause. If this happens, the nation will be glad that it was designed in a way to self-destruct when no longer meeting its objectives.
3. National Service may move to an even higher plateau by growing to an enrollment of several million young people. This growth may result from the virtual exclusion of young people from the competitive labor market, from a gradual blurring of the lines between National Service and higher education, or possibly from the perception of National Service by young people as a rite of passage as important to them as getting a driver's license.
4. The National Service program may branch out to the 25 to 65 year old population in a way that fosters large-scale exchanges among different occupational groups. When Haverford College President and Federal Reserve Board member John Coleman went to work incognito as a garbage collector in the early 1970s, the experience generated newspaper articles and a book.[5] Given a combination of certain technical arrangements (e.g., health care, living quarters, pension plans) and individual perceptions of such radical departures as valued experiences, it may become possible to facilitate wholesale shifts among academicians, laborers, businessmen, technicians, and bureaucrats.
5. National Service may reach out even further to embrace senior citizens. Given their generally good health, their increasing share of the population, their effective lobbying efforts, and their genuine desire to continue to serve, Eberly has predicted that "a national senior service program, constructed from such present small programs as Foster Grandparents and Green Thumb, may well be in place before National Youth Service."[6]

6. National Service may become denationalized. It is clear from Irene Pinkau's (chapter 4) and Roger Landrum's (chapter 5) descriptions that a
   number of national service seeds have germinated under very different
   historical, political, economic, and social conditions. It is not very likely,
   however, that these seeds will somehow coalesce into a comprehensive,
   internationally sponsored program. Such a program, called the United
   Nations Volunteers (UNV), has been attempted. It was created about
   1970 and grew in 10 years to only 300 volunteers. Its size has been
   consciously restricted by a perception that, for the program to survive
   even on such a small scale, great political and bureaucratic caution in the
   recruitment and placement of volunteers must be exercised. Part of the
   problem with UNV has been its origins and administration in the UN
   itself, where diplomatic caution is so important. By contrast, a grassroots
   denationalized program could begin with the swap of, say, 500 members
   of the Nigerian National Youth Service Corps to teach Yoruba, Ibo, and
   Hausa in U.S. schools, while 500 members of the U.S. National Service
   who have learned and practiced automechanics go to Nigeria to teach
   automechanics in the vocational schools. In time, such bilateral swaps
   could evolve into multilateral exchanges and some kind of international
   body would be needed to coordinate such exchanges. Such a body would
   have its roots in the needs of the participating countries and in the interests of young people, and would exist only as long as it continued to serve
   a genuine purpose.

While it is interesting to think about future possibilities of National Service,
the more immediate question is: "How do we move toward National Service
from where we are today?" We have suggested a five-step approach in chapter 7. Other avenues are possible; perhaps they would prove to be more
effective.

CONCLUSION

We do say without equivocation that a vacuum exists in the relationship
between the nation and young people, and that something similar to what we
have called National Service is needed to fill that vacuum. Whatever it is
called, it is essential that the government take the first step by telling young
people that their help is needed, offering them dignified stipends and educational benefits, and asking them to step forward and lend a hand. It is
essential that young people perform needed services and that the public
recognizes that tax dollars are being spent productively. Only if participants
are engaged in genuinely productive work can they reap the benefits of the

service experience. Finally, recruitment must be truly universal, with either deliberate or accidental discrimination strictly prohibited.

To embark on a new course requires more than a simple analysis of the pros and cons, and a reckoning of the costs and benefits. To some extent, it also requires a leap of faith. A country that undertakes a national service compact with its young people will demonstrate faith in itself, faith in young people, and faith in the future.

NOTES

1. Melvin Laird, "It's Time for a Big Pay Raise," *The Washington Post* (March 10, 1980), p. A27.

2. Earl Latham, *The Philosophy and Policies of Woodrow Wilson* (Chicago: University of Chicago Press, 1958).

3. Jennifer Boyd, "The Draft: A Change in Priorities," Letter to the Editor, *The Washington Post* (March 16, 1979).

4. National Service Secretariat, "Washington State Creates Youth Service Corps," *National Service Newsletter* (September 1977), p. 2.

5. John Coleman, *Blue Collar Journal: A College President's Sabbatical* (Philadelphia: Lippincott, 1974).

6. Donald J. Eberly, "National Service: Alternative Strategies," *Armed Forces and Society* 3, no. 3 (May 1977): 448.

Annotated Bibliography

ACTION. "National Service, Action for Youth." *Synergist* 6, No. 3 (Winter 1978). Sam Brown, Donald J. Eberly, Dennis Gallagher, Evelyn Ganzglass, Layton Olson, and Robert Sexton cover a range of national service issues.

American Friends Service Committee. *In Place of War.* New York: Grossman, 1967. This book recommends nonviolence as the basis for national defense, together with voluntary national service.

Ball, Colin, and Ball, Mog. *Education for a Change.* Baltimore: Penguin Books, 1973. From a British perspective, the authors suggest a modernization of community service activities by students, and suggest how it might be done.

Bingham, Jonathan B. "Replacing the Draft." *The New Republic,* January 16, 1971. Bingham presents the case for the limited national service bill (HR 18025) which he introduced on June 10, 1970.

Black, Algernon. *The Young Citizens: The Story of the Encampment for Citizenship.* New York: Frederick Ungar, 1962. This book describes a voluntary service program started in 1940 to promote patriotism, leadership, service, and education. Trustees included Mary McLeod Bethune and Eleanor Roosevelt.

Botstein, Leon. "The Debate over the Draft: We Need a Fresh Approach." *The Chronicle of Higher Education,* September 2, 1980. A young college president argues in this article that mandatory national service "would demonstrate that America's leadership is capable of more than short-term political dexterity and astuteness. . . ."

Brown, B. Frank. *The Transition of Youth to Adulthood: A Bridge Too Long.* Boulder, Colorado: Westview Press, 1980. Several educators and youth experts analyze major youth issues and strongly recommend a national service program.

Carnegie Council on Policy Studies in Higher Education. *Giving Youth a Better Chance: Options for Education, Work, and Service.* San Francisco: Jossey-Bass, 1979. The Council, headed by Clark Kerr, recommends voluntary national youth service to combat a condition identified as "compulsory youth . . . , a twilight zone of uncertainty and ambiguity of status."

Commission on Voluntary Service and Action. *Invest Yourself.* 475 Riverside Drive, New York, New York. This annual publication lists openings for volunteers in hundreds of projects, both in the United States and overseas.

Committee for the Study of National Service. *Youth and the Needs of the Nation.* Washington: The Potomac Institute, 1979. Co-chaired by Harris Wofford and Jacqueline Grennan Wexler, this foundation-funded Commitee calls for the United States to move toward universal service by incentives but without compulsion.

Commitee for the Study of National Service. *National Youth Service: What's at Stake?* Washington: The Potomac Institute, 1980. This volume is the report of a 1979 national service conference sponsored by the Commitee. Included are addresses by Bernard Anderson, Sam Brown, Representative John Cavanaugh, Peter Edelman, George Gallup, Jr., Senator Paul Tsongas, Jacqueline G. Wexler, and Harris Wofford.

Control Systems Research, Inc. *The Program for Local Service: Summary Findings.* Seattle: Control Systems Research, 1973. This report is a summary description of the ACTION-sponsored Program for Local Service (PLS) in Seattle. As a major national service pilot project, PLS is found to be highly successful.

Crook, William H., and Ross, Thomas. *Warriors for the Poor: The Story of VISTA: Volunteers in Service to America.* Clifton, New Jersey: William Morrow, 1969. The origins and early years of VISTA are described in this book.

Dickson, Mora, ed. *Alec Dickson, A Chance to Serve.* London: Dennis Dobson, 1976. This is a
biographical account of the man who founded the British equivalent of the Peace Corps
(Voluntary Service Overseas) in 1958 and the British equivalent of VISTA (Community Service Volunteers) in 1962.

Eaton, Joseph W., and Chen, Michael. *Influencing the Youth Culture.* Beverly Hills, California:
Sage Publications, 1971. Several youth programs in Israel which, in combination, approximate
national service are described and analyzed.

Eberly, Donald J. *A Profile of National Service.* New York: Overseas Educational Service, 1966.
This publication is the report of the national service conference of May 7, 1966.

Eberly, Donald J., ed. *National Service: A Report of a Conference.* New York: Russell Sage
Foundation, 1968. This 600-page report contains commissioned papers by Eli Ginzberg,
Charles Benson, and others, and a series of discussions on national service at a conference
keynoted by Margaret Mead.

Eberly, Donald J. "Service Experience and Educational Growth," *Educational Record,* Spring
1968. This article reports on the first nationwide survey of service-learning programs and sets
forth an agenda for colleges to follow in establishing them.

Eberly, Donald J. "A Universal Youth Service." *Social Policy,* January/February 1977. Eberly
begins with a description of ACTION's Program for Local Service and goes on to suggest
essential elements for a nationwide youth program.

Eberly, Donald J. "National Service: Alternative Strategies." *Armed Forces and Society* 3, no. 3
(May 1977). Several features of national service are compared with military service, and the
author suggests a set of evaluation criteria for national service.

Eberly, Donald J. "A Call for National Service." *Voluntary Action Leadership,* Summer 1979.
This article presents a case for national service and reviews selected U.S. milestones related to
national service.

Edelman, Peter B., and Roysher, Martin. *Responding to Youth Unemployment: Towards a National
Program of Youth Initiatives.* New York: State Division for Youth, 1976. Edelman and Roysher
view youth unemployment as damaging to society and as a compelling interest of the state.

Etzioni, Amitai. *Toward Higher Education in an Active Society: Three Policy Guidelines.* New
York: Center for Policy Research, 1970. Etzioni's first policy guideline proposes a year of
national youth service and discusses its social, educational, and military consequences.

Gingerich, Melvin. *Service for Peace.* Abron, Pennsylvania: The Mennonite Central Committee,
1949. This is a detailed account of the Mennonite-sponsored Civilian Public Service Camps for
Conscientious Objectors during World War II.

Glick, Edward Bernard. *Peaceful Conflict: The Non-Military Use of the Military.* Harrisburg,
Pennsylvania: Stackpole Books, 1967. Viewing demobilization in the foreseeable future as not
feasible, Glick argues for assigning civilian tasks to military personnel as a constructive
alternative.

Hanning, Hugh. *The Peaceful Uses of Military Forces.* New York: Frederick A. Praeger, 1967.
Sponsored by the World Veterans Federation, Hanning gives examples of governmentally
sanctioned civilian activities by military service personnel in 16 countries.

Hedin, Diane; Arneson, Janis; Resnick, Michael; and Wolfe, Howard. *Minnesota Youth Poll:
Youth's View on National Service and the Military Draft,* Misc. Report No. 158. St. Paul:
Agricultural Experiment Station, University of Minnesota, 1980. Hedin and her colleagues
describe the views of Minnesota young people on national service and military conscription.

Human Environment Center. *Youth Conservation Jobs and Service—A New National Corps?*
Washington: Human Environment Center, 1981. This conference report examines the performance of the Youth Conservation Corps and Young Adult Conservation Corps. Sydney
Howe, speaking for the Center, concludes that "diffident and unorganized constituencies must
be informed, inspired, and convened in support of these programs."

Humphrey, Hubert H. "Plan to Save Trees, Land, and Boys." *Harper's Magazine* 218 (January 1959). Humphrey proposes a program very similar to the Civilian Conservation Corps of the 1930s.

Humphrey, Hubert. *S 3675: A Peace Corps.* A bill introduced in the U.S. Senate, June 15, 1960. In this original version of the Peace Corps, a three-year stint in the Peace Corps would have fulfilled peacetime military obligations except for Reserve requirements.

Isaacs, Harold R. *Emergent Americans—A Report on Crossroads Africa.* New York: John Day, 1961. This is a study of Crossroads Africa, a significant precursor of the Peace Corps, founded by the Rev. James Robinson to enable American young people to spend the summer on a service project in Africa.

James, William. "The Moral Equivalent of War." *International Conciliation*, no. 27 (February 1910). This seminal essay, first given as a lecture at Stanford University in 1906, is often cited as the psychological basis for the concept of national service.

Janowitz, Morris. "American Democracy and Military Service." *TransAction* 4, no. 4, (March 1967). Janowitz puts forth a national service proposal to reduce social injustices in military service.

Jordan, Vernon E., Jr. "Black Youth: The Endangered Generation." *Ebony,* August 1978. Jordan argues for structural changes that "go beyond inadequate piecemeal programs." He advocates a "National Youth Service, open to all, but with emphasis on aggressively recruiting young people from economically disadvantaged backgrounds."

Katz, Michael B. "Missing the Point: National Service and the Needs of Youth." *Social Policy* 10, no. 4 (January-February 1980). Katz argues that national service proponents are misguided idealists.

King, William R. *Achieving America's Goals: National Service or the All-Volunteer Armed Force.* Washington: U.S. Government Printing Office, 1977. In this report, prepared for the Senate Armed Services Committee, King finds national service an attractive alternative to the All-Volunteer Force.

Korten, David C., and Korton, Frances F. "The Impact of a National Service Experience Upon Its Participants: Evidence from Ethiopia." *Comparative Review* 13, no. 3 (October 1969): 312–24. The authors find that most members of the Ethiopian University Service were skeptical about their year of mandatory civilian service when they entered, and enthusiastic about it when they left.

Landrum, Roger. "Voluntary National Service: An Alternative to the Draft." *Transatlantic Perspectives*, no. 3 (September 1980). This article describes the West German civilian service program for conscientious objectors. The program currently enrolls some 35,000 young men performing a variety of social services at a cost of $200 million per year.

Landrum, Roger. "Serving America: Alternatives to the Draft." *USA Today,* January 1981. Landrum suggests that "We need a broader conception of national security and, instead of a military draft, many forms of national service."

Lash, Joseph P. *Eleanor and Franklin.* New York: The New American Library, 1973. Chapter 45 of this best seller describes Eleanor Roosevelt's keen interest in, and actions in behalf of, the national service concept.

Lindley, Betty, and Lindley, K. Ernest. *A New Deal for Youth—The Story of the National Youth Administration.* New York: The Viking Press, 1938. This is a report on the largest of the New Deal youth programs.

Marmion, Harry A. *The Case Against a Volunteer Army.* Chicago: Quadrangle Books, 1971. Marmion predicts that a volunteer army will produce soldiers from the nation's underclasses and will increase the influence of the defense industry on national policy.

McKee, Robert L., and Gaffney, Michael J. *The Community Service Fellowship's Planning Project: Final Report.* Washington: American Association of Community and Junior Colleges, 1975.

Under a grant from ACTION, the authors examine the feasibility of a GI Bill for National Service and recommend a series of grants to states to test different models.

McNamara, Robert S. Speech to the American Society of Newspaper Editors. *The New York Times*, May 19, 1966, p. 11. The then Secretary of Defense, in the midst of the Vietnam War, caused a great stir with his espousal of voluntary national service.

Mead, Margaret. "The Case for Drafting All Boys—and Girls." *Redbook Magazine*, September 1966. Mead suggests that all young people "would benefit from the kind of life, for a limited period, in which obligation, privilege and responsibility were combined. . . ."

Moskos, Charles C. "National Service and the All-Volunteer Force." *Society*, November-December 1979. Moskos concludes that "Now is the time to consider a voluntary national service program—in which military duty is one of several options—which would be coupled with post-service educational benefits."

Moskos, Charles C. "Saving the All-Volunteer Force." *The Public Interest*, Fall 1980. Moskos says the answer is to restore the GI Bill for military service, link federal aid for higher education to voluntary national service, and establish pay differentials between short- and long-term military personnel.

Muller, Stephen. "The Case for Universal National Service." *Educational Record* 52, no. 1 (Winter 1971). Muller recommends a national service program concentrating on four major areas: day care, neighborhood preservation, health, and education.

National Advisory Commission on Selective Service. *In Pursuit of Equity: Who Serves When Not All Serve?* Washington, 1967. Appointed by President Johnson and chaired by Burke Marshall, the Commission recommends changes in selective service and briefly reviews several national service issues.

National Association of Secondary School Principals. *25 Action Learning Schools.* Reston, Virginia: National Association of Secondary School Principals, 1974. This is one of several NASSP publications which have helped to promote student community service as an integral part of the educational process.

National Child Labor Committee. *Rite of Passage: The Crisis of Youth's Transition from School to Work.* New York: National Child Labor Committee, 1976. The Committee, founded early in the twentieth century to campaign for child labor laws, now advocates a broad program of youth participation, work, and service.

National Commission on Resources for Youth. *New Roles for Youth in the School and the Community.* New York: Citation Press, 1974. This publication describes numerous youth involvement projects.

National Council of Women of the U.S. *Women in National Service.* New York: National Council of Women of the U.S., 1967. This conference report recommends that national service be open to women as a means "of finding alternate roles, of finding channels of service, and of self-fulfillment."

National Interreligious Service Board for Conscientious Objectors. *The Reporter for Conscience' Sake.* 550 Washington Bldg., 15th Street and New York Avenue, Washington, D.C. 20005. This monthly newsletter reports on matters of concern to persons interested in conscientious objection to military service.

National Service Secretariat. *National Service Newsletter.* 5140 Sherier Pl., N. W., Washington D.C. 20016. Published since 1966, this occasional newsletter reports developments in the area of national service.

National Society for Internships and Experiential Education. *Experiential Education* 1735 Eye St., Suite 601, N.W., Washington, D.C. 20006. This newsletter carries articles, book reviews, and conference announcements on such topics as national service and service-learning.

Panel on Youth of the President's Science Advisory Committee, James S. Coleman, Chairman. *Youth: Transition to Adulthood.* Washington: U.S. Government Printing Office, 1973. This report explores the trend toward passive education and recommends national service and other forms of experiential education.

"Peace Corps—Wishful Thinking." Editorial, *Michigan State News,* January 25, 1961, p. 2. This editorial emphasizes the importance to college students of the Peace Corps as an alternative to the military draft, a provision contained in President Kennedy's first Peace Corps proposal but later dropped.

Pinkau, Irene. *Service for Development,* three volumes. Dayton, Ohio: Charles F. Kettering Foundation, 1978. The author conducts a detailed, comparative study of youth service programs and youth issues in such countries as Costa Rica, Indonesia, Kenya, Nigeria, and the United States.

Preiss, Jack J. *Camp William James.* Norwich, Vermont: Argo Books, 1978. This book details the efforts of a small band of Harvard and Dartmouth men to turn the Civilian Conservation Corps into a form of national service.

President's Task Force on Manpower Conservation. *One-Third of a Nation.* Washington: U.S. Government Printing Office, 1964. Created in 1963 by President Kennedy out of his concern that so many young men were failing preinduction examinations, the Cabinet-level Task Force recommended universal examination of 18 year old men and remedial education, training, and health services for those who failed the examinations.

Quarmby, Andrew, and Fussell, Diana. *Study-Service Newsletter.* P.O. Box 1883, Gaborone, Botswana. The editors of this newsletter have helped to design and operate study-service programs in such countries as Indonesia, Nepal, and Botswana.

Ritterbush, Philip C., ed. *Let the Entire Community Become Our University.* Washington: Acropolis Books, 1972. With 29 contributors, this book explores a broad range of ideas and examples related to experiential education.

Salmond, John A. *The Civilian Conservation Corps, 1933–1942: A New Deal Case Study.* Durham, North Carolina: Duke University Press, 1967. Salmond's book on the CCC is perhaps the best single source on this popular New Deal program.

Sanders, Marion K. "The Case for a National Service Corps." *The New York Times Magazine,* August 7, 1966. A participant in the first national service conference assesses the likely size and cost of national service.

Sherraden, Michael. "The Civilian Conservation Corps: Effectiveness of the Camps." Ph.D. dissertation, The University of Michigan, 1979. This study looks at effectiveness of CCC camps, specifically in the areas of work productivity, enrollee satisfaction, and camp-community relations.

Sherraden, Michael. "Youth Employment and Education: Federal Programs from the New Deal Through the 1970s." In *Confronting Youth Unemployment in the 1980s: Rhetoric Versus Reality,* edited by Ray C. Rist. New York: Pergamon Press, 1980. The role of education in federally-sponsored youth employment efforts over a forty year period is reviewed in this article.

Sherraden, Michael. "Military Participation in a Youth Employment Program: The Civilian Conservation Corps." *Armed Forces and Society* 7, no. 2 (Winter 1981). Sherraden evaluates the Army's role in managing CCC camps in the 1930s. In general, the Army did a satisfactory job and was able to function effectively in a program under civilian control.

Swomley, John M., Jr. *The Military Establishment.* Boston: Beacon Press, 1964. Swomley presents the antimilitaristic case against the draft.

Tax, Sol, ed. *The Draft: A Handbook of Facts and Alternatives.* Chicago: University of Chicago Press, 1967. National service is a major topic of discussion in this volume whose contributors include Donald Eberly, Erik Erikson, Milton Friedman, Lewis Hershey, Morris Janowitz, Edward Kennedy, Margaret Mead, Donald Rumsfeld, and others.

Taylor, Eugene. "Camp William James: Historic Model for a Self Imposed Draft." Unpublished paper, Cambridge, Massachusetts, 1980. This present-day student of William James examines current national service proposals in the light of James' philosophy and the CCC camp which bore both his name and his philosophy.

Teachers College Record 73, no. 1 (September 1971). This issue contains national service articles by Morris Janowitz, Charles C. Moskos, Jr., Jack R. Butler, Adam Yarmolinsky, Albert D. Biderman, Margaret Mead, Donald J. Eberly, and Gayle Janowitz.

Tyler, Ralph W., ed. *From Youth to Constructive Adult Life: The Role of the Public School.* Berkeley, California: McCutchan, 1978. Youth socialization is examined and national service, action-learning, and other youth involvement ideas are put forward.

U.S. Civilian Conservation Corps. *Final Report of the Director of the Civilian Conservation Corps, April 1933 through June 30, 1942.* Washington: U.S. Civilian Conservation Corps, 1942. Among other information, this final report on the CCC contains summary statistics on work projects and program costs.

U.S. Comptroller General. *Additional Cost of the All Volunteer Force.* Washington: U.S. General Accounting Office, 1978. This study finds the additional cost of the AVF for each of the fiscal years from 1973 to 1977 to be $3 billion or more.

U.S. Congress, House, Commitee on Armed Services, *Hearings on Military Posture and H.R. 1872 CH.R. 4040,* 96th Congress, 1st sess., 1979. Includes testimony in support of national service by Majority Leader Jim Wright, Representatives John J. Cavanaugh, Paul N. McCloskey, Jr., and others.

U.S. Congress, Senate, Committee on Labor and Human Resources, *Hearings on Presidential Commission on National Service and National Commission on Volunteerism,* 96th Congress, 2nd sess., 1980. Most of the 606 pages in this hearing on the Tsongas bill are devoted to rich testimony on all sides of the national service issue.

U.S. Congressional Budget Office. *National Service Programs and Their Effects on Military Manpower and Civilian Youth Problems.* Washington: U.S. Congressional Budget Office, 1978. This study considers three different types of national service and finds their costs, largely a function of size, would range from $2 billion to $23 billion.

U.S. Congressional Budget Office. *Costs of the National Service Act (HR 2206). A Technical Analysis* (Washington: U.S. Congressional Budget Office, 1980). This study of the 1979 McCloskey bill estimates that three million worker-years of national civilian service from 1982-1986 would incur a net budgetary cost of $13.1 billion in 1981 dollars.

U.S. Military Academy. *Senior Conference on National Compulsory Service, June 16–18, 1977, Final Report.* West Point, New York: U.S. Military Academy, 1977. Includes papers on national service by Richard Cooper, William King, Adam Yarmolinsky, and a summary of conference discussions.

U.S. National Youth Administration. *Final Report of the National Youth Administration, Fiscal Years 1936–1943.* Washington: U.S. Government Printing Office, 1944. This final report on the NYA contains much useful information and is perhaps the best introduction to this large New Deal program, which was a forerunner to modern youth employment and work-study programs.

Wexler, Jacqueline Grennan. Testimony before the Congress in U.S. Congress, Senate, Committee on Labor and Human Resources, *Hearings on Presidential Commission on National Service and National Commission on Volunteerism,* 96th Congress, 2nd sess., 1980, pp. 22–29. One of the most articulate advocates of national service presents national service as a citizenship responsibility.

White House Conference on Youth. *Recommendations and Resolutions: 1971 White House Conference on Youth.* Washington: U.S. Government Printing Office, 1971. Five of the conference's 10 task forces made recommendations related to national service.

Willenz, June A. *Dialogue on the Draft.* Washington: American Veterans Committee 1967. This is the report of a 1966 conference which examined the draft and went on to consider proposals for the future by Donald Eberly, Harry Marmion, Joseph McMurray, Bayard Rustin, and Harris Wofford.

Wirtz, Willard, and the National Manpower Institute. *The Boundless Resources: A Prospectus for an Education/Work Policy.* Washington: New Republic, 1975. Wirtz recommends an array of policies, including Education and Work Councils, to foster linkages among work, service, and learning.

Wofford, Harris. "Toward a Draft Without Guns." *Saturday Review,* October 15, 1966. Wofford suggests that voluntary national service can approach universality as virtually all young people recognize a responsibility to contribute some form of service.

Woods, Dorothea. *Volunteers in Community Development.* Paris: United Nations Education, Scientific and Cultural Organization, 1971. Woods assesses the contributions made to the development of Third World countries by volunteers from overseas.

Yarmolinsky, Adam. "National Service Program." In *Final Report of the Senior Conference on National Compulsory Service.* West Point, New York: U.S. Military Academy, 1977. Yarmolinsky suggests that "the greatest unmet needs in the United States today are for human services delivered by relatively untrained but caring people at the local community level."

Index

About the Authors

Donald Eberly is employed by the Selective Service System to develop plans for Alternative Service for Conscientious Objectors in the event of a draft. He circulated his first proposal for national service in 1958 and founded the National Service Secretariat in 1966 to conduct research and serve as a national service clearinghouse; he has been Executive Director of the Secretariat since it was founded. Eberly was a consultant on national service to the National Advisory Commission on Selective Service in 1966–67 and was Program Manager of ACTION's national service test project in Seattle in 1973–74. He has testified on national service before committees of the Congress, has authored numerous articles, and has edited two books on national service, *A Profile of National Service* (1966) and *National Service* (1968).

Peter Edelman is a partner in the Washington, D.C. law firm of Foley, Lardner, Hollabaugh & Jacobs. He was formerly Director of the New York State Division for Youth and, before that, Vice President of the University of Massachusetts. He served in 1979 as counsel to the Vice President's Task Force on Youth Employment and in 1980 as Issues Director for the Presidential campaign of Senator Edward Kennedy.

Diane Hedin is Assistant Director and Associate Professor at the Center for Youth Development and Research, University of Minnesota. She directs the Minnesota Youth Poll, a qualitative opinion poll which regularly asks teenagers their views on issues of central importance to them, such as work, success, school, friendship, health, and national service. She has just completed the first nationwide study of experiential learning and youth participation in secondary schools.

Roger Landrum conducts policy research with the Potomac Institute in Washington, D.C. and was Study Director for the Committee for the Study of National Service, which in 1979 published the landmark report, *Youth and the Needs of the Nation*. Landrum also recently published a study of the Peace Corps' role in education in developing countries. He has taught at the University of Nigeria, Yale, and Harvard.

Charles Moskos is Professor of Sociology at Northwestern University. His research interests deal with the enlisted ranks of the military and national youth service. One of the nation's leading experts on military personnel,

Moskos was a Fellow at the Woodrow Wilson International Center for Scholars during 1980–81.

Irene Pinkau directs the Development Services Cooperation project in Washington, D.C., which is coordinated by the Charles F. Kettering Foundation, Dayton, Ohio. She is author of *Service for Development*, a report of a multinational project which evaluated 30 volunteer and development services in 15 countries. Previously a management consultant, teacher, and director of a rural youth program, Pinkau has also served as Director for Evaluation and Research of the International Secretariat for Volunteer Service and headed its North American Regional Office. More recently her studies have focused on the role of private sector organizations in building a sense of world community.

William Ramsay is Vice President for Labor and Student Life at Berea College, Berea, Kentucky, where he is responsible for Berea's unique program of student labor and student industries. Ramsay, who originated the phrase "service-learning," has been active in service-learning and student work programs for many years and participated in the development of service-learning internships in the 1960s. Practicing what he preaches, he is active in community and church, continues to read and study, and makes sorghum molasses with his family on a Kentucky mountain farm.

Michael Sherraden is Assistant Professor at The George Warren Brown School of Social Work, Washington University, St. Louis, where he teaches graduate courses in social welfare administration and employment policy. He has been director of a residential youth program in Arkansas and a work camp for teenagers in Nova Scotia. With support from the U.S. Department of Labor and the Eleanor Roosevelt Institute, Sherraden has undertaken a major study of the Civilian Conservation Corps of the 1930s. His research interests are youth employment, national service, and organizational behavior.

Harris Wofford is counsel in the law firm of Schnader, Harrison, Segal and Lewis in Philadelphia and Washington, D.C. He is author of *Of Kennedys and Kings: Making Sense of the Sixties*, and was Co-Chairman of the Committee for the Study of National Service. In the 1960s Wofford was Special Assistant to President Kennedy and Associate Director of the Peace Corps. From 1970–78 he was President of Bryn Mawr College.